Ron's World

All the Times I Died

Ron Autrey

JSA Publishing
Ponte Vedra Beach, Florida

Book and cover design by Sagaponack Books & Design

ISBNs
979-8-9881881-0-0 (softcover)
979-8-9881881-1-7 (hardcover)
979-8-9881881-2-4 (e-book)

Library of Congress Control Number: 2023907002

Summary:
Ron's World: All the Times I Died is a recollection of personal and geopolitical events occurring during the life of the author in the 20th and 21st centuries.

BIO026000 Biography & Autobiography / Personal Memoirs
HIS027130 History / Wars & Conflicts
PHI008000 Philosophy / Good & Evil
HIS037030 History / Modern

AutreyResearch.com

JSA Publishing
Ponte Vedra Beach, Florida

Printed and bound in the United States of America
First Edition

Acknowledgments

I could not have accomplished the work required to complete my first book without the professional assistance provided by my copyeditor Beth Mansbridge and the skills and guidance of publishing consultant Fran Keiser. My endless thanks go to my research assistant Christen Sinquefield at InSinq, LLC. For the confidence to forge ahead, I thank my dear friends Dr. Priscilla Berry, Dr. Stephen Wallace, and the late Walter Mayberry Lee.

To my wife Hilah, who tolerated four decades of my up-and-down moods and behavior. I am here to share my life because of her love and perseverance.

Never think that war, no matter how necessary,
nor how justified, is not a crime.

—Ernest Hemingway

Contents

Introduction

The ability to look back and remember the events and developments in my life with some level of accuracy is a personal blessing for me. As I reviewed the historical events occurring around the world during my lifetime, I could see clearly that my knowledge of world events was a mere sliver of all that has transpired. It also became apparent that a large portion of Americans in my generation and those that followed in the next were equally deficient in their limited frame of reference to the past. I quickly learned that many transformational things happened around the globe in my early years and before I was born. A study of the years spanning from 1950 to 2022 provided a fascinating chronology of life-changing events and larger-than-life people who built the foundation for the complex world we live in today.

Sadly, the reviews of each year include what seems like endless wars between good and evil, and greed and oppression. Death and destruction take on a new meaning when we look beyond the tabulations and statistics of war and discover the wretched impact on people and families. That we measure the loss of war tools such as tanks and planes on the same charts and pages with human lives and suffering paints a portrait of mankind that is not benevolent or divinely inspirational. Skipping through the years, there was no break in the cycle of events that built up to warfare, nor in the repetitive conduct of fighting and dying for opposing ideologies and territories.

Although darkness prevails, the history of conflict and social injustices provided a stage for some of the most inspiring leaders the world has ever seen. Recognizing that all men and women are short of perfection, the greatness of 100 men and women, among thousands, stands out as a vestige of hope for mankind. Goodness and grace, integrated with strength and determination, are qualities that emanate from great leaders. We must recognize and develop these voices to counter the antipathy from the hostile and destructive forces that surround us.

The timely emergence of people like Nelson Mandela and Dr. Martin Luther King Jr. changed the dynamics of racism and moved people toward freedom and justice. Winston Churchill and Franklin Delano Roosevelt brought the vision and fortitude to lead allied nations to victory over the tyranny of Adolf Hitler in World War II. Iconic figures, including President John F. Kennedy, Margaret Thatcher, Mother Teresa, and Ronald Reagan, were in the right place and time when their leadership qualities were needed. Behind the first tier of well-known names are tens of thousands of great leaders who have advanced the well-being of humanity. Their relative anonymity, compared to other names that are well-known, is stratified not by a lack of equal greatness, but by their access to media attention.

The Millennials of today, and Zoomers of Generation Z who follow, live in a world that is determined to ignore, deny, or rewrite history, rather than learn from it. The approach taken by ultra-liberally-minded factions of the new classes of young citizens is to ban or destroy the sources of what they consider to be wrong or deviant from their beliefs. Freedom of speech and conservative platforms are suppressed on many college campuses and in some business forums. Books and other media that are deemed to be racist, homophobic, or that promote ideologies which do not support the latest unfounded whimsical views of life and how to live it are shunned or banned. Historic statues and monuments are indiscriminately destroyed—not because they are grossly offensive, but as a form of rage and protest. The message from the misguided young anarchists is that they are disgusted by our past and want to neutralize its influence. If they are successful, what remains will be a world devoid of any moral values or social constraints on behavior. We are seeing microcosms of this predictable outcome in major cities including Portland, Oregon; Chicago, Illinois; Seattle, Washington; and San Francisco, California.

The daunting challenge which the new generations will face is how to successfully and beneficially fit into a world that, by some measures, is already in social and economic decline. Visionary young leaders hoping for a utopian one-world order will see that the variances among 195 nations are simply too great to bind everyone into a homogenous assembly of states. The sustainability of Mother Earth and her support systems for advanced societies of people cannot be produced by or measured in gigabits and teraflops. It is time to remove the earpieces and virtual goggles and get to work. Before the world can reach Maslow's idyllic definition of self-actualization, we must first master the lower rungs of physiological needs for food, health, and security. We are far from achieving any level of consistency worldwide. Some countries enjoy and share excess production of goods and resources, while others struggle with poor health and insufficient water and food sources. The third level of Maslow's Pyramid of Needs prescribes love and togetherness. As you read through the chapters in this book, you will discover, as I did, that we are extremely far from achieving a world that has overcome the hate and evil which precludes the formation of a loving global society.

1950–1952

The story begins in the 950th year of the second millennium. Important events that year laid a foundation for the geopolitical landscape we live in today. In the beginning of the year, in a move that would have far-reaching impact, the United Kingdom, Finland, and Israel recognized the People's Republic of China (PRC) as the established governing body of China. This move was not earth-shattering at the time. China's largely agrarian population was just under 540 million. Today it exceeds 1.4 billion people. After nearly a decade of war with Japan, the PRC was established, in 1949, with a mission to stabilize the country's economy and rebuild China's infrastructure. Party leaders set out to accomplish a long-range goal of building a powerful Socialist industrial state. In a bold move, the Chinese government redistributed nearly half of all farmlands to individual farm families that previously only worked the land for other, more prosperous landlords. China was on the move, but did not pose a threat to Western or European countries.

In 1950 the Israeli legislature established Jerusalem as the capital city of Israel. This action, taken 72 years ago, had a lasting global effect on the course of history for the next seven decades. Israel controlled the oldest city in the world and claimed it as their capital. The Palestine National Authority declared that Jerusalem was the rightful capital city of Palestine. Because of the controversy, the rest of the world did not endorse the claims of either party. Sixty-eight years later, on Israel's 70th anniversary, President Donald Trump made a historic landmark decision to move the US Embassy from Tel Aviv to Jerusalem, thereby recognizing Jerusalem as the capital city of Israel. The violent conflict between the Jewish and Arab nations was ongoing then and it continues today.

The decade of the 1950s brought transformational developments in the scientific world. Scientific research conducted in the 1942 Manhattan (nuclear bomb) Project led to the commissioning of work on the peaceful use of nuclear energy. The use of nuclear fission power was first established in 1951 when scientists at the Argonne National Laboratory in Idaho connected a series of light bulbs to an electrical source generated by an experimental breeder reactor. Within days the reactor was providing power to the entire reactor facility. With that success, the US Atomic Energy Commission and the Argonne Laboratory provided the foundation for the design and commissioning of commercial power reactors around the world.

The first commercial utility to use distributed nuclear power was developed by Russian scientists in Moscow in 1954. This was entirely due to one of the most empowering intelligence failures at the Los Alamos National Laboratory in 1944. A German physicist named Klaus Fuchs, working with British scientists assigned to the lab, confessed to the United Kingdom's MI5 (Military Intelligence, Section 5) that he was a Soviet spy, and for seven years had passed US and British nuclear weapons research to the Soviets.

The Soviets tested their first atomic bomb in 1949. Soon after the Soviets' test, President Harry S. Truman commissioned the development of the first hydrogen bomb. Testing of this new generation of atomic weaponry proved it to be 1,000 times more powerful than the earlier atomic bombs. In 1950, the US federal government partnered with the DuPont Corporation to build the Savannah River Site in South Carolina. The highly secretive plant produced heavy water that was used in the process of building hydrogen bombs. The plant, completed in 1956, was the first tritium facility used for the extraction of plutonium and uranium from irradiated materials in nuclear reactors. Twenty years later, seven countries had developed nuclear weapons. A prescient Albert Einstein appropriately warned the world that mutual nuclear destruction was a real possibility.

In the lower regions of the planet, in a move that would attract global attention for the next seven decades, South Africa passed the Group Areas Act, mandating the segregation of the races in that region. Apartheid laws denied non-White South Africans access to cities, crushing their opportunity for education and economic growth. The ensuing conflicts and protests eventually brought South Africa international attention and focused the world view on the inequity of systemic racism. Protests were met with unbridled police brutality. The bloody conflicts cost the lives of more than 1,000 Black South Africans. The oppressive policies of apartheid continued for half a century, before ending in 1990. The struggles over racism, poverty, and injustice continue today in South Africa. While segregation is no longer mandated by law, it is maintained by the boundaries of diminished opportunity and poverty.

Overshadowing most current events of the decade, June of 1950 was the beginning of the Korean War. North Korea aligned with the Soviet Union and China, and waged war with South Korea. The United States and combined forces of the United Nations provided crucial support to the South Koreans. Typical of most modern wars, the atrocities of battle were remarkable. In deadly battles with many casualties, North Korea captured Seoul, the largest metropolis of South Korea. Lacking remorse, South Korea bombed the Han River Bridge with hundreds of refugees fleeing across the span connecting South Korea to the north. In the Bodo League massacre, the South Korean Army executed more than 100,000 North Korean sympathizers. The act was so horrific, they denied it and tried to hide the truth for four decades. In smaller numbers, but no less tragic, North Korean troops executed 41 United States Army POWs in the battle for Hill 303 in Waegwan, South Korea.

The US Air Force made aeronautic history with the first jet to jet dogfight, shooting down two North Korean MiG-15 jets over the Yalu River border between North Korea and China. When not contemplating nuclear destruction, American legislators successfully passed the 22nd Amendment to the US Constitution, which (thankfully) limited elected presidential service to two four-year terms.

The ability of civilized nations to conduct deadly warfare while simultaneously celebrating national events at home is a puzzling conundrum for modern society. With the deadly Korean conflict raging across the sea from our homeland, we joyously celebrated the first 12 Hours of Sebring automobile race in Florida. Simultaneously, as General Douglas MacArthur was threatening to use nuclear weapons in the Korean conflict, more than 4 million American households watched their favorite television shows on their very own black-and-white TV. *I Love Lucy* and *The Twilight Zone* trumped the news of death and war in Korea. The Baby Boom Generation was well on its way, with 4 million newborns added to the US population every year through the 1950s.

In the confusing, piecemeal, but rapidly escalating development of modern society in America and around the globe, it was timely that J. D. Salinger released his novel, *The Catcher in the Rye*. The book sold more than 65 million copies. The fictional character Holden Caulfield is cast in a story depicting the superficiality of modern society. The youthful minds in the '50s and the decades that followed pondered the futility of life. Wars competed with other major events like the "Shot Heard 'Round the World" when New York Giants baseball player Bobby Thomson hit a still-famous home run to win the National League pennant. Meanwhile, our nation's sons continued to die in foreign conflicts—without a compelling and well-defined purpose.

The decade of the 1950s provided us with sociological and technological achievements that laid the foundation for 50 years of phenomenal advancements in technology, medicine, transportation, and space travel. Despite the plethora of new products and pleasures that made life easier, it was as though we had never advanced from the medieval warring mentality of past centuries. Developed nations around the globe continued seamless conflicts over territories and morally deficient religious beliefs and ideologies. As Sonny and Cher sang in 1967, "The Beat Goes On."

1952: Escape from the Womb

Before my first spontaneous breath, I was doomed. Not yet physically developed enough to sustain life, my lungs collapsed and were not ready for normal respiration. For reasons beyond the control of the normal gestation process, my mother's womb was ready to expel its contents after 32 weeks in lieu of the prescribed 40 weeks. The normal pale pallor expected for a four-pound newborn baby was quickly replaced with the cyanotic blue tinge of asphyxiation.

I was born three days after Christmas. The year was 1952. Twenty-seven-year-old Dr. Richard Skinner was six years past his graduation from Emory University's medical school. He was the attending pediatric physician at Saint Luke's Hospital in downtown Jacksonville, Florida. Fortunately for me, Dr. Skinner was brilliant and aspirational in both senses of the word.

After what was likely a very quick medical assessment of respiratory distress, and without the benefit of modern imaging tools, Dr. Skinner devised a treatment that involved the insertion of a large syringe into the air cavities surrounding my lungs. He removed air and fluids, allowing my infantile lungs to slowly recover their normal shape and function. I was going to live.

During my six-week recovery, the initial blue skin color took on an alarming yellow discoloration. Infantile jaundice became another one of the first words and multisyllabic phrases I heard in the early weeks of life. The yellow-green light illuminating my incubation crib probably looked more ethereal than therapeutic. This obstacle, like many to follow in my life, was not an insurmountable challenge for me and my new best friend, Dr. Richard Skinner. We had been to the sacred mountaintop together and returned with repair and bold ambition.

While the first weeks of my life were challenging, the next 10 years maintained a nearly normal developmental pattern. My environment was at least as normal as one could expect on the Northside of Jacksonville in the early '50s. We were fortunate to have my mother volunteering at the local kindergarten. I attended to the playground while my mother shared her love and caring nature with dozens of children too young to begin the first grade of elementary school. Singing, swinging, and rolling in the sandbox with nameless children of working dads and nurturing moms, I learned many of the important lessons needed for my life ahead. Our basic childhood experiences taught us that to steal was wrong. To physically hurt someone without cause would bring dire consequences. Telling adults something that is not true was also wrong, and it would likely bring about some form of age-adjusted corporal punishment. One important lesson I still remember is that if you punch a bully, hit him really hard. You will hopefully cause him to not want to harm you again, and at the very least it will give you some time to run.

My first year at Riverview Elementary School (later renamed Henry F. Kite Elementary School) was not traumatic or remarkable. Except I did discover a set of new emotions. I was in love with my first-grade teacher, Mrs. Rose. Given the significant difference in our ages, I resorted to a desperate but time-proven method to win her attention. Through my labors, I collected a monetarily significant number of discarded Coca-Cola bottles. Each bottle represented a refundable deposit amount that was paid to the holder of the assets upon redemption at the local five-and-dime (retail store).

Having placed two cases of the bottles on Mrs. Rose's front porch, I knocked on the door and paused, awaiting the arrival of my prize. She was very tall, beautiful, and smelled of lilac. She quickly understood my intentions and was very pleased with her gift. Mrs. Rose took me in her arms and kissed the top of my head. She said something about what a special little boy I was and thanked me with a flash of her dark eyelids and a swirl of her long dark hair. After our brief interlude and having ensured that I knew my way back home, she waved a thankful goodbye and I walked proudly up the tar roads and hill toward my house in Riverview, a changed man forever.

In December of 1952, aside from my remarkable birth coinciding with the introduction of the astronomical Big Bang theory as the origin of the universe, the real news was that the first Chevrolet Corvette prototype was created by famed designer Harley J. Earl. The first Vette left the assembly line on June 30, 1953. The model reached greater importance and notoriety when it was upgraded to a V8 engine in 1955. I vowed to own such a car one day, but never actually did.

On February 6 in the year of my birth, Princess Elizabeth, then 25 years old, ascended to the throne of the British Empire following the death of her father, King George VI. Queen Elizabeth II continued her reign for 70 years. In 1952 *The Diary of a Young Girl*, also known as *The Diary of Anne Frank*, was published in English, and Charlie Chaplin was denied reentry to the United States by Joe McCarthy and his House Un-American Activities Committee. The United States tested the first hydrogen bomb—1,000 times more powerful than the first atomic bomb.

Many historically significant events continued to unfold in the early '50s. Nelson Mandela was arrested in South Africa. India held its first general election. Americans watched nationally televised live atomic bomb testing in Nevada. Puerto Rico became a self-governing commonwealth of the United States. Kentucky Fried Chicken opened its first franchise. *Mad* magazine published its first issue. Ban Roll-On Deodorant was introduced to the worldwide battle against body odor. The first Holiday Inn opened in Tennessee. Jonas Salk introduced the polio vaccine to the world. Following Harry S. Truman, Dwight D. Eisenhower defeated Adlai Stevenson to win the presidency of the United States.

The first year of life is not something we remember as a child, or in adulthood. Today it is generally accepted that major life events are not recalled in adult memory until after the age of two or three. In 1952, photography was limited to Polaroid cameras, and not readily available to many families. I learned the details of my birth and my experiences as a toddler from my parents and other relatives and family friends. I also suspect that in these pre-Facebook years, not so much importance was placed on the daily or hourly chronicles of life and its myriad childhood activities.

I am still amazed at the long list of major events that changed the lives of people across the world in 1952. It was a good year for me. I made it, and I am still here and breathing just fine.

1953–1959

When I first evaluated the year 1953, I thought it might be unremarkable, given the lengthy list of major events logged in the previous year. I was wrong. This year brought about several changes that still shape the world we live in today, among them the first issue of *Playboy* magazine and Ian Fleming's first James Bond novel. The first color television sets appeared for sale at prices beginning above $1,200 ($12,000 in 2019 dollars). Color televisions in 1953 brought us *The Perry Como Chesterfield Show*, *The Guiding Light*, and *The Adventures of Superman*. Our afternoons and evenings were enlivened by the antics of Jackie Gleason, Milton Berle, and Lucille Ball. Box office hits included *Gentlemen Prefer Blondes*, *Peter Pan*, and *From Here to Eternity*.

Looking back to 1953, the nationalization of the Anglo-Iranian Oil Company in Iran started a series of events that still reverberate through modern international diplomatic relations. In 1951, Mohammad Mosaddegh was elected as Iran's prime minister. Iran severed ties with Great Britain in 1952, after Britain embargoed Iranian oil. In 1953, Mosaddegh was removed from office and the shah, Mohammad Reza Pahlavi, became the authoritarian shah, and remained in power until the Iranian Revolution in 1979.

Today's news cycles include frequent mentions and discussions about the state of affairs in Iran. President Barack Obama, like many prior presidents, was faced with Iran as a threat to peace in the Middle East, as well as potential harm to Americans and other allies. His successor and 45th president, Donald Trump, took a hard-line stance against the threats and acts of terror sponsored by Iran. Today, Iran continues to be a serious threat to the region and other US interests. The determined efforts to develop nuclear weapons and long-range missiles are the foremost threat to all nations seen as adversaries of the Iranian regime.

Following the dismissal of General MacArthur in 1951, President Eisenhower informed the Chinese that he would not be afraid to use nuclear weapons to end the Korean conflict. In this undeclared war, 33,629 American troops lost their lives, along with 1.5 million Communists from China and North Korea. In July of 1953, an armistice closed the conflict and established the demilitarized zone. At a historic summit 68 years later, North Korean leader Kim Jong-un and South Korea's President Moon Jae-in officially declared an end to the Korean War.

If the world was not already more dangerous than ever before, in 1953, after the Soviet Union announced it had successfully tested a hydrogen bomb, the arms race was officially on and escalating. The Cold War would continue for 36 more years, to the fall of the Berlin Wall in 1989. After a 30-year reign of death and the death of more than 10 million of his own people, Joseph Stalin, the leader of the Soviet Union, died on March 5, 1953. He was succeeded by Nikita Khrushchev and his era of de-Stalinization. Today a new Cold War is ramping up, but not against Russia. China has emerged as the world's greatest threat, militarily and economically. Russia remains engaged in nefarious acts, but NATO and the sheer strength of the US military is, hopefully, a significant deterrent to future conflicts between Russia and NATO member countries.

On the list of good news events, a polio vaccine was ready for field trials. Jonas Salk first immunized his own family in 1953, followed by 1.3 million children in 1954. By 1955, the vaccine would be 90 percent effective against this paralyzing disease. Today, in 2022, the disease has been nearly eradicated, with the only remaining outbreaks contained to remote parts of Afghanistan.

British physicist Francis Crick and US biologist James Watson unveiled the famous double helix model of DNA. This scientific discovery provided the basis for genetic research and scientific advancements for the next seven decades. Our children are not only studying genetic science, but they will also personally benefit from genomic medical advances and discoveries in profound and life-changing ways.

Whether we look at entertainment, science and technology, or international political affairs, the events in 1953 and all the early years in the '50s provided starting points and important advances in worldwide affairs and the quality of our human existence.

Drowning

My dad was very resourceful. We lived in a custom home designed to be similar to a prefabricated model offered by Sears, Roebuck & Co. It was a conventional 1,100-square-foot home that was delivered at a cost of just under $11,000. Dad, along with help from my uncle Roy White, Granddad White, and a neighbor, James Moody, also built a new swimming pool next to our stately handcrafted home.

The hole for the pool was dug by hand, and wire mesh reinforcing steel and rebar rods were carefully placed in the excavated shell of the pool. The placement of the concrete to form the walls and bottom of the pool was a day to remember. My dad and his team of volunteer craftsmen worked frantically to spread and shape the concrete mixture before it solidified.

The gleaming white finish of the pool was remarkable, but slightly abrasive to the soft feet and buttocks of the swimmers. Dad obtained a diving board that had been discarded from use at a much larger pool. It was almost as long as our 30-foot pool's length. Fifty or more concrete blocks were stacked on the back end of the board. I remember that when I bounced on the pool end of the diving board, the blocks bounced up several inches with each jump.

Dad and his crew constructed a room addition overlooking the pool, complete with footings and floor joists. As a young six-year-old athlete, I naturally assumed I possessed innate gymnastic talents. The narrow edge of the parallel two-by-10-inch floor supports made a perfect balance beam for my exhibition. After a few short steps, my foot caught the side of the board and I slipped into a perfect V-shaped position, straddling the floor joist. The squared edges of the upright pinewood beam met harshly against the soft underpinnings of my youthful manhood. I cannot adequately describe the newfound level of pain I experienced. Most future abrasions and bruises would be dismissed as minor in nature, compared to the baseline of excruciating pain in my testicles. In a quick visit to our local physician, Dr. Thomas Meldrum confirmed that I was not actually going to die, and that my future abilities and fertility remained promising.

One sunny day as we played and swam in our luxurious pool, I again faced down death in an encounter that I would remember for life. I was at one moment laughing and swimming with my older sister and her friend from across the street, and in the time it takes to blink, I was underwater, praying for a breath of air.

My sister and her friend playfully pushed me under the water and found humor in the way I was struggling. I don't think they fully understood the peril they were imposing. After what seemed much longer than the actual time that elapsed, I knew I was at the end of my struggle. It was the ultimate dilemma. I'd have to open my mouth and breathe the water or simply pass from consciousness. At that moment my uncle Roy White noticed the scene and plunged into the water and rescued me from what could have been a tragic drowning. Despite this near-death experience, I still loved the beautiful pool. The hot summer months on the Northside of

Jacksonville were bearable with frequent afternoon swims. The pool marked the advancement of our family into America's lower-middle-class.

1958

In December of 1958 I celebrated my sixth birthday. I recall that a birthday three days following Christmas was often not so memorable. My mother even offered to move the December celebration date from December to May. In the early years, she was always careful to label the birthday gifts and separate them from the other Christmas gifts. The efforts and gifts were eventually merged by time and frugality.

The early '50s were transformational for life in America. When I began investigating the events occurring in 1958, I thought that life would have plateaued or slowed down on the world stage. I could not have been more wrong. President Eisenhower created NASA, and the race for space was up and running. Russia had already launched the first satellite, Sputnik 1, from the Sputnik rocket the previous year. The United States followed with our first satellite and the Explorer 1 rocket. The US continued the year launching Pioneer 1 and Vanguard 1 rockets. Over the course of the year, Russia blasted off Sputnik 2 and Sputnik 3.

The world of technology was also transformed when scientist Jack Kilby and Texas Instruments invented the first microchip. The creation of integrated circuits started an exponential rate of change in the world of technology. Space travel, future computers, industrial systems, communications, and every aspect of modern society would be changed beyond the imagination of people living in the 1950s.

Aside from great scientific advances in the Western world, disparity in the human condition raged for the Chinese populace. The Great Chinese Famine was in full swing. In the short years between 1958 and 1961, 30 million Chinese died of starvation. The People's Republic of China, led by Communist Party Chairman Mao Zedong, launched the Great Leap Forward campaign. The abrupt transformation of China's agrarian economy to a Communist society was a disaster. Some investigators today place the death toll as high as 45 million. Failed political leadership and the fear of reprisal kept the truth about food and grain production hidden from public view.

On the home front, and perhaps a thousand years too late, 1958 was the year the United States outlawed female genital cutting, or female circumcision. As astonishing as that appears, worldwide today (2021), there are more than 200 million circumcised women still living.

In an event that would change life in the neighboring country of Cuba for the next 60 years, Fidel Castro's Revolutionary Army attacked Havana. For two years Castro waged guerrilla warfare in Cuba, attempting to overthrow the military regime of Fulgencio Batista. The battles started when Castro and his 81-man army sailed from Mexico to crash-land in Los Cayuelos, Cuba. Batista's forces reduced Castro's army to 19 survivors. The remaining force eventually grew to more than 300 guerilla soldiers and remained hidden in the Sierra Maestra mountains on the southeast coast of Cuba. Ultimately, Castro's guerilla army defeated the 10,000 warriors led by Batista's General Eulogio Cantillo.

The Arab world was also changing. Egypt and Syria unified to create the United Arab Republic (UAR). Egyptian President

Gamal Abdel Nasser became the first leader of the UAR. Three years later, Syria seceded from the union. Turmoil was the state of Arab affairs in the late '50s. Jordan aligned with Iraq to counter the strength of the United Arab Republic. In July of 1958, Iraq's military officers led a successful coup and overthrew the Kingdom of Iraq. The United States sent marines, along with the British special forces, to protect Lebanon and Jordan from the UAR forces. Later in July, Lebanon President Fouad Chehab met with UAR leader Nasser and forged an agreement to end the crisis and impending conflict. The volatility and complex fights for geography continue in the region today.

The world of exploration and transportation took a giant step. Britain's Sir Edmund Hillary completed the Commonwealth Trans-Antarctic Expedition, crossing the South Pole in tractors and sleds. Not to be outdone, later in the same year the United States traveled under the North Pole in the submarine USS *Nautilus*. Private air travel also took a leap forward with the first transatlantic flight in a Pan American Airways Boeing 707. Ruth Carol Taylor became the first African American flight attendant. The world was no longer flat, and our international neighbors just got a lot closer to the New World.

Before the chronicling of my next near-death experience, let's look at a couple of other interesting moments in 1958. You remember Elvis Presley and his amazing musical and movie career. Elvis was drafted into the United States Army in 1958. He served in the 1st Medium Tank Battalion, 32nd Cavalry Regiment, 3rd Armored Division. Elvis was stationed in Germany, where he met his wife, Priscilla. Priscilla went on to star in the film *Naked Gun*, and the *Dallas* television series. Sadly, while in Germany, Elvis was also introduced to the drugs that eventually led to his untimely death in 1977, at the age of 42.

On July 12 of 1958, The Quarrymen—later renaming themselves The Beatles—had their first recording session, belting out the song "That'll Be the Day," written by Buddy Holly and Jerry Allison. Ten years later The Beatles released the *White Album* under the Apple Records label. They brought us the *Magical Mystery Tour* album, the song "Yellow Submarine" from the *Revolver* album, and *Sgt. Pepper's Lonely Hearts Club Band* album, among many more. Other notable stars included Jerry Lee Lewis performing "Great Balls of Fire," while married to his 13-year-old cousin, Myra Gale Brown. Johnny Cash performed at the San Quentin State Prison, while singer-songwriter Merle Haggard served a two-year sentence there for burglary. Marty Robbins, Don Gibson, Ricky Nelson, The Everly Brothers, and Ray Price all contributed number one musical hits in 1958.

The Fall

In the summer of 1958, my father built a homemade swing set. It was an impressive design, and 30 years later I would re-create the structure for my own children. As I previously mentioned, at six years of age I was an experienced and fully developed athlete. Climbing the structural bones of this monstrous swing and slide assembly presented no real challenge for me. Sitting on the highest point, on a four-by-four timber extending parallel to the ground from one A-frame end to the next, I first felt accomplished, but not quite certain how I would descend from this new height—10 feet above the earth.

My sisters and younger brother, along with another neighborhood friend, were raucously swinging and playing on the new swing set below me. The slight movements of the structure added to my stress and escalating fear as I struggled to hold my balance at the top of the wooden monster. Things were happening quickly. And as I looked down, I lost my stability. Maintaining good balance on the beam was no longer possible. My only option was to climb down the framing. At such an elevation, it was simply too high to jump. I shifted to the end of the beam and attempted to extend my short legs to the cross brace of the framing. The distance was too great to span with my six-year-old legs. Climbing back to the uppermost position on the beam, I began to feel disoriented and dizzy. My center of gravity shifted, and I moved my body to adjust and gain balance. The change was fatal.

I began falling and the total time from leaving my perch to striking the ground seemed like slow motion. As my body soared straight toward the ground in a head-first orientation, I was having cognizant thoughts of my impending death. I hit the hard ground—perfectly perpendicular to the flat surface. The force at impact was equal to my mass times the speed of light squared and it caused no movement of the earth's surface. The cervical joints of my upper spine were compressed, with C1 and C2 permanently fused. I lay there on the ground, without tears or crying. Only shock. I feared movement, not knowing if I was alive, dead, or paralyzed.

The '60s

In response to the Soviet Union's successful dog in space launch onboard the Sputnik 2 rocket in 1957, President Dwight Eisenhower created the National Aeronautics and Space Administration (NASA). In November of 1958, the newly created Space Task Group opened the book on space travel. They created the human space flight program called Project Mercury. In April of 1959, military test pilots were selected for the program. They had the newly created title of star travelers, now known as astronauts. The seven original astronauts were Navy Lieutenant Scott Carpenter, Air Force Captain Gordon Cooper, Marine Lieutenant Colonel John Glenn, Air Force Captain Gus Grissom, Navy Lieutenant Commander Wally Schirra, Navy Lieutenant Commander Alan Shepard, and Air Force Captain Deke Slayton. The Mercury Seven crew ranged in age from 32 to 37. Primates Baker and Able were successfully launched and returned from space, and the Space Age had officially begun. Just months later, in February of 1959, NASA successfully tested the first Titan intercontinental ballistic missile. In June, the USS *George Washington* was commissioned as the first submarine to carry ballistic missiles.

Meanwhile, the international front was changing daily. Unrelated and geographically distant events continued to weave the fabric of life on planet Earth. In January of 1959, Fulgencio Batista fled Cuba as Fidel Castro and his forces entered the city of Havana. Very soon afterward, the United States and the Soviet Union recognized Castro as the leader of the Cuban government. As the People's Republic of China celebrated its 10th anniversary, the Chinese government tried to arrest the Dalai Lama. The Dalai found asylum in India. In March, Hawaii was granted statehood by the Eisenhower administration. Later in the year, the Vietnam War escalated with armed conflict between the Army of the Republic of Vietnam and the Viet Cong.

The technological revolution continued with Bell Lab's invention of the first metal-oxide-semiconductor field-effect transistor. The MOS transistor would become the foundation for the digital revolution. The first mass-produced electric car was introduced as the Henney Kilowatt. In the combustion engine world, the iconic 1959 Cadillac, with its prominent tailfins, was produced along with the first Chevy El Camino.

In January of 1960, Senator John F. Kennedy announced his candidacy for president. His term of leadership would face the Cuban Missile Crisis and the failed Bay of Pigs invasion, along with escalation of the ongoing Cold War with Communism. Twenty-three months later, JFK was assassinated in Dallas, Texas, by Lee Harvey Oswald.

The National Football League announced the addition of expansion teams for Dallas and Minneapolis-Saint Paul. With *Ben-Hur* in the theaters and Elvis Presley pining away the lyrics of "Are You Lonesome Tonight," the newly named Beatles were formed in Liverpool, England.

The year 1960 ushered in the Supreme Court decision ending segregation in public transportation. It also ruled Louisiana's segregation laws to be unconstitutional. Woolworth's served its first Black customer on July 25, 1960, starting demonstrations across the Southeast. The year was also known as the Year of Africa: South Africa became an independent republic, along with 16 other newly established African countries. As the Nixon-Kennedy debates raged in the fall and the Space Race continued, the world's population grew to more than 3 billion people.

In 1962 we encountered Taco Bell, Johnny Carson, *The Lucy Show*, the US embargo against Cuba, the Cuban Missile Crisis, and the Navy SEALs. John Glenn became the first American to orbit the Earth. The iconic Marilyn Monroe died of an overdose from sleeping pills. Soviet missiles in Cuba were aimed at the United States, while Bob Dylan belted out the tune of "A Hard Rain's a-Gonna Fall." The Soaring '60s were off and running.

Human rights were advanced in 1963. Dr. Martin Luther King Jr. wrote the "Letter from Birmingham City Jail" and delivered his "I Have a Dream" speech at the Lincoln Memorial. South Carolina, the last state to hold out for segregation, admitted Black student Harvey Gantt to Clemson University. James Meredith became the first Black student to graduate from the University of Mississippi. Meanwhile, George Wallace was elected governor of Alabama, and proclaimed, "Segregation now, segregation forever." Later that year, he reluctantly stood aside, and the first Black students enrolled in the University of Alabama.

In 1964 the United States passed the 24th Amendment, outlawing the poll tax. After a 75-day filibuster by Democratic senators, the United States also passed the 1964 Civil Rights Act. As the Ku Klux Klan continued murdering Black people in the South, Dr. Martin Luther King Jr. was awarded the Nobel Peace Prize, and Sidney Poitier won the Academy Award for Best Actor. In the two-year span of 1963–1964, women gained the right of suffrage in Algeria, Afghanistan, New Guinea, The Congo, Iran, Fiji, Kenya, Morocco, Monaco, and Sudan.

In the summer of 1962, the Autrey family moved from the hills of Riverview on the Northside of Jacksonville to sunny Jacksonville Beach. Our newly constructed ranch home on a canal of the Isle of Palms would be our home base for the next 15 years. In the Isle of Palms, the Autrey family enjoyed their new pool and fished from the floating dock, catching mullet by the bucketful.

We made new friends and enjoyed life at the beach. I learned to body-surf the ocean waves while my mother dutifully watched from shore. One Saturday morning as I was swimming through the waves next to the Jacksonville Beach Pier, I saw another young fellow with only his head above water. He was caught in a rip current that was dragging him slowly into deeper water. I could see the terrified look on his face. On shore, my mother could see the situation developing and knew I was contemplating a move that might well drown both the other boy and me. She ran from her beach lounger to the shore, yelling, "No, no, don't do it!" I was faced with a life-changing dilemma. As a good swimmer, I might have saved him. I also knew that his larger size and frantic condition could have led us both to our death. Before I had to make the final decision, the volunteer lifeguards had entered the water with their life-saving buoy dragging behind them as they swam to the drowning boy. I would always remember that incident. Life-and-death decisions leave a scar on your psyche.

I'm not sure if one's IQ is fixed at birth or if it develops along with the collection of life experiences. I do know that in the summer of my 11th year, mine was at an all-time low. I had recently had the surgical removal of a benign fatty tumor removed from my right shinbone. The incision was deep and cut into the bone. At the time, I was addicted to surfing. My childhood friend Archie and I built rickshaws out of wood and old wagon wheels—not the wagon wheels of the Wild West. They were small, hard rubber wheels taken from our little red childhood wagons. We strapped our surfboards to the contraptions and towed them behind our bicycles.

Rather than wait for the surgical leg wound to heal, I bandaged it and pedaled to Atlantic Beach and proceeded to surf the waves in a Seminole Beach surfing contest. As a normal-thinking person would expect, the motions and activity caused a breach in the wound's stitching, and blood flowed freely into the ocean surrounding my surfboard. I caught the next wave with the intention of heading safely into shore. As I glided the face of the wave, I could clearly see the outline of a shark swimming alongside my board and the streaming flow of blood running into the water. The shark was not more than six feet in length, but it could have inflicted serious trauma to my bloody leg. While probably not a near-death experience, it affirmed without debate that sharks are indeed attracted to blood.

By my 13th birthday my intelligence quotient had risen significantly, but apparently not quite to the level of normal cognition. My friend Eddie, from Fletcher Junior High School, showed me new depths of stupidity that were both reckless and illegal. We did some things which could be considered normal delinquency, but also recklessly pushed into a new level of juvenile criminality.

We skipped school to go surfing. Our surfboards were hidden in the shrubs on a wooded lot near the ocean. We were always back in time to catch the bus home. Eddie showed me how to pencil in the back side of a paper bearing my mother's signature. I could then trace the signature with the paper placed over a forged note excusing me from school for an illness or doctor's appointment. The transferred leaded signature was a perfect match, but Eddie and I were eventually caught when the school called my mother to inquire about my illness.

Skipping school was just an introduction. Eddie had more serious offenses planned for his newly acquired and mentally deficient friend. At the age of 13 I did not smoke cigarettes or drink alcoholic beverages. Eddie was one year older than me and more experienced in truancy and delinquent behavior. We drove our bicycles to Jacksonville Beach, Neptune Beach, and Atlantic and Seminole beaches, as far as 15 miles from my house.

One day in the lunar cycle of the lowest possible brain function, Eddie introduced me to smoking cigarettes while hiding under an elevated and overturned boat in his neighbor's yard. With the equivalent of a phrase like "Hold my beer," Eddie said to go with him. We ran to a parking lot surrounding a small independent liquor store on Third Street. As the car in the drive-through-window lane exited and the bartender and cashier turned their backs, Eddie reached in and grabbed a fifth of J&B Scotch. He ran, and I ran behind him as fast as I could. I ran, knowing I would never hear the shotgun blast that could end my short life.

The Vietnam War

Vietnam's history goes back 20,000 years. A book covering just the last 1,000 years would need to be 10,000 pages long. The country was under the name Dai Viet in the Golden Age, spanning AD 900 to AD 1500. Dozens of dynasties controlled or fought to control the region. As Europe moved toward capitalism, Dai Viet's evolution was impeded by a failing and weak Confucian ideology locking the feudal regimes into civil wars through the 16th century. The French began the colonization of Vietnam in the 19th century. Their attempts to bring about Western-style reforms were continuously rejected by the Nguyen dynasty and ultimately failed. One significant event was the establishment of the Communist Party of Vietnam in February of 1930. Another notable milestone, in 1945, was the takeover of the Democratic Republic of Vietnam by Communist Party leader Ho Chi Minh. Occurring in the first half of 1954, the Battle of Dien Bien Phu brought an end to Vietnam's conflicts with French colonists.

At the Geneva Conference in 1954, the country of Vietnam was divided at the 17th parallel by the Geneva Accords. The Geneva Conference that year was attended by Cambodia, China, France, Laos, the United Kingdom, the United States, the Soviet Union, and North and South Vietnam. The nonbinding treaty and declarations set forth a ceasefire and withdrawal plan for the forces from the north and the south. The cease-fire line at the 17th parallel divided the north and south regions of Vietnam. The temporary division was to last 300 days to facilitate the withdrawal of forces on each side. The division was not meant to be a permanent geographic or political boundary. Despite the Accord's formal declarations and provisions for a unifying Vietnamese election, the country would spend the next three decades fighting—not for unification, but for dominance by North Vietnam.

Back in the United States, the Korean War was still fresh in the mind of President Dwight Eisenhower. The French were appealing to the US for air support in Dien Bien Phu, but Eisenhower remained reluctant to get involved in the Indochina conflict. Americans wanted no more to do with wars like the Korean conflict. The official position of the United States was to support the dividing partition set forth in the Geneva Accords, as a way to contain the Communist forces and divide the country into North Vietnam and South Vietnam. President Ho Chi Minh led the Communist regime in the north, and the unifying national elections planned for 1956 never occurred. The framework for the Vietnam War that would follow was firmly in place.

The Communist government of Ho Chi Minh's Democratic Republic of Vietnam was entrenched in Hanoi. The Republic of Vietnam, led by Ngo Dinh Diem, was supported by the United States and positioned in the capital city of Hanoi. The divergent ideologies of the north and south can be distilled to a battle for the north's centralized bureaucratic control versus a more distributed, personalized form of governance in the south. In 1963, Ngo Dinh Diem was killed and his government was overthrown by General Duong Van Minh. Only three months later, General Minh was deposed in a coup led by General Nguyen Khanh. After one year in power in South Vietnam, the despised General Khanh was deposed and forced into exile.

The United States was intertwined into the upheavals in South Vietnam. American civilian and military leaders, including the Pentagon and US Commanding General Paul Harkins, thought highly of General Khanh, but were opposed to the overthrow of Diem. The State Department and US Ambassador Henry Cabot Lodge were in favor of the coup overthrowing Ngo Dinh Diem. As a result of the conflict, Secretary of Defense Robert McNamara saw our US Command in Vietnam as a weakness, with poor leadership. Ambassador Lodge and President Johnson also had their differences in the assessment of the situation in Vietnam. Johnson was seeking reelection as the US president, and Lodge was seen as the front-runner for the presidency in the Republican Party.

The turmoil in the management of the US support effort in Vietnam and the upheavals in leadership in South Korea are far more complex and impactful than this summary represents. The discouraging aspect of the prewar diplomacy and planning is that conflicting political beliefs and opposing strategies ultimately became the catalyst for escalating military actions, enormous human suffering, and economic losses. The disparate civilian-driven military strategies would carry through the 10-year war and three US presidencies with poorly defined and inconsistent objectives. The cost was measured in billions of dollars and the lives of 58,281 American warriors. In addition, more than 300,000 US military personnel were wounded in battle.

In 1964, with 21,000 US military advisors in Vietnam, US aircraft carriers *Ticonderoga* and USS *Constellation* bombed North Vietnam in retaliation for attacks on US destroyers in the Gulf of Tonkin. This was an official start to a war that would continue 12 more years, to 1975. The following year was a pivotal point in the Vietnam War. In March of 1965, the first 3,500 US Marines were dispatched to Da Nang. By July, the troop levels were increased to 120,000. Following the first major Battle of Ia Drang, in November, President Lyndon Johnson announced that the number of American troops in Vietnam would ultimately be increased to 400,000. In December of 1964, in a significant step that escalated and intensified the conflict, the Soviet Union began supplying rockets to the North Vietnamese.

Meanwhile, at home, what started as a few thousand protesters marching against the war, had grown to hundreds of thousands across the country. In contrast, an October pro Vietnam War march in DC attracted 25,000 people. The country was philosophically and politically split over the Vietnam War. The number of young men being drafted into the US Armed Forces increased to 25,000 per month. Small numbers of draft dodgers publicly burned their draft cards in protest and others escaped the draft by moving to Canada. South Vietnam was not without protests: 20,000 Buddhists marched in protest of the Vietnamese government's military policies.

As the US began bombing the North Vietnamese cities of Hanoi and Haiphong, the Warsaw Pact, consisting of seven Eastern Bloc countries, declared their promise to support North Vietnam. In October of 1967, 70,000 war protestors gathered at the Lincoln Memorial, with 50,000 marching on to the Pentagon. As the battles in Vietnam raged on with heavy casualties on both sides, President Johnson futilely looked for ways to build support for the war.

Two months prior to the major setbacks that would come from the Viet Cong's Tet Offensive of 1968, US Army General William Westmoreland assured the public that we were winning the war. In a coordinated offensive, the North

Vietnamese attacked 100 cities and outposts in South Vietnam. The two-month Tet Offensive was over in February of 1968, after the North Vietnamese captured the city of Hue, in central Vietnam, at the border between the north and south. It was the longest and bloodiest battle of the war. In the Tet attacks, 4,000 US soldiers were killed and 45,000 were wounded. The North Vietnamese saw a 60 percent casualty rate in the conflict. With 485,000 troops stationed in Vietnam in 1968, total US deaths in the war exceeded 20,000. In October, only weeks after ordering 24,000 American troops back to Vietnam for second tours, President Johnson announced that the bombing campaign in North Vietnam would cease and that progress was being made in the Paris peace talks.

That same year, approximately 500 unarmed villagers were killed by US soldiers in the hamlet of My Lai. That tragic black mark in our history is indexed by the name Lieutenant William Calley. He was later found guilty of leading and ordering the massacre, and served 42 months under house arrest. Other officers, including high-ranking officers, were charged; Calley was the only one ultimately incarcerated.

On March 16 in 1968, the US Army's 11th Infantry Brigade ordered Charlie Company to search and destroy the Viet Cong guerrillas who had reportedly occupied a small village in the Quang Ngai Province. Charlie Company had been engaged in combat throughout the Tet Offensive that had ended a month earlier. Twenty-eight C Company soldiers had been killed or injured in the Tet battles, reducing their forces to 100 men. When they arrived at the village, they found no Viet Cong forces. The village was quiet and inhabited by women, children, and old men. After finding no significant caches of weapons, Lieutenant Calley ordered his men to shoot the villagers.

Between the hours of 7:00 a.m. and 11:00 a.m., Lieutenant William Calley and his platoon killed more than 350 noncombatants—men, women, and children. News sources reported the deaths to include 182 women, 117 children, and 56 infants. The soldiers slaughtered livestock, molested women, and burned the village huts. Occupants fleeing their thatched homes were shot. The American forces received no return gunfire. The expanded details of the massacre are detailed and gruesome, and too difficult to summarize.

If there is a positive aspect of the event, it rests with the actions of Army Warrant Officer Hugh Thompson Jr. He was on a reconnaissance mission in his Scout helicopter, accompanied by two gunship choppers. In Thompson's airborne surveillance of the village, he and his crew saw large numbers of bodies. Dead civilians were piled in ditches. They witnessed US infantrymen shooting women and children and executing the wounded victims. In his words, "We kept flying back and forth … and it didn't take long until we started noticing the large number of bodies everywhere … these were infants, two-, three-, four-, five-year-olds, women, very old men, no draft age whatsoever."

The massacre ended when Thompson landed his helicopter between a group of fleeing civilians and ordered his door gunner to aim the M60 machine gun at the approaching US Army soldiers and to open fire if they attempted to harm the fleeing villagers. Thompson directed the gunships to land and begin evacuating the civilians. His heroic actions went largely unrecognized, in part because there were fewer than a dozen evacuated civilians, and because of the enormity of the massacre and the efforts to cover it up higher in the chain of command.

In 1970, the war in Vietnam raged on. South Vietnamese leaders implored the United States to continue their support with munitions, training, and US soldiers. US troop levels were more than 335,000, and 6,173 US warriors died in ongoing combat.

When President Richard Nixon was inaugurated in January of 1969, his initial evaluation of the war left our strategy relatively unchanged, and our US forces continued to rise, peaking at 549,000 in May of 1969. In what sounds like a movie title, the Battle of Hamburger Hill, in May of 1969, had substantial impact back home. The news of the fruitless bloody battle was a watershed moment for the US military and political leaders, the American public, and hundreds of thousands of war protestors.

By itself, Hamburger Hill had very little to no strategic value. The general plan for what was named Operation Apache Snow was for five battalions to clear the enemy in the larger, remote A Shau valley, by engaging the North Vietnamese Army (NVA) and cutting off their supply routes to South Vietnam. The hill, now known as Hamburger Hill, is marked on military maps as Hill 937, accurately reflecting its elevation in meters. It was part of the valley's terrain and heavily fortified by NVA forces. The terrain and the fortified enemy bunkers had sustained little damage in the pre-assault bombing and napalm raids.

Three airborne infantry battalions from the 101st Airborne Division were assigned to the operation to clear the valley and take the hills. Marine forces along with the 3rd Squadron of the 5th Army Cavalry were assigned and ordered to provide reconnaissance and block the enemy's escape routes into Laos. The 3/5 Cavalry is a historically heralded force originating in 1861, known as the Black Knights.

The NVA repelled multiple assaults on both sides of Hill 937 and suffered heavy casualties. The 3,074-foot elevation of Hamburger Hill (937) was surrounded by rugged jungle canopies and bamboo thickets. The NVA also occupied nearby Hills 900 and 916, giving them a significant strategic advantage over the tactical movements of the American forces. After sustaining hundreds of casualties and the loss of experienced company commanders and platoon leaders, the US Army's commanding general of the 101st Airborne Division, Melvin Zais, considered calling off the operation. Marine Corps and US Army commanders convinced him to continue the attacks and he called in three replacement battalions.

The American and South Vietnamese forces prevailed in their mission in the A Shau valley. On May 20, 1969, between 10:00 a.m. and 3:00 p.m., the US Army crested Hamburger Hill 937 and destroyed the enemy bunkers. During the 10-day battle, after barrages from 10 batteries of artillery and 272 Air Force missions dropping 500 tons of bombs, 72 US soldiers were dead and 372 more were wounded. Two weeks later, on June 5, 1969, the US military silently abandoned Hill 937.

The Battle of Hamburger Hill brought about a change in US strategy in South Vietnam. The military policy of maximum pressure was simply too costly in terms of American lives being lost. The commanding generals shifted to a more defensive policy of "protective reaction." Following the controversial battle, President Richard Nixon announced the first withdrawal of American troops from Vietnam. Later that year, on November 3, 1970, in a televised evening broadcast, President Nixon outlined his plans to end the United States' participation in the war. His plan would be to favor the desires of the American people, while protecting the image of America and not frame the withdrawal as a defeat. History has not complied with his vision of victorious withdrawal.

In 1970, the conscription lottery for the military draft was in full force. In 1967, President Lyndon Johnson had signed into law a bill granting 2-S deferments from the military draft for students enrolled in university studies. In 1970, President Nixon announced that new legislation would be introduced that would end deferments for students. The law was implemented the following year. This action, coupled with news of an escalation in the Vietnam War with incursions into Cambodia, sparked a new wave of war protests.

On May 1 at Kent State University in Kent, Ohio, students held an anti-war protest that included attacks on police with rocks and bottles. The protesters broke windows and looted nearby stores. The next day, the mayor of Kent declared an emergency and requested the governor to provide National Guard troops to secure the city. When the Guardsmen arrived that evening, they found the university's ROTC building on fire. Cheering protesters harassed the firefighters as the building burned. The crowd was dispersed by the Guardsmen using tear gas.

On day three, amid rising tensions, 1,000 National Guard troops were deployed on the Kent State campus. Classes resumed, but more protests were planned for the next day. The school intervened and attempted to stop the planned protests. On May 4, the following day, students and nonstudents gathered and confronted the Guardsmen. A platoon of 29 armed members of the National Guard were surrounded and feared for their lives when they opened fire on the protestors. Nine students were injured and four others were killed in the barrage of rifle fire.

After a decade of conflict and the death of 58,281 Americans killed in action, the US military left Vietnam. From 1954 to 1975, the South Vietnamese suffered longer and in greater numbers, with the loss of life estimated to be between 700,000 and 1.2 million military and civilian casualties. The totals for North Vietnam approached 1.5 million civilian and military deaths. The total deaths in the Vietnam War from 1954 to 1975, including both sides and from all countries involved, military and civilian, lies somewhere between 2.5 and 3.5 million lost souls. The Paris Peace Accords in January of 1973 ended the fighting and restored a tentative state of peace in Vietnam. In April of 1975, 7,000 Americans and South Vietnamese were evacuated and the South Vietnamese government officially surrendered to North Vietnam. A new all-time low was set for human evolvement, but unification of North and South Vietnam was finally achieved.

Near-Death at Sea

In 1968, life in the Isle of Palms was active and sporting. Surfing, fishing, and hunting were regular activities. We regularly mowed the high grass in the wide easement on the south side of Beach Boulevard. It was a baseball diamond in the spring and a football field in the fall. There were enough kids in the neighborhood to field two opposing teams at any time. I used the grass clippings from the mowing to stuff landing bags for a high jump and pole-vaulting pit in the outfield. Several years later, that sport turned out to be my ticket to Western Carolina University.

My dad always had boats. In the beginning we had a wooden skiff that I rowed with two oars. The next boat would be a fiberglass 14-foot boat, with a nine-horsepower outboard engine. That vessel took me to the St. Johns River jetties and the Atlantic Ocean. A few years later, with the arrival of a new 19-foot fiberglass bowrider and a huge 115-horsepower Evinrude engine, the ocean was mine to explore.

My friend Buz Livingston and I fished after school and on weekends for sheepshead, trout, and redfish, in the Intracoastal Waterway and the St. Johns River. In the ocean we caught cobia, kingfish, bonito, tarpon, jacks, and sharks. My mother would not allow me to take the boat into the ocean alone.

One Saturday morning I talked my younger brother Tom into a trip to the jetties to catch tarpon and kingfish. It was a blustery yet tolerable day, with three- to four-foot seas and a northeast wind.

The fish started biting immediately. Through the day we caught kingfish, jacks, and cobia. In the afternoon as we were preparing to head home, Tom hooked something very big. The line screamed from the heavy reel. I thought something as powerful as this must be a large shark. After a half hour had passed, we could see the large hammerhead shark in the waves as they rose beyond the boat. Tom pumped and reeled for another 30 minutes and got the shark alongside the boat. It was at least 10 feet in length and perhaps 300 pounds. We tail-roped and wrestled with the shark and managed to cut the steel leader, releasing the great hammerhead shark. He swam ominously away from our little boat.

We were now more than an hour late for the return trip home. I secured the fishing tackle and started cranking the engine. It turned over and over but would not start. The sun was getting low in the western sky above the shoreline, six miles away. I cranked and cranked the engine, but it would not start. After the battery became too weak to turn the starter, I removed the engine cowling and tried the manual pull rope. The engine was too large, and we could not manually start the 115-horsepower Evinrude outboard by hand-pulling the flywheel with the short crank rope.

Handheld VHF radios and cellular telephones had not been invented in 1969. The 19-foot bowrider was primarily designed for rivers and lakes and water skiing. We had handheld flares, but the striking surfaces were wet and did not ignite the flares. I put the boat's anchor out with all the line that we had. In 40 feet of depth, the 100-foot anchor line did not have enough rope to securely anchor the boat. It held for a time and broke free, and the outgoing tide from the ocean inlet and the northerly ocean current slowly dragged the boat farther out to sea.

Mayport and the St. Johns River jetties are on the northeast side of Jacksonville. Airplanes took off from the Jacksonville Airport and flew over the ocean in northerly and southerly routes. The sun was just above the horizon and daylight was slipping toward dusk. While not yet frantic, I was becoming very concerned. I knew my mother had expected us to be home two hours earlier. She would be both angry and terrified that we were not safe.

As I hopefully predicted, a small jetliner appeared in the western sky and its route brought it directly over our position. The plane's altitude was high, but low enough that I thought they could spot us. Tom frantically waved the bright orange life vest over his head in a manner that conveyed our distress. I grabbed the portable fire extinguisher and pressed out three blasts of the white fire retardant in an abbreviated SOS Morse code sequence: a short blast followed by a long one, then a short one—short, long, short—short, long, short—short, long, short. The jetliner flew over our heads and was quickly soaring to the south and away from our view. Then I saw it. The plane dipped its wings, rocking left and right as it disappeared in the cloudy sky.

I knew we'd be rescued. I did not know when or how, but I knew the US Coast Guard was based in Mayport and they would be contacted by the airline's pilots. They'd dispatch a boat to save us. I also knew that my mother and father had very likely already called the Coast Guard about our delayed return. Standard procedure in a vessel-in-distress situation is for the Coast Guard to put out a radio message to other boats and ships in the area to be on the lookout for the distressed vessel. The response to the radio message came quickly. A 700-foot steel-hulled freighter was cruising from the Port of Jacksonville and heading northeast in a route that would take it directly to our position. The ship was high in the water and making good time with its empty holds. As it approached from a quarter of a mile away, the draft and wake of the moving ship pulled us off our anchored position and we drifted toward the big ship.

As we approached the ship's side, about midway down its length, we were waving frantically. The noise of the sea and the ship's engines drowned out our voices. The ship's crew was foreign and did not speak English. The ship had not come to a full stop, and we continued to slide along the steel sides of the ship toward the stern. One hundred feet away I could see and hear the large slow-turning propeller as each blade cut the water.

The propeller—or screw, as it is called on large ships—is guarded by large flat steel platforms on each side of the spinning shaft and propeller. The lightly loaded ship was high enough in the water that they were exposed just above the waterline. I had previously tethered my brother Tom to the boat to prevent him from being washed overboard in the rough seas. I yelled to him to untie his line and that we would now have to jump from the boat to the exposed steel platforms or be crushed by the still turning propeller. The churning water surrounding a spinning screw is like a waterfall. The circulating forces would suck us under the water to certain death by drowning and blunt force trauma.

The ship's crew realized our predicament and acted quickly by lowering a very large mooring rope to our boat. The three-inch-diameter line was too large to make simple knots. I looped it through the bow rails of the 19-foot bowrider ski boat. Just as the large screw finally stopped turning, our small boat jerked forward just 30 feet from what would have been our stairway to heaven. The big ship slowly turned back toward Jacksonville, and we rode the pitch and yaw of the waves alongside the steel hull. I will always remember the reverberating sound of the engines through the steel hull, and the *crush, crush, crush* sound of the propeller cutting the water with each revolution.

It was dark as we approached the St. Johns River sea buoy position four miles from shore. We were met by a Coast Guard boat with four crew members. They illuminated the area with a large spotlight. It was too rough for the smaller RIBs (rigid inflatable boats), so a larger 50-foot cutter-type boat had been dispatched for our rescue. As I removed the large line from the bow rail of our boat, I tied a smaller rope to the large line and stringered two large kingfish on the smaller line. The fish and the line were hoisted to the freighter's deck and several smiling crew members. We drifted away from the freighter and the deck crew of the Coast Guard cutter secured our boat for a one-hour tow back to the boat ramp in Mayport. We arrived after 11:00 p.m., and my dad and mom were waiting with flashlights and relieved but weary faces.

MCMLXIX (1969)

Except for the horrendous ongoing war in Vietnam, 1969 was unremarkable if you are looking for world wars or other international upheavals. However, peering with a finer lens, you'll find it packed with significant daily events that changed the shape of the world: deaths and murders, rocket launches, elections, assassinations, and new music hits topped the list.

The Soviets launched a probe to Venus in January, and it successfully landed on the planet's surface in May. A second, sister probe arrived the next day, only to be crushed by Venus' atmospheric pressure. Not to be outdone by the Soviets, the US *Mariner 7* probe flew by Mars, and the Apollo's *Eagle* spaceship landed on the Moon's surface, where American astronaut Neil Armstrong took the first historic steps for mankind.

Richard Nixon was sworn in as the 37th president of the United States, and, two days later, Soviet leader Leonid Brezhnev survived an unsuccessful assassination attempt by a disgruntled deserter. Two months following the execution of nine Israeli spies in Baghdad, Golda Meir became the first female prime minister in Israel. Meanwhile in Cairo, Yasser Arafat was elected to lead the Palestine Liberation Organization (PLO). The list of events in 1969 is densely packed. Former President

Dwight Eisenhower died in March, Charles de Gaulle took office in April, and Zakir Husain died in India.

On the domestic front, Mary Jo Kopechne tragically drowned in a Chappaquiddick pond while Ted Kennedy fled the scene. After marrying Yoko Ono, John Lennon recorded the song "Give Peace a Chance." This timely release was followed by 300 students taking over Harvard University's administration building; 184 students were arrested. In Chicago, the National Guard was deployed to control the Days of Rage demonstrations by the radical militant Weathermen organization. In a more deadly and gruesome event, the "Manson Family" killed Sharon Tate and her unborn child, and four others.

On the brighter side of life in America, 1969 brought us the opening of the first Walmart, along with Wendy's, Fish and Chips, Long John Silver's, and Captain D's eateries. Elvis Presley was in Memphis to record "Kentucky Rain," "In the Ghetto," and "Suspicious Minds." The Beatles finished their North American tour on the rooftop of Apple Records, with a live recording of "Let It Be." In the literary world, Mario Puzo published the novel titled *The Godfather*.

In the same year as the first Boeing 747 flight, the United States Defense Department created the Advanced Research Projects Agency Network (ARPANET), and successfully demonstrated a packet-switched network of interconnected computers that allowed emails, file transfers, and remote login. Initially under government control, in 1981 the National Science Foundation and the Computer Science Network interconnected supercomputers at several universities. By 1990, the government-run ARPANET was decommissioned, and the private sector's telecommunications industry took over the commercialization of what became a worldwide network.

The Wingmaster Incident

B ack in the Isle of Palms, life was calm, but not without incidents! My older sister graduated from Fletcher High School and ran away to North Carolina with her piano teacher. As you'd expect, that trip was short and did not end well. At the time, I was deeply in love with the junior high school principal's daughter. That tumultuous relationship lasted three years and also lacked a happy ending. For the most part, life was typical for this healthy, working, and upwardly mobile middle-class American family.

We celebrated life with regular family dinners and weekly television viewing of National Geographic's *Wild Kingdom*, *The Andy Griffith Show*, *Bonanza*, *Gunsmoke*, and *The Rifleman*. Holidays were festive, celebrated with food, laughter, and Dad playing his guitar and belting out Johnny Cash songs. On big holidays like the Fourth of July and New Year's Eve, at the stroke of midnight we'd fire off a few rounds into the night sky from my dad's 16-gauge, double-barrel Stevens Savage shotgun.

My dad made a swap with our grandad Roy White and traded our 14-foot outboard-powered fiberglass skiff for a 12-gauge Remington Wingmaster pump-action shotgun and a .22 caliber semiautomatic rifle. One afternoon during a summer school break, I removed the Wingmaster from a gun cabinet in our den and was showing it to my younger sister. Whether she dared me, or I was just showing off, is not significant to the outcome.

I opened the top half of the French-style door leading out to the pool. I had a clear view to the large uninhabited sandlot across the canal from our house. The shotgun held three rounds which could be fired successively with the pump action of the gun. I fired two very loud blasts through the open door and over the canal to the empty lot. (See "diminished IQ" in previous chapters.) My sister wanted to shoot the gun. I saw no harm in it and secretly knew that the recoil of the gun would cause her some unexpected surprise and pain.

I chambered the third round and eased the safety to the off position. I carefully handed the gun to my sister and positioned it against her shoulder, with the barrel pointed through the opened door. Instead of pulling the trigger and firing the gun, she took a step backward and turned her body and the shotgun barrel toward my face. Two feet away from my forehead was what could have been the instrument of my destiny and instant death. Her finger was on the trigger and she was smiling. It was not an evil act. She was trying to be funny. We had a normal and playful sibling relationship.

My sister had never fired a gun before, and I knew she had no knowledge of the miniscule amount of pull required to discharge the weapon. I also didn't want any sudden movement on my part to startle her. I moved slowly while pleading with her to raise the barrel away from my head. At what may have been mere luck in timing, I grabbed the barrel and placed my finger behind the trigger, preventing it from inadvertently firing. I twisted the shotgun from her hands. It would be many years before we fully understood and talked about the danger that incident had presented both of us that day. We still don't dwell on the details of what was the result of my poor judgment, and we have since remained very close.

The '70s

The '70s continued our global human evolution, punctuated with steady and unwarranted deaths around the globe. Drug overdoses took the lives of 27-year-old Jimi Henricks and Janis Joplin. A Buenos Aires rail disaster killed 236 passengers and crew. From 1970 to 1972, five commercial airline crashes killed more than 500 people. The Tutsi-dominated army in Burundi committed genocide against the Hutus, killing more than 150,000. Some estimates placed the number at more than 300,000. A nightclub fire in Osaka, Japan, killed 115 patrons. The list seems endless, and what is represented here is a mere sampling of the souls lost in the early '70s. Wars and other massacres around the world increased the death toll immeasurably.

The political scene is marred by the Watergate scandal. President Nixon and chief of staff H. R. Haldeman were caught on tape with damning evidence of the cover-up of the break-in at the headquarters of the Democratic National Committee, located in Washington, DC, in the Watergate Office Building. Avoiding impeachment in 1974, Nixon became the first US president to resign from office. Later that same year, his successor, Gerald Ford, granted Nixon a full and unconditional pardon.

The war in Vietnam escalated again when President Nixon ordered the mining of harbors and increased bombing in Hanoi and Haiphong. Meanwhile, at home, 100,000 protesters marched on Washington, protesting the escalation. In July of 1972, actress Jane Fonda made the headlines and added to the war's scars when she toured North Vietnam and was photographed sitting on a North Vietnamese antiaircraft gun.

The global death spiral continued at the 1972 Summer Olympics in Munich, where 11 Israeli athletes were murdered by members of the Arab terrorist group Black September. The murderous act may have been retaliation for the bombing of a primary school in the Egyptian village of Bahr el-Baqar. Forty-six children were killed and the school was demolished. To close out 1972 and to put life and death into an even broader and desperate perspective, in December, 11,000 people perished in a Nicaraguan earthquake in the capital city of Managua.

On the upside, the year provided the first opportunity for women to compete in the Boston Marathon. President Nixon signed a bill ending the military draft and vowed to send no more draftees to the Vietnam War. Technology took a leap forward with the introduction of the first scientific handheld calculator, offered as the HP-35 for $395. The Nixon administration ordered the development of the Space Shuttle program, the Apollo 17 mission landing on the Moon, and *Pioneer 10* became the first spacecraft to successfully travel beyond our solar system. Back on Earth, the first Popeye's Fried Chicken restaurant opened in New Orleans.

Where Is the Body?

In the fall of 1971, I was driving my brand-new Ford Pinto from Jacksonville Beach to Cullowhee, North Carolina, to begin my sophomore year at Western Carolina University. The car was comfortable and fully equipped with air conditioning, automatic transmission, and cassette tape player. While driving, I sang along with Grand Funk Railroad, Johnny Cash, and Peter, Paul and Mary.

About seven hours into the trip and as I entered the foothills of the Great Smoky Mountains of North Carolina, I had the good sense and prescient urging to fasten my seat belt and shoulder harness. I cinched it tight for no apparent reason. I continued along the highways that made up the well-established route known as the Woodpecker Trail. There were no other cars on the rural roads in the southern approach to Franklin, North Carolina. The rolling hills provided a smooth track for my speedy little car as I cruised along at 90 miles per hour. (See "diminished IQ" in previous chapters.)

It was dark. My headlights casting dim light on the road's surface were the only illumination. Up and over the foothills I drove, and while speeding down the long backside of a hill, my windshield was instantly filled with the image of a large, dark rear end of a Buick four-door sedan. No lights were illuminated inside or outside the car. I later found out that the car had stalled and the driver had turned the lights off to conserve the battery while he tried to restart the engine. He had been drinking and stepped out of the car to enjoy a cigarette.

I struck the stalled car with the force of a 2,370-pound steel-and-plastic projectile traveling at 117 feet per second (80 miles per hour). My seat ripped from the floor of the car, and I flew, attached to the seat, up and over the steering wheel and into the windshield. The impact had compressed the front end of the car so severely that the windshield was already shattered as my head approached the point of impact. The compression of the impact folded the driver and passenger doors into wedged shapes. The other car was launched 100 yards down the dark road.

A family living downhill from the impact heard the crash and came to investigate. The first man to approach asked if I could speak and told me the doors were jammed. He also said that fuel was leaking and we needed to act quickly. By then, another car had approached and the driver supplied a lug wrench that was used to pry open the sharply folded driver-side door. My body was curled into a fetal position over what was previously the steering wheel. The two men wrestled me out of the car. I was able to stand and, miraculously, was not seriously injured. I was not bleeding significantly and was fully conscious and aware of my surroundings. When the police and ambulance arrived, the police officer walked up to me as I leaned against the ambulance, and asked, "Where is the body?"

The gentleman who first found me was a local Baptist preacher. After some time in the ambulance where I was checked out for possible head trauma, I declined to be transported to the nearest hospital. (See "diminished IQ" in previous chapters.) The local minister offered to drive me to Cullowhee and the Western Carolina campus located one hour away. We arrived at Jacobs Hall on the hill above the campus at about 10:00 p.m. I thanked the man and offered him money for gas, and he declined. I called my mother and father and shared the news of the harrowing event. My mother insisted I go to the school clinic and stay for observation. While I did not consider that necessary, I complied and visited the clinic, where I rested on a gurney for a couple of hours before returning to my dormitory room. I was okay, and my once new 1971 blue Ford Pinto was totaled and never seen again.

1973

Like most years, the days are packed with life-changing events. In 1973, the renowned artist Pablo Picasso died. His iconic paintings will be exhibited and esteemed around the world for many years to come. Human sociological changes that were notable included an assessment by the American Medical Association that homosexuality would no longer be considered a mental disease. On a less notable front, boxer George Foreman knocked out Joe Frazier in the second round to win the WBC and WBA heavyweight championship titles. The top story in the category of longest-lasting and consequential changes was produced by the United States Supreme Court. The Roe v. Wade decision overturned all state bans on abortions. A close second was the introduction of the first portable cellular phone.

To demonstrate how opinions and judgments change over time, consider that in March of 1973, Paul and Linda McCartney were cited and fined £100 for growing cannabis. Meanwhile, John Lennon and Yoko Ono formed their own micro-nation named Nutopia. News of this sort was introduced in the newly established "CBS Radio News on the Hour" report. It was the beginning of 7 x 24-hour news programs.

On the political front, the Shah of Iran, Mohammad Reza Pahlavi, nationalized all Iranian oil assets. This change had long-lasting economic effects in the region and in the United States. His 53-year imperial dynasty amassed a fortune estimated to be more than $20 billion. Not to be outdone, Ferdinand Marcos was named the 10th president of the Philippines. He declared his term to be for life. He was deposed after 20 years of corrupt authoritarian rule and exiled to Hawaii with $10 billion of stolen government funds. In the more violent arena of war, the fighting in Vietnam ceased with the signing of the Paris Peace Accords. In February and March of 1973, a total of 531 American prisoners of war were released. More than 1,200 POWs never returned. The war would officially end in 1975 with the memorable rooftop evacuation and the fall of Saigon to the North Vietnamese.

The most tragic dates in 1973 were the span of 20 days, from October 6 to the 25th. The Ramadan War, better known as the Yom Kippur War, once again demonstrated the lethality of armed conflict. The war brought to the forefront the horrific capacity of human beings to inflict immoral and inconceivably evil torture to fellow members of our modern society.

As it was in the past and would be in the years ahead, the October war was about land—the Sinai Peninsula. Anwar Sadat, the president of Egypt, wanted the Sinai returned to Arab control. In the 21-day battle over sand, Israel lost 2,800 soldiers and suffered 8,800 wounded. Much higher than Israel's casualties, Egypt and Syria lost a total of 16,000 lives, with 18,000 more wounded. History provides a range of numbers for this conflict, but given the short three-week duration, it was a tragic setback for the karmic humanity of mankind. The enormity of the conflict can be indexed by lives lost and fighting equipment that was destroyed. One thousand Israeli tanks were destroyed or damaged, along with 102 airplanes. The Arabs lost 2,300 tanks and more than 500 airplanes.

The inhumanity of man was at a peak in this war. The Syrians ripped off fingernails and burned prisoners with cigarettes. Beatings, electric shocks, and the targeted wounding of body parts like the ears and legs were common. Syrian soldiers were rewarded for killing Israelis. One Syrian killed 28 prisoners with an axe and decapitated several of the prisoners. Other Israeli prisoners were simply executed. In a preplanned action described in pamphlets distributed before the war by Egyptian General Shazly, Egyptian soldiers followed Shazly's orders and killed as many as 200 Israeli prisoners. One captured Arab fighter carried a bag of severed Israeli body parts as war souvenirs. For a conglomerate of countries that professed to follow Allah, "The one and only God," the reality of their God's supposed forgiving and merciful nature was lost to the minds of the terrorist warriors.

A notable parameter of the short war was the identification of allies that stepped up to defend each side. While the conflict is identified as a war between Israel and the combined forces of Egypt and Syria, it was the presence of the United States on the side of Israel, and the Soviet Union aligned with the Arab States, that took center stage. The Soviets openly condemned Israel's actions and deployed two destroyers after Israel sank a Soviet merchant ship. They also put seven airborne divisions on alert and deployed 40,000 naval infantrymen to the Mediterranean Sea.

With President Nixon's authorization, Secretary of State Henry Kissinger convened a meeting with White House Chief of Staff Alexander Haig, Defense Secretary James Schlesinger, and CIA Director William Colby. The meeting produced a message that was sent on behalf of President Nixon to Soviet Leader Leonid Brezhnev: "If the Soviets were to intervene, so would the United States." The increase in America's defense posture did not go unnoticed by the Soviets. Presidium Chairman Nikolai Podgorny, KGB Chief Yuri Andropov, and Soviet Premier Alexei Kosygin all agreed that a third world war was not a reasonable response to the causes sought by Egypt and Syria.

The commitment and resolve of the United States and the Soviet Union were parked in the Mediterranean Sea, with 97 Soviet ships and 23 nuclear-capable submarines. All of these were in hostile positions against the United States' Sixth Fleet, with its 60 ships, three aircraft carriers, two helicopter carriers, and nine submarines. This would be recorded as the largest naval standoff in the Cold War. The ships ultimately disengaged after a cease-fire was successfully negotiated in the Arab-Israeli War. The Soviets and Americans were not alone. On the sidelines of the Yom Kippur War, Algeria, Cuba, East Germany, North Korea, Pakistan, Saudi Arabia, Libya, and five other countries in the region sent troops to support Egypt and Syria.

Sigma Nu's Stetson

After my sophomore year at Western Carolina University, I successfully fooled myself into thinking I possessed an intellect that commanded the attention of more worthy educational institutions. I gave up my prestigious and parentally appreciated pole-vaulting track team scholarship and transferred to Stetson University in DeLand, Florida.

Stetson was a small Baptist school with 3,000 undergraduate students. The Baptist influence was waning, but still required first-year women to be inside their locked dormitories by 10:00 p.m. on weekdays and 11:00 p.m. on weekends. Chapel attendance on Wednesday mornings was mandatory. This was an incongruous mix of social mores in the world of fraternal life at the university. Certainly, the drinking and dancing habits of the students did not comply with the loosely guarded standards of the historically religious campus community.

Several significant events changed the direction of my life in the fall of 1973. First and foremost was the predictable breakup of my high school romance with the junior high school principal's daughter. Our plan was to continue our pre-med school education at the University of Florida, and lustfully cohabitate at my parents' lake house in the nearby city of Keystone Heights. Under her parents' wise influence, she went to Mercer University in Macon, Georgia, and studied nursing. The enormous class sizes at the University of Florida were unappealing to me and I opted for a transfer from Western Carolina to Stetson University. The breakup was emotional trauma for me, and it simultaneously kicked off my singing and dancing career at the local pub in DeLand, known as the Elbow Lounge. My newfound Sigma Nu fraternity brothers and I drank our way through the fall of my junior year, singing along to Frank Sinatra's "Summer Wind" and Dean Martin's mellow voice, "In the Chapel in the Moonlight."

Debauchery has consequences in the world of academics. It was apparent that I would receive an unsatisfactory grade in Advanced Organic Chemistry and Physical Chemistry 401. So I applied for, and was granted a withdrawal-passing status for the organic chemistry course and a WF (withdrawal from college while failing) status for physical chemistry. Neither course was available in the second semester. This would mean repeating the courses the following year, thereby delaying graduation one full calendar year. This undesirable outcome would require me to confront my parents and admit to my failures.

In the fall conclusion of my junior year at Stetson, I successfully completed the short winter semester in January of 1974, and submitted my senior project titled "Mercury Contamination in Estuarine Shrimp in the Lower St. Johns River." While my grade on the paper was an A, and my competency in the operation of Stetson's National Science Foundation–supplied atomic absorption spectrophotometer was exemplary, the likelihood of gaining admission to any English-speaking medical school was now nonexistent. With my father's approval and a reluctant recommendation from the chair of Stetson's Chemistry Department, I transferred to Florida Technological Institute to pursue a bachelor's degree in electrical engineering. Three weeks into the semester, I became very ill with pneumonia. I missed three weeks of classes, and the lost tutelage in computer science and the physics of materials was not recoverable. I was distraught to the point of being clinically depressed.

Unsure of my next steps, I dodged confrontation and took an unscheduled leave of absence back to Cullowhee, North Carolina, to reassess my options. I secured a job with a large general contracting company that was building a new football stadium for the Western Carolina Catamounts. After reading my impressive résumé that included courses in calculus, chemistry, and two years of German language, the project superintendent assigned me to the gas-operated tamper machine that pounded down the clay and dirt for the rows of stadium seats that were to be poured in successive concrete tiers. My first paycheck paid for my company-issued gloves, earmuffs, and hard hat.

My past relationship with the university's Baptist Student Union and the local Baptist preacher and his family provided me with a private room in a student union dormitory below the chapel. After three weeks of working, I came to realize that this was not my life. I had to face reality and my parents. I phoned my dad's office and found out that he was on a business trip in Charlotte, North Carolina. It was a short drive and I showed up unannounced. I told the desk clerk it was a surprise for my dad. Indeed it was, yet he was happy to see me and made me feel welcome. That important milestone set the tone for what would later become an amazing relationship and the cornerstone for my career in the electrical industry.

The US Army

It was not by chance that I found myself in the Army Recruiting Office in Jacksonville, Florida. A sharp-looking, highly decorated army NCO filled me full of new aspirations of greatness and patriotic duty. Based on my prior college attendance and my superior military entrance examination scores, I'd surely be picked for Officer Candidate School after my initial training. Moreover, with my apparent knowledge of electronics, I'd be assigned to the Army Security Agency for advanced training. This would, as he told me, make me a sure bet for assignment to the State Department and duty at the US Embassy in Washington, DC.

In February of 1974, I thanked my distraught mother, and boarded a chartered bus at the Downtowner Inn in Jacksonville. Other than a school bus, I had never set foot on a bus that wasn't yellow. It was a long, quiet ride to Columbia, South Carolina, and the start of Basic Combat Training in the US Army at Fort Jackson. I would never forget that bus ride. The compilation of past deeds, good and bad, were extinguished by the new world of intrigue and apprehension that I was stepping into.

Fort Jackson today is the largest army training base, with 52,000 acres and more than 1,000 buildings. Half of all soldiers entering the army are processed through Fort Jackson.

My name is inconspicuously missing from the list of notable soldiers that were trained there. The list may surprise some, and included singer Jim Croce, Congressman Jason Crow, *Star Trek*'s Leonard Nimoy, and film producer Geoff Ramsey. The post was created in 1917, at the beginning of World War I. It was later closed and then reopened with the start of World War II. The Korean conflict kept the base open, and it continues its mission today. The base maintains the motto "Victory Starts Here," and trains 35,000 new soldiers each year to keep the ranks of the army filled with new warriors.

My three-month Basic Combat Training began in a typical way, with medical exams and inoculations against diseases I had never heard of. We were instructed how to dress, how to make our bunks, and how to clean and maintain the barracks. The buildings in the early '70s were a vintage design left over from the war years. The white wood-lapped siding and polished wooden floors kept recruits busy painting the siding, waxing and buffing the floors, and scrubbing the 50-year-old tile bathrooms.

Physical training was part of a daily routine that started before breakfast each morning. We would fall out in green fatigues and boots, and work through basic calisthenics and mile-long runs. We trained in platoons, marching to a four-count cadence provided by the drill sergeant, who recited decades-old marching songs and prose. The mess hall was right out of the scenes from old war movies.

Our training company consisted of mostly volunteer enlistees. Some recruits were serving at the direction of their local judicial systems as an alternative to incarceration. About one-fourth of the company's population were young Puerto Rican males who were volunteers or were compelled by other circumstances to join the army. Even though they were nationally disenfranchised, Puerto Ricans were US citizens.

While not able to vote in US elections, they were subject to the military draft, and later qualified for voluntary enlistment in the US Armed Forces. They generally kept to their own in the social silos of the military base.

I point out the Puerto Ricans because their behavior over my three-month training course was distinguished by late-night infighting and multiple attempts to murder each other using shovels or dull butter knives stolen from the mess hall. A significant number of the troublesome recruits were transferred to a "Special Training Company," where they carried heavy 60-foot-long wooden power poles over their heads while marching to the cadence of not-so-happy drill instructors.

We received training in advanced first aid methods and procedures and were instructed in the grotesque methods one would utilize to replace the intestines of a fellow soldier back into his blown-apart stomach cavity. The proper use and handling of splints, stretchers, and body bags was also included in the training curriculum. Map reading and hikes to overnight bivouacs were a highlight in the program. Hand-to-hand combat training and up-close bayonet skills were part of the curriculum.

Sometime around the midpoint of the training cycle at Fort Jackson, we received lectures and training on biological, chemical, and nuclear weapons. The newfound knowledge was equally fascinating and terrifying at the same time. We learned how to deploy and fit our gas masks, and performed group firing exercises in which we advanced on and entered a small three-room building. Once inside the building we were immediately exposed to multiple detonating tear gas canisters. We were required to remain exposed in the building for several minutes, before putting on our gas masks. After experiencing the breath-saving features of the protective masks, we were then instructed to remove the masks and make our way to the exit.

Outside we found more gas and continued violently coughing and gasping for air.

The tear gas experience was not terrifying, but it did cause some physical harm. My coughing and nausea did not subside. While in formation a couple of days later, my commanding officer (CO) stood in front of me with his silver captain's bars shining in the sunlight. He looked at my pale, drawn face and said, "Private! You don't look well. Fall out and report to sick bay." I reported as ordered and sat in a waiting room for several hours, coughing up sputum and bits of trachea and bronchial tissue.

A male army nurse interviewed me and took my vitals. He left and returned with a young army doctor who asked me a few more questions and told me I would be moved to the Moncrief Army Clinic. It was a modern 12-story facility that had opened in 1972. Like Fort Jackson, it was a training facility. An "army" of medical trainees and other young physicians would attend to my care as they explored my body and medical history, and every rash or ailment that I could recall in my life.

After two days of lying in a hospital bed, a seasoned older doctor, maybe 40 years of age, came to my bedside and informed me that I had double pneumonia. He also told me about several current cases of viral equine encephalitis on the base, and that my symptoms, while common with pneumonia, also matched those caused by the encephalitis. The rumor was that the others with the infection had died. My hospital roommate had it and he did not look so good. The doctor asked if he could call anyone for me. God only knows what he told my mother, and I can only imagine the lively response she gave him.

I remained in the hospital for 24 days. Army regulations prescribed that if a soldier or recruit was hospitalized for more than 14 days, he or she would receive transportation home and 30 days of paid recuperative leave. I was going home. The military rules of conduct in 1974 required all personnel to be dressed in their Class A uniform when traveling privately outside of their military duty station. I took the bus home in my impressive olive drab US Army uniform, which was devoid of medals or commendations of any sort. The simple chevron of a private's rank was my only distinguishing mark. I wore it to every bar in Jacksonville Beach. I returned to Fort Jackson expecting to resume my training where I had left off. I quickly discovered that it wasn't the army way. I had to start basic training all over from the beginning. I was okay with that. I now knew the ropes and I knew they would not actually kill me.

The premier component of the combat readiness training at Fort Jackson is riflery instruction. In the second week, we were each provided a standard army service rifle, the M16, a 5.56 mm, lightweight, fully automatic weapon with a detachable 20-round capacity clip. Now, understand that we were not walking around base with loaded automatic weapons. We did keep our weapons in the barracks, but were not allowed to possess ammunition unless we were receiving instruction on the firing of the weapon at the rifle range. It was a "brass-in, brass-out policy." Each day of riflery training, we received a prescribed number of rounds of live ammunition, and at the end of the training session we returned the exact number of expended shell cartridges.

It is important to note that the M16 rifle was the successor to the World War II era M1 rifle and the M14 version adopted in 1959. The M16 is often confused with the model made popular by the movie industry and the news media's distorted reporting on deadly "assault rifles." The term "assault rifle" does not exist in military vernacular. It is derived from the acronym AR-15, which was a designation created by the manufacturer. ArmaLite was a small arms manufacturing company that sold the brand and the right to build the ArmaLite rifle (AR-15) to the Colt Manufacturing Company.

Rifle training spanned a six-week period. We would fall out in fatigues and backpacks with our rifles, and fast march to the rifle range. Each phase of rifle training required the use of a different range. Each range was a couple of miles farther away. By the end of the training the last range was 21 kilometers (13 miles) in distance from our barracks. The marathon-length trek to and from the range took all day. Fast marching was like jogging with a heavy pack, carrying a rifle, and was physically arduous. We would soon be in the best physical shape of our lives. My portly college profile of 230 pounds was now measuring in at just under six feet and 198 pounds.

Having been taught to shoot rifles at a young age by my dad gave me a measurable advantage over recruits who had never held or fired a gun of any kind. Toward the end of rifle training, a post-wide competition was held. Targets at 25 meters, 50 meters, 100 meters, and 300 meters (984 feet) were set for the match. I had a perfect score hitting all targets multiple times with open iron sights. The trophy was awarded to our platoon, and it resides in the Command Building display case at Fort Jackson Army Base in Columbia, South Carolina.

You may recall the movie *Full Metal Jacket*, when a delusional Vincent D'Onofrio nicknamed "Private Pyle" has a psychotic break and threatens his fellow soldiers with his rifle loaded with live 7.62 mm full metal-jacketed ammunition. He kills Gunnery Sergeant Hartman and then commits suicide in front of the other soldiers trying to disarm him. I witnessed a very similar scene in my barracks, when a mentally depressed soldier marched into the bath area with his rifle, shouting loud obscenities at no one in particular. He showed us live ammo in his clip and threatened to kill everyone. The NCO on night barracks duty subdued the weeping recruit and secured his rifle. We never saw our Private Pyle again.

After rifle training, we moved to the hand grenade pits. Having been a world-class Little League baseball pitcher, I possessed arm strength and coordination that I demonstrated by throwing the M67 fragmentation grenade farther than most instructors had previously seen. A group of drill sergeants gathered around the throwing pit to watch me hurl the round steel grenade into the treetops just beyond the training field in front of the pits. We also received hands-on training and use of the M203 grenade launcher that mounted under the barrel of the M16 rifle. It fired salt-shaker sized 40 x 56 mm high-explosive grenades that could disable a moving jeep 400 yards away.

Training on the iconic M60 machine gun was an experience I will always recall. The rifle fired 600 7.62 NATO rounds (.308 Winchester) per minute, using belt-fed 100-round belts and was accurate and effective out to 1,200 yards. The tracer rounds placed in each belt made the appearance of "walking the fire" to the enemy or target. The powerful rounds heat the barrel of the weapon to a visibly red-hot hue. Occasionally the weapon jams, and the cartridges cannot advance the belt through the receiver. The heat of the barrel and the receiver can reach temperatures that cause the cartridges in the receiver's chamber to discharge uncontrollably, erratically jerking the rifle barrel up and down, and left and right, placing everyone around it in danger. The proper procedure in an M60 "cookoff" is to keep the weapon pointed downfield and let it cool for 15 minutes.

I was firing the M60 machine gun from a prone position, and after several minutes and hundreds of rounds of ammunition fired, a malfunction occurred, and the belt of rifle cartridges could not advance as designed. The drill instructor cursed and picked up the heavy searing-hot weapon. The firing

range is like an amphitheater with a control tower. As soon as
the drill instructor picked up the overheated gun, I heard a loud
booming voice coming from the rifle range control station:
"Put the gun down! Sergeant, put the weapon down *now!*"

The next thing I heard was the sound of dozens of .308
caliber automatic machine gun rifle cartridges firing and
striking the soil 12 inches from my exposed head, face, and
ears. The sound was deafening. My M1 steel helmet kept
the exploding bullet fragments and the sand and clay from
destroying my vulnerable cranium. My eyes were turned
away from the pulsating blasts, but my left ear was not as
fortunate. The tinnitus and partial hearing loss would prove to
be permanent. After my basic training and assignment to duty
at Fort Devens, near Boston, Massachusetts, an examining
medical officer suggested that I could take a medical discharge.
I refused.

I survived another brief but memorable boot camp
experience while serving as the platoon night guard, along
with the assigned night duty officer. The staff sergeant was
charged with monitoring the barracks and trainees, and served
as a first responder for any disturbances that might occur. Like
many of the NCOs at Fort Jackson, he had recently returned
from combat duty in Vietnam. As the night officer he was
issued a Vietnam-era sidearm. It was an M1911 .45 caliber
semiautomatic pistol. He pulled it out and began inserting and
removing the magazine, which was fully loaded with seven
rounds of ammunition.

We sat together at the standard issue gray metal desk in
the duty officer's office. After an hour of rambling on about
army life and some of his personal issues, he racked the slide
of the weapon, and a live round was jacked into the chamber
of the gun. He raised the pistol and placed the barrel against
his temple. I do not know if he was intoxicated or mentally

disturbed or both. He mumbled something unintelligible to me, and abruptly pointed the gun at my forehead, now less than two feet away. I do not recall what was said next. At the time, I did not really think he would pull the trigger. After he settled down and placed the pistol on the desk, he told me that if I ever said anything about that night, he would kill me. I never uttered a word to anyone.

Fort Devens, Massachusetts

The Vietnam War was over for all practical fighting purposes. The Paris Peace Accords in 1973 brought an end to the fighting and the loss of American lives. Two years earlier I would have probably been shipped to Vietnam after completing Military Occupational Specialty Training (MOS). My orders after leaving Fort Jackson were to report to Fort Devens in Worcester County, Massachusetts. I was assigned to the Army Security Agency and my MOS was Intercept Systems Electronics Maintenance.

The history of Fort Devens extends from the Civil War, through the World Wars, Vietnam, and the Gulf and Afghanistan Wars. It has been the home of dozens of military battle groups including the Fourth Infantry, the Seventy-Sixth Artillery, the Thirty-Fourth Armored Division, and the Fifth Cavalry. The base was closed in 1996, after 79 years of service. The Army Security Agency (ASA) was housed there for 25 years. Veteran agency members have constructed a museum on the site.

During my time there in the ASA, we shared space and time with Special Forces soldiers returning from Vietnam. The agency also trained language specialists in the Russian, Vietnamese, Chinese, and Turkish languages. Army intelligence personnel and Special Forces were trained in languages, electronic surveillance, and traffic analysis. The ASA mission was to train specialists in electronic traffic interception and analysis. The traffic analysts, known as "dee dots," could be spotted unconsciously tapping out Morse code on their chair armrests or bar counters. The mix of nerdy ASA types and the Special Forces guys was uniquely challenging, yet provided a fun and rewarding experience for both parties. The stories and lies told at the post's PX over Shaefer Beer abuse were memorable.

Conflicts on base were rare, but when they occurred it raised the interest of the entire post of fewer than 400 enlisted personnel. One evening after a weeklong dispute, a planned fight was to end in a battle to the death between a Special Forces E-5 and a similarly ranked Army Intelligence NCO. They were both veterans of war and tough as nails. It was sophomoric in its origin, and a waste of the intelligence and experience they both possessed. At dusk in a wooded area surrounded by onlookers, the two faced off. After minutes passed, nothing happened. I know they were thinking and exchanging the common thought that each was capable of killing the other. After the silent pause, they shook hands and turned and walked away.

My initial training was centered around the maintenance and repair of large R-390A radio receivers. The jeep-and-rack-mounted radios were the size of a suitcase and weighed 85 pounds. They were the most reliable vacuum tube type shortwave radio receivers available. With 26 vacuum tubes and a transmitter and receiver range of 0.50 MHz to 32 MHz, we listened to Russian traffic intercepted at the ASA base on Simiya (or Shemya) island in the Aleutian Islands chain southwest of Alaska. It was mostly fast transmissions of encrypted Morse code. The base had top secret rooms with hundreds of 50-track magnetic tape recorders that recorded the intercepted code, and used computers the size of a bus to decode the intercepted traffic. It was fascinating work.

Life in Massachusetts was different than my upbringing in sunny Florida. In the winter months our education was paused briefly each morning by snow shoveling activities. Our army uniforms were augmented with long underwear, heavy field jackets, and wool scarves. I felt as though I was living in a movie set. The spring came, with frequent outings to Walden Pond in nearby Concord, Massachusetts, only 14 miles away. My platoon was known as "F Troop." We were a mix of trainees with varied military occupational specialties (MOS). Some were training in electronics maintenance, others in intercepted radio traffic analysis, and language specialties.

The presence of the Women's Army Corps (WAC) at Fort Devens was another very positive aspect of military life at Fort Devens. Many of the women stationed there were training to be traffic analysts or language interpreters. I developed a close relationship with one female member of the ASA, named Stacy. She was from Miami, Florida, and was studying and simultaneously teaching other soldiers the Vietnamese language. Like many of my platoon members, I smoked cigarettes. I had borrowed a butane cigarette lighter from my dad without his knowledge. It wasn't the modern plastic Bic-style lighter. This was a classic, silver steel lighter with a top that flipped open. It was a James Dean movie prop kind of lighter. It was inscribed with my dad's nickname, "Buck." So, Stacy frequently referred to me as Buck. After I separated from the army, I returned to my family home. Stacy called my house to check on me, and when my mother answered the telephone, she inadvertently asked for Buck. This required some significant follow-up and explanation from me to my mother. To this day, I'm not sure she bought the storyline.

One day after class, as I was standing casually outside my barracks, Bob, a six-foot three-inch-tall White friend of mine was also outside enjoying a smoke. Another acquaintance from an adjacent barracks caught the eye of my friend, and Bob yelled out, "Hey, n—! Don't drink that cheap wine, you know it makes you mother—rs crazy." Both of them were used to the daily back-and-forth racist jibes, but today was different. My Black friend Lavon smashed his jug of wine onto the concrete curb and advanced toward Bob while waving the glass bottle neck. Its sharp blade-like edges were now a deadly weapon.

I approached the escalating standoff and yelled at Lavon to return to his barracks, right now! He responded that I had no authority over him and he was going to cut this White trash to shreds. I repeated my command for him to stand down. He knew my words had no standing, but his better judgment kicked in and he lowered the glass bottle. It was then that Bob had to have the last word and uttered, "Just like a n—." Lavon rushed him and, as I stepped between them, the bottle jabbed my right forearm. Another slash caught Bob in the neck below his jaw. Blood was saturating our white T-shirts and faces.

Someone who had witnessed the violent exchange called the Military Police. The MPs showed up quickly and took the three of us into custody. We were detained in a holding cell at the Criminal Investigative Division (CID) headquarters. After individual interrogations, it was evident what my role was in the altercation, and I was released. The DIS report was sent to my CO and shared with my platoon sergeant. They both commended my efforts.

Only a couple of weeks later, I was haphazardly placed in another racially tense situation. This time a small group of young Puerto Rican soldiers were arguing over an attitude problem of one of the other guys. I was initially friendly to the gathering and exchanged jovial conversation. They continued their badgering and one of them pulled out a pocketknife with a five-inch blade and flipped it open. He lunged at his opponent with the intent to stab him in the stomach. My left hand reflexively grabbed the blade before it could penetrate the victim's midsection. The knife was abruptly withdrawn, neatly slicing my fingers at mid-joint.

The MPs from CID took us into custody, and we were moved to CID headquarters. After the initial questioning and corroboration of my role in the incident, I was released, without charges, to the medical clinic. The CID reports of my bravery and stupidity reached the CO and he ordered that I be put in charge of a newly formed race relations effort. We were to hold weekly meetings in the barracks lounge to discuss and defuse potentially tense interracial interactions.

My life at Fort Devens was as picturesque as it was satisfying. Having previously attended college for 3½ years, I was slightly older than my fellow soldiers in Charlie Company. As the elder, I gained some inherently awarded and possibly misplaced respect in my platoon and company. My company commanding officer and platoon sergeant gave me additional responsibilities and "acting jack—nonpaid" rank advancement from corporal to sergeant. I wore the three chevrons on my hat only when leading the morning fall out and physical training sessions for the ASA's 100-man Charlie Company. I was also appointed by the company's top sergeant as a Race Relations Specialist for the company. We held beer-and-bitch training sessions in the evenings and hashed out any racial tensions that were brewing in the ranks. The standard-looking canned drink machines in our barracks dispensed 25-cent Schmidt's beer in lieu of soft drinks.

Each weekday morning at Fort Devens, we walked casually to a 50-year-old complex of brick buildings. It was like a college campus, except that our classroom building was surrounded by a wire fence 20 feet in height with barbed wire at the top. We were prohibited from bringing any paper products in, and we did not leave with any papers or books. The topics and material we were discussing and being taught were classified by the Defense Department.

Each of us, including the cooks, had a Top-Secret security clearance with "Limited Access to Special Intelligence." Any deviant behavior, arrests, or unbecoming indiscretions could be grounds for losing "Access to S.I.," along with any hope of advancement in the agency. Prior to my activation to active duty, the Department of Defense (DOD) conducted a background investigation into my life in college. They interviewed past church pastors and bartenders, and researched state and federal databases for arrest records. I was subsequently interviewed and allowed to offer mitigating explanations for any issues considered significant or borderline reasons for denying a Top-Secret security clearance. I had several, but all were considered benign youthful offenses.

I had an advanced competency and understanding of AC and DC electrical theory. I must have gotten it from my dad. He was an apprenticeship instructor and self-taught electrical engineer. We were being trained to transition the army and the agency from the older tube set radios, to the Top-Secret VHF (very high frequency) portable radio sets. The new radios used transistors and integrated circuit chips instead of large power-consuming vacuum tubes. The reception and transmission signal waves were limited to "line of sight." So, the sea level range was limited to eight miles or less by trees and mountains, and the curvature of the earth. In Vietnam the Army Corps of Engineers was busy constructing radio towers that would significantly extend the effective range of the lightweight portable radios. They called the antenna towers "elephant cages" because of their towering cagelike structure of bamboo stilts and braces. Within 15 years, the Top-Secret VHF radio would be a standard feature on every oceangoing vessel and most pleasure boats.

Nearing the completion of my electronics MOS (military occupational specialties) training, I received official orders to report to the US Army facility and listening post on the Black Sea coast of Turkey. It was a NATO logistics base in Sinop, Turkey. Situated just opposite Sevastopol in Crimea, it was known for its geodesic domes and parabolic satellite dishes. The 400 army and ASA (Army Security Agency) personnel stationed there were isolated from most social frivolities and local ambience. We also believed the escalating rumors that we might end up in a new war with Turkey.

Upon receiving my disappointing orders, I requested a meeting with the commanding officer of ASA's F-Troop. Instead of meeting with the CO, I spoke with the sergeant major. He was the highest-ranking NCO on the post. I pointed out to him that my enlistment contract specifically provided that my assignment upon completion of training was to embassy duty in Washington, DC. He pointed out to me the disputable fact that I had voided the embassy option when I selected my electronics MOS at the ASA. He assured me I had "the army by the balls" and I should ride it out and make the best of it.

Following my meeting with the sergeant major and a little research at the JAG office library, I sent a well-crafted, handwritten letter to the commanding officer of our company. I clearly recited his responsibilities in what was an "erroneous enlistment" case. He was required to "right the wrong or pass the case to his superior officer."

The next orders I received directed me to report to Shemya, Alaska, on the western end of the Aleutian Islands chain, and 1,200 miles from Anchorage. The small group of techies on the island of Shemya was lacking in any comforts found on any other military depots around the globe. Women, whiskey, and song were not known benefits in the tour of duty in the frozen Aleutian Islands.

I was disappointed, but I really liked army life. I was in a holding company with 100 other soldiers that were slated to attend Officer's Candidate School. If accepted, we would complete training at the Fort Benning military base in Georgia, and be commissioned as 2nd lieutenants in the Regular Army of the United States of America. We voluntarily enlisted and had been inducted into the US Army as "Regular Army" with four-year enlistment contracts, not the Army Reserve status assigned to draftees serving two-year stints.

In the fall of 1974 I was standing in an informational assembly of the entire company. After a command from the CO, "Company, at ease," the commanding officer yelled my name and ordered me to come forward. He told me I should report immediately to the Fort Devens post commander, who was also the brigade commander of the army unit that the ASA was assigned to.

The ASA was a conglomeration of standard platoons that made up each company. The combined companies constituted a battalion, and the battalions formed a brigade. The highly unusual difference was that the commanding generals and other high-ranking ASA officers did not report directly to the Secretary of the Army. The Defense Secretary bypassed his Army Secretary and sent directives and received intelligence reports directly from the Officer Corps of the ASA.

The Defense Secretary apparently did not trust the generals running the Vietnam War to provide accurate reporting of the progress in the conflict. This mistrust was evident from the often inflated progress reports in international press briefings and presidential speeches. It was increasingly difficult to determine if we were winning the war or just fueling the machines of war. The Defense Department's ASA policy was cumbersome on the battlefield, with some combatant units taking orders and reporting up the standard chain of command, while

ASA attachments withheld collected intelligence from the field officers until it had been submitted and cleared by the Defense Secretary. The level of mistrust between ASA forces and the other field units was a distraction and destructive to the common war effort.

I was not going to Simiya, Alaska, or Sinop, Turkey. I was also apparently not going to Officer Candidate School or embassy duty in Washington, DC. After the Paris Peace Accords in 1973, the troop withdrawals in Vietnam continued to escalate, with 400,000 soldiers in the process of being repatriated. The demand for 1st and 2nd lieutenants was at an all-time low. With my lowly enlisted status and preferred assignment in limbo, I was not a priority for anyone but me, and possibly my mother back home.

I went to the post commander's office, wearing my best highly starched fatigues and self-administered haircut. I reported sharply and addressed the brigade colonel with the utmost of respect. He said, "Son, I have read your letters and I understand your frustration. What is it you really want to do? Do you want to go home? Do you want a promotion and reassignment?" I replied, "Sir, I love the army and the opportunity it provides for me. I will serve as I am ordered." He paused and said, "Son, if you have a job at home, you can go home." I replied, "Sir, if you have a phone, I have a job." A few days later, in full company formation, the CO again called me to the front of the assembly. He said, "Congratulations, you are going home."

After a week of separation activities, I was provided $900 in cash and an airline ticket to Jacksonville, Florida. A physical exam was provided as part of the separation from service. It confirmed my hearing loss, and the medical specialist informed me that I would probably not be able to reenlist. That bothered me because I felt an affinity for the army that I cannot explain. It was a sense of duty and obligation that I felt like I had avoided while in school. I only served 10 months of my four-year enlistment. I was on inactive reserves for an additional six years, but barring a world war, I would not be recalled to service. Today I proudly display my wall plaque with the honorable discharge certificate and the embossed seal of the United States Army. It was one of the most rewarding experiences of my life.

1975

With the global population exceeding 4 billion souls, the year 1975 would be remembered for human actions and events that shaped the decades that followed. A notable invention produced by Steven Sasson, of Eastman Kodak Company, was the first self-contained portable digital camera. It would become the technological father of billions of photographs produced in the following five decades.

Perhaps the most significant announcement was the introduction of the microcomputer. The Altair 8800 was designed by a company in New Mexico named Micro Instrumentation and Telemetry Systems (MITS). Ed Roberts and his partner started the company in his garage, where they made model rockets and radio transmitters. The microcomputer utilized an 8-bit processor created by Intel in 1973. Microprocessors were already in use for calculators, cash registers, and computer terminals. The Altair computers were sold as kits for hobbyists, in *Popular Electronics* magazine, at a cost of less than $500. Later in November of the same year, and also in New Mexico, Bill Gates and Paul Allen founded a company named Micro-Soft and laid the groundwork for the popular operating system OS/2 (Operating System/2). Their partnership with IBM led to the introduction of the software suite, Microsoft Windows. Today the Microsoft Company employs 130,000 people worldwide and generates $87 billion in annual revenue.

When you turned on the television in 1975, you'd find the premiere of the popular game show, *Wheel of Fortune.* The evening news brought you the tragic news of the sinking of the SS *Edmund Fitzgerald.* More breaking news added to the sorrow. President Ford's successful Operation Babylift evacuation of 3,300 Vietnamese orphans was unjustly marred by the crash of a C-5 military plane carrying orphans to safety—138 people, mostly young orphans, perished in the crash. Closing out the night, you watched the first episode of *Saturday Night Live* hosted by George Carlin. In the global mix of humanity, the world took steps toward peace and cooperation.

The birth year of professional golfer Tiger Woods was 1975. It was also the year that President Gerald Ford posthumously restored the citizenship of Confederate General Robert E. Lee. Eighty-six hundred miles away, South Africa announced that all Black children would be provided free and compulsory education. The Helsinki Accords document was signed in Finland and provided European nations and the United States with sovereign equality and territorial integrity. The act prescribed respect for human rights and fundamental freedoms, along with a cardinal principle of self-determination. To cap the year of influential events, Wally Smith Broecker, a geochemist and "grandfather" of climate science, first used the term "global warming."

The Vietnam War officially ended on April 30, 1975, with the fall of Saigon to the North Vietnamese. American officials and military personnel, along with many of our South Vietnamese allies, were part of a massive evacuation in Operation Frequent Wind. The iconic photograph taken on April 29, 1975, by Dutch photojournalist "Hugh" van Es, of what was assumed to be the last helicopter leaving the roof of the abandoned US Embassy, became the hallmark the world would remember as the end of the Vietnam War.

In mid-April, C-130 and C-141 aircraft evacuated thousands of Vietnamese from Saigon's Tan Son Nhut airport. On April 27, rockets hit Saigon, damaging the runways and leaving 5,000 people homeless. The airlift that began April 1 evacuated 45,000 people, including 5,000 Americans. The evacuation continued around the clock with the use of CH-53 helicopters that could carry as many as 65 passengers. While 150,000 enemy soldiers surrounded the city, F-4 and A-7 fighter jets protected the helicopter flights.

During the last days of the mission, 65 US Marine and Air Force helicopters continued the evacuation. They ferried Vietnamese and other non-US evacuees to the navy fleet offshore. On the afternoon of April 29, 30-year-old pilot Col. Gerry Berry was dispatched to pick up US Ambassador Graham Martin at the American Embassy. Instead of the ambassador, he was besieged by dozens of Vietnamese and other non-US personnel. He airlifted and deposited them on the USS *Blue Ridge* naval ship waiting offshore in the South China Sea. His efforts to evacuate the ambassador were delayed; he flew a dozen more trips evacuating hundreds more people escaping Saigon. Finally, at 4:50 a.m. on April 30, Berry removed the remaining evacuees from the chopper and demanded that the ambassador be placed on the aircraft. Colonel Berry's six-hour mission was now in its 18th hour. He radioed the code words "Tiger, Tiger, Tiger," and headed to the USS *Blue Ridge* with Ambassador Martin onboard.

Back in Washington, Secretary of State Henry Kissinger was anxious for a positive political moment and, in what was considered a "horrendous screw-up," he announced that the last US chopper had left the US Embassy. However, 11

US Marines were still on the embassy rooftop and 420 more non-US citizens that were promised airlifts were lined up to depart. The marines barricaded themselves on the rooftop and prepared for an inevitable attack.

After sunrise the USS *Hancock* sent a final chopper to rescue the stranded marines. Above the embassy, the crew could see the 420 people left behind and 10,000 more who had overrun the compound desperately hoping for a way out of Saigon. Three hours later, North Vietnamese tanks entered the gates of the presidential palace. Saigon would now become Ho Chi Minh City. After 20 years and 58,220 American deaths, the Vietnam War was finally over for the United States.

1976–1978

Computer science again takes the stage and the first commercially available supercomputer is introduced by Cray Research, Inc. A quiet genius from Wisconsin, Seymour Cray brought the world a computer that was 10 times faster than any other model. It cost as much as $10 million and used the power equivalent to 10 residential homes. The Cray-1 housed densely packed integrated circuits interconnected with more than 60 miles of wiring. Dovetailed into the Cray release, Apple Computer Company was formed by Steve Jobs and Steve Wozniak. On July 11, 1976, the last slide rule was manufactured in the United States.

The tragedy of 1977 was not a war. It was an episode of Mother Nature breaching the gap between the natural world and our man-made world. The result yielded an insight into human nature and the depth of our depravity. Much like the gonging of an alarm bell, the state of New York received three strikes which opened a wound that would never heal.

Strike one came at 8:37 p.m., when an electrical substation on the Hudson River was hit by lightning. Westchester County was plunged into darkness. Five minutes later came strike two. A substation on the Hudson River received a lightning strike that took down the 900-megawatt Indian River nuclear power plant. Attempts to start backup generation of power failed. Three minutes passed, and strike three took out the major transmission lines of power to Upstate New York. The overload on the balance of the system started a cascading failure of other electrical substations. At 9:27 p.m. the largest generator in New York City failed. New York City, the city of bright lights, was plunged into darkness.

The entire Con Edison power system was shut down. LaGuardia and Kennedy airports were closed. Television stations and many radio stations were off the air. About 4,000 people were stranded in the city subways. It was the peak of summer, and the streets and buildings were dark. There were no humming sounds coming from running air conditioning systems. The large fans on cooling towers were quiet. What happened next redefined darkness.

The sirens from police cars and fire trucks came quickly. The apocalyptic human tragedy had begun. Looting and vandalism spread through the neighborhoods. Arson and violence added to the crescendo of mayhem. More than a thousand stores were looted and damaged. About 550 police officers were injured as they arrested 4,500 looters. The next day, the 25-hour-long battle was winding down. It was not a struggle with the environment; there were no hurricanes, tornados, or floods. The earth didn't shake and fissure and swallow up people on the street. The mayhem was not God's doing. It was a short and tragic play, and we wrote the script. We, the people, acted out the parts.

It was the first year of Jimmy Carter's presidency. He represented hope and change. It was not the same politically coined phrase used by politicians today. He truly believed in the advancement of human rights and providing relief for suffering nations. He was the son of a farmer from Plains, Georgia. He and his wife Rosalynn worked in the farm and feed business.

Our nation was suffering, and the voters decided he was our best hope for the country.

President Carter's giving nature yielded a pardon for the Vietnam War's draft dodgers. He received the Nobel Peace Prize for his work in peace negotiations between Egypt and Israel. He may have reached a fault point when he turned over a 50-mile-long waterway that connects the Atlantic Ocean to the Pacific. The Panama Canal has provided a 10-hour passage for over 1 million ships since it was opened in 1914. The canal earns more than $2 billion per year in revenue. Its strategic value is immeasurable.

Today everyone has a computer or a handheld communication device. In the '70s every family had a record player. The music was as diverse as the 220 million people in the country. Elvis Presley topped the charts until his death in 1977, at the age of 42. The Bee Gees sang "How Deep Is Your Love," while Stevie Wonder released "I Wish" in his 18th album. Barbra Streisand climbed the charts, right along with Fleetwood Mac and Rod Stewart.

The world of technology was not slowing down. The US Defense Department developed and began using the Navstar Global Positioning System (GPS). In the greatest breakthrough in modern medicine, a New Yorker went from playing the violin at the Julliard School of Music, to graduate from the Albert Einstein College of Medicine as Dr. Steven W. Smith. He invented the first full-body scanner. The use of nuclear magnetic resonance was packaged as the first MRI scanner. NASA launched the first space shuttle off the back of a jetliner. Introduced several years earlier and clocking in at 1,354 miles per hour, the 100-passenger Concorde jetliner began regular commercial service from London to Washington, DC, and New York.

The Organization of the Petroleum Exporting Countries (OPEC) gained worldwide attention as it pushed oil prices up

70 percent to $5 per barrel. Later in the year, OPEC, along with Egypt, Syria, and Tunisia, raised the price to $12 per barrel. Prices at the pump soared to 65 cents per gallon. In the US, the timely opening of the Trans-Alaska Pipeline System occurred on May 31, 1977.

The year of 1978 started with tragedy and death as frontrunners. A Boeing 747 crashed in Bombay, killing 237 passengers and crew. In British Columbia, a Boeing 737 crashed with 50 people onboard. Miraculously, there were six survivors. In the category of things not expected in the modern world, 170 people perished in a blizzard that spanned two weeks and covered the Ohio Valley and New England. Human depravity raised its ugly head when serial murderer Ted Bundy sexually assaulted four students and beat to death two young coeds at the Chi Omega sorority house at Florida State University. Bundy was convicted and executed in 1989. Four thousand miles away, the Hillside Stranglers assaulted and killed 10 young women in the hillsides of Los Angeles.

The Mideast was in turmoil. Afghanistan's President Daoud Khan and his family were killed in a Marxist coup d'état. This marked the start of a 43-year civil war that continues today. In Iran, university students were rioting and in conflicts with the Iranian army. Opposition to Mohammad Reza Pahlavi brought riots and protests in hundreds of towns and villages. On what is labeled Black Friday, the army squelched the riots in Tehran by opening fire and killing 122 and wounding 4,000 others. The Iranian Revolution replaced the shah with Ayatollah Khomeini. The number of casualties in the revolution varies widely. Khomeini said 60,000 martyrs perished in the conflict. Others suggest that approximately 3,000 protesters were killed.

In the Yemen Arab Republic, President al-Ghashmi was the second Yemen president in six months to be killed. His death marked the beginning of a four-year war with more than

1,000 soldiers killed in action. It would be 12 years before North and South Yemen would see unification. Yemen's north-south conflicts began in 1962 and the 60-year war continues today.

As much as the world wanted to leave wars and death behind, the victor in the Cambodian civil war and Khmer Rouge leader Pol Pot began his totalitarian leadership with a social engineering plan that imitated China's disastrous "Great Leap Forward." The Chinese effort yielded 20 million deaths from starvation between 1958 and 1962. Pol Pot's collectivist agricultural reforms led to the starvation deaths of hundreds of thousands. The total Cambodian genocide deaths exceeded 1.5 million and eliminated one-fourth of the Cambodian population.

Under the guise of promoting communal living and abolishing personal interests, the Khmer Rouge (the Liberation Army of Kampuchea), supported by the Communist Chinese Party, executed hundreds of thousands of people who were perceived to be political opponents. The new Democratic Kampuchea was an atheist state. Buddhist monks were forced to defrock and work as peasants. As many as 25,000 Buddhist monks were killed by Pol Pot's regime. Islamic leaders were also executed. Christians were accused of spying for the United States and were taken away and killed.

The Communist Party closed schools and hospitals. Factories were closed and banking was abolished. Cities were evacuated and the people were sent to work in agricultural communes. Technically-skilled citizens were returned to work on reopening the factories. Other professionals and military leaders were sent to reeducation camps where they were tortured and executed. All private interests and enterprises were prohibited, and violations were punishable by death. Attempts to privately farm and feed yourself and your family were not allowed. Only work for the common good was allowed. In a plan to destroy the family unit, marriages were arranged by government officials. Sex outside of marriage was punishable by execution. The Khmer Rouge arrested, tortured, and eventually killed anyone connected to the former Cambodian government. Professionals, intellectuals, artists, Muslims, Catholics, and ethnic Vietnamese were all killed. New research completed on mass graves now estimates the death toll may be as high as 2.5 million.

In 1978 Pol Pot invaded the border town of Ba Chuc. He suspected that a Vietnamese invasion was coming. With the exception of two survivors, the entire population of 3,157 civilians was massacred. Peace talks between Pol's Kampuchea and Vietnam collapsed in December of 1978, and with support from the Soviet Union, Vietnam invaded Cambodia and the Khmer Rouge retreated to the west.

Crossing the Road

In 1978 I was three years into a white-collar job in the electrical construction industry. My work at Miller Electric Company in Jacksonville, Florida, was the beginning of a rewarding 45-year career. I followed my father into the executive ranks and served as president and CEO of a highly successful electrical contracting company with work in all the southeastern states and beyond. Life was good.

Jacksonville is a city on the St. Johns River, where boating was a regular pastime. My cadre of friends included professionals and novice businessmen who, like me, enjoyed the outdoors. We also enjoyed the indoor features of the Florida Yacht Club. The bar scene was right out of the Roaring '20s. We told stories and laughed our way through the evenings, with Robin the piano player banging out tunes for the not so talented kazoo hummers huddled around the deck of the baby grand piano.

Bronson Lamb III was from a family of boaters. They owned the local marina, and he had access to a stately 35-foot Bertram Express sport yacht. One evening we collectively decided to cruise the Bertram down and across the river to a restaurant on Julington Creek. The booze flowed as freely as the water parting our bow. One unfortunate fellow lost his balance and grip on the flybridge of the small yacht. He sailed over the railing and, grasping the now broken fiberglass radio antenna, fell 10 feet to the dark water below. He survived.

We were well into the cocktail hour when we docked the boat in the tributary just off the main river. From there we marched up the embankment, toward the two-lane State Highway 13 and the restaurant. I walked slowly, with my head down, drearily thinking about why I was alone and not with a suitable mate. We approached the roadside and the others paused. Unaware that they had stopped, I continued to cross the highway. As I neared the center line, I saw headlights approaching very fast in the southbound lane. As the car sped toward my precarious spot in the center of the road, I glanced to my right. Another fast-moving vehicle was approaching, northbound. The two cars passed each other at the precise spot where I was standing. The sound was deafening and the wind gust nearly caused me to lose my balance.

In an instant the cars were gone and the scene was pitch-black and dead quiet. I walked to the far side of the road and bent over and threw up violently. I had just seen the miniscule time and distance between living and breathing and instant death. The memory would remain entrenched in my psyche for life. The group gathered and we continued a carefree stroll to another evening of dining and dancing the night away.

1979–1981

The event most remembered in 1979 is the Iran hostage crisis. On November 4, the US Embassy was taken over by 3,000 militarized Iranian Muslim students. Sixty-three US diplomats and citizens were taken hostage. Three more American diplomats were seized at the Iranian Foreign Ministry. Khomeini later ordered the release of 13 hostages. They were either Black or female and not judged to be American spies. An additional hostage with medical problems was released in July of 1980. The remaining 52 hostages were held in captivity for 444 days. It was an act of revenge against America for its attempts to undermine the Iranian revolution. The regime of Shah Mohammad Pahlavi was overthrown in the revolution led by the Ayatollah Ruhollah Khomeini. The shah was granted asylum in the US and checked into a hospital for cancer treatments. In April of 1980, President Carter conducted a failed hostage rescue attempt that killed one Iranian civilian and eight American servicemen. The Americans were killed in a helicopter collision with a US transport aircraft.

The Iranian "Muslim Student Followers of the Iman's Line" were demanding the return of the shah for trial and execution. In December of 1979, Shah Pahlavi was granted asylum in Egypt, where he died from cancer seven months later at the age of 60. In an agreement brokered by the Algerian government, the hostage crisis ended on January 19, 1981, with the signing of the Algiers Accords. The agreement provided that the US would remove the freeze placed on $8 billion of Iranian assets and remove all trade sanctions. Iranian debts to US institutions would also be paid. All litigation between the US and Iran would cease and be referred to international mediation. Future relations between the US and Iran would prove this one-sided agreement structure to be the norm for dealing with Iran.

The day after the signing of the Algiers Accords, and just minutes after President Ronald Reagan was sworn into office, all 52 hostages were released. The release may have been solely the result of the Algiers agreement, or perhaps it was also the knowledge that our new president would take a far more hawkish posture to resolve the crisis.

November of 1979 proved to be a period of student-led violence in the Mideast. Hundreds of anti-American protesters, led by Islamic students from Quaid-i-Azam University, filled buses and stormed the main gate to the American Embassy in Islamabad, Pakistan. They climbed the walls of the compound with ropes. They set fire to the lower floors with Molotov cocktails.

US Embassy officials would not authorize the embassy Marines to use lethal force to repel the protestors. Tear gas did little to stop the invaders as they kidnapped several American civilians. The Pakistan army watched the burning building from a helicopter. They decided to let it burn and not engage the rioters.

Steve Crowley, a 20-year-old US Marine, was shot on the rooftop and transported to a vault with steel doors. The Americans hid behind the vault doors and waited to be rescued from the smoke-filled building. The rioters fired shots through ventilation openings in the walls. After nightfall, several marines were able to escape the room from a rear exit. Finding the building empty, the marines led 140 Americans and other embassy personnel to the embassy courtyard.

The building was burned to the ground. The Iranian Ayatollah Khomeini praised the attack, while Pakistan President Muhammad Zia-ul-Haq condemned the attack as a violation of Islamic codes of discipline and forbearance.

Continuing the human stain of violence in 1979 and marking the start of a 10-year war, on Christmas Eve of 1979 the Soviet Union invaded Afghanistan. At midnight, 280 transport planes deposited 8,500 Soviet soldiers at the Kabul airport. Two days later, after fierce but futile efforts by the Afghan army, Babrak Karmal, the leader of Marxist People's Democratic Party of Afghanistan, became the country's new government leader. As the battle reached beyond the capital city stronghold, the Islamic mujahidin resistance fighters proclaimed a *jihad* (holy war) against the Christian and atheist Soviet invaders. Toward the end of the 10-year conflict, with the aid of antiaircraft Stinger missiles supplied by the US, the mujahidin gained the advantage by regularly shooting down Soviet planes and helicopters. On February 15, 1989, newly installed Soviet leader Mikhail Gorbachev ordered the retreat from Afghanistan.

Meanwhile, back in the United States, we were dealing with a potentially disastrous nuclear incident now known as Three Mile Island. A study of the events revealed five days in crisis for Middletown, Pennsylvania, and the south-central area of the state. A nuclear meltdown generated fears of a nuclear explosion that would release lethal levels of radiation. Wednesday, March 28, and day one of the crisis, began with the declaration of a general emergency. On day two, engineers and public health officials established that a cooling water valve that was closed for maintenance had stuck in the closed position. This caused major damage to the nuclear reactor and the potential for a release of large quantities of radiation.

On day three, Pennsylvania Governor Richard Thornburgh recommended that young children and pregnant women evacuate the area. The FDA ordered 250,000 bottles of potassium iodide to be administered as droplets to prevent the thyroid glands of exposed victims from absorbing the radiation. By Saturday, March 31, it was concluded by the Nuclear Regulatory Commission (NRC) that a hydrogen gas explosion was imminent. The NRC told reporters that a 20-mile-radius evacuation may be necessary. Later, after being assured that the explosion was now several days away, President Jimmy Carter and Mrs. Carter toured the nuclear facility. Later that afternoon the experts concluded that a hydrogen explosion was not possible and the crisis was over.

There was no "China syndrome." There were no injuries or immediate health impacts from the incident. Inadequate training and instrumentation led to the melting of one-third of the nuclear fuel core. Radiation was released from the plant, but the containment building worked as it was designed. Completed studies revealed that people living within 10 miles of the plant were exposed to a level of radiation that was equivalent to a chest X-ray. US citizens receive three times that amount from natural exposure to the earth's background radiation. The greatest harm caused by the incident was the loss of public confidence in nuclear energy as a viable alternative to fossil fuels. The construction of nuclear power plants steadily declined over the next two decades.

In tragic juxtaposition to the Three Mile Island nuclear event, 11 people did die from asphyxiation and 26 others were injured when they were trampled by concertgoers frantically trying to get into a concert to be performed by The Who, in Cincinnati, Ohio. About 18,000 fans were expected to attend the concert, and 15,000 of those tickets had unassigned—first come, first serve—seating. A crowd of 7,000 assembled two hours early, expecting to be let in for a mad rush to select premium seating. People outside could hear the warm-up and instruments tuning, coming from inside the coliseum. The sound check for The Who's *Quadrophenia* movie could also be heard and was interpreted by the crowd as an early start to the concert.

The fans pressed against the people standing in front of the locked doors. Two doors located away from the main entrance were found to be unlocked and some fans began entering the event. This caused an abrupt surge of people to press against the crowd and the closed doors. Helpless fans were crushed against each other and trampled as the desperate crowd tried to enter the coliseum.

As singer Donna Summer belted out "Hot Stuff" and "Bad Girls," Margaret Thatcher shored up the women's movement by being elected prime minister of the United Kingdom. Oblivious to any such movement, the "guys" were glued to cable television by the launch of the Entertainment and Sports Programming Network (ESPN), and the airing of the first *Sports Center*, anchored by George Grande and Lee Leonard.

May of 1980 brought natural disasters to the front page. In Washington State, after a month of small earthquakes, the Mount St. Helens volcano erupted, killing 57 people. Summertime brought even more tragic death as a heat wave reduced the US population of 226,504,825 souls by 1,117. In August of 1980 in Haiti, Hurricane Allen killed 200 people. Earthquakes in Algeria and southern Italy took the lives of more than 5,000 people. The ironic human condition allows us to remember the shooting death of the iconic musician John Lennon, while obscuring and erasing the disastrous deaths of thousands more.

In the arena of national and state governance, 1981 culminated the FBI's Abscam investigation of more than 30 political figures in the US. One US senator from New Jersey and five congressmen from South Carolina, Florida, New York, and Pennsylvania were also convicted of bribery and conspiracy. Five additional state officials were convicted.

The year 1981 brought the world new mobility with the launch of the first Space Shuttle. *Columbia* carried astronauts John Young and Robert Crippen on a successful two-day test mission. A month earlier, three workers were accidentally killed in a launch test of the spaceship. Reaching even farther into space, the USSR sent the *Venera 13* spacecraft to Venus, and successfully placed a lander on the planet's surface. The lander took color panoramic photographs and collected subsurface rock samples for analysis.

Our 40th president, Ronald Reagan, filled the news throughout the year. Replacing President Jimmy Carter in January, Reagan punctuated his first term by being shot in the chest in an assassination attempt by John Hinckley Jr. In July, President Reagan nominated the first female Supreme Court Justice, Sandra Day O'Connor. He is also remembered for his executive order firing 11,000 striking air traffic controllers for their refusal to return to work. In November he kicked off what would later become the Iran-Contra scandal, when he authorized the CIA to recruit and support Nicaraguan Contra rebels.

The world, and certainly people in the United States, were weary and distraught from the onslaught of deaths.

My life-changing event in 1981 was not a near-death experience. It was, however, the end of "me" and the introduction of "us." Two souls became as one with the marriage of Mr. Ronald Andrew Autrey to Miss Hilah Francis Hillyer. The July 11 wedding was the starting block for what is now an ongoing

42-year journey through life. The joyous occasion started a cascade of large-scale changes in our lives.

We moved into a charming three-bedroom house in "Old Ortega." I immediately and lovingly adopted Hilah's eight-year-old daughter, Hilah Gray, and gave her my last name forever. She is married now, and I moved to the middle name position. After 14 months of marriage, Hilah was due to deliver our second child, Jacquelyn. While Hilah was in labor at the Riverside Clinic in Jacksonville, Florida, I struck a deal on the purchase of a beautiful modern four-bedroom ranch home in Ortega Forest, in the Westside area of Jacksonville. Jacquelyn was born on August 20, 1982. She was six weeks premature and spent her first two weeks apart from her mother, in an incubator at St. Vincent's Hospital, in respiratory distress. In 1984 our third and final child, Ronald Andrew Autrey II, joined the clan, and we continued an adventure that is a living depiction of the American dream. As the title song originally recorded by Waylon Jennings and sung by a dozen more iconic artists says, "We Had It All."

1982–1985

The New Year did not bring many positive events to the forefront. The economy was overshadowing most good news. The yearly inflation rate dropped from 14 percent in 1980 to 6 percent in 1982, and interest rates also dropped, from 21.5 percent to 11.5 percent. The average cost of a new home soared from $68,000 to $82,000 in 24 months. Unemployment surged to a record high of 11 percent, with 12 million Americans unemployed. The United States was headlong into the greatest economic downturn since the Great Depression. To tighten the money supply, the federal funds rate was allowed to increase to 20 percent, while long-term interest rates also continued to rise.

Ironically and coincidental to the 1981–1982 recession and following a 1974 antitrust case against the company, the US Justice Department ordered AT&T (Ma Bell) to break up into seven Baby Bells. At the time, AT&T controlled the entire market for telephones and phone services. The breakup reduced the book value of AT&T by 70 percent. Lessons can be learned from the AT&T breakup. Applying similar measures against Google and Facebook today would likely create multiple new distributed monopolies.

While the third mission of the Space Shuttle *Columbia* orbited the Earth, the machines of war continued the mission of death and destruction. Kicking off a 74-day aggression to gain sovereignty, Argentina invaded the Falkland Islands. A battle started with Exocet missiles sinking the guided missile cruiser HMS *Sheffield* and ended with the nuclear sub HMS *Conqueror* sinking the Argentine cruiser *General Belgrano*. Argentina surrendered in mid-June of the same year. Tragically the conflict produced the deaths of 649 Argentine soldiers and 255 British military personnel. Three Falklanders also perished in the short war.

On the war front, man's inhumanity to man was exemplified again in February of 1982. Syrian President Hafez al-Assad ordered his army to invade the town of Hama and stop a Muslim Brotherhood uprising. The month-long campaign ended a six-year revolt by the Sunni Muslims. One thousand Syrian soldiers were killed along with thousands more Syrian civilians. Amnesty International put the war's death toll between 10,000 and 25,000 people. It was the deadliest massacre in history inflicted by the Arabic government against its own people. More than 100,000 citizens were displaced by the violence.

As border clashes with the Palestine Liberation Organization flared continuously in June of 1982, Israel invaded Lebanon to drive out the PLO's terrorist army. Some 120,000 Israeli soldiers seized a quarter of the country in a period of a few days. The invasion created several hundred thousand refugees. The military blockade imposed on July 2 cut off food, water, and fuel to Arafat's PLO fighters and forced the end of the aggression from PLO forces. Lebanon could now be maintained as a stable buffer between Israel and Syria. Multinational ground forces from the US, France, and Italy were dispatched to facilitate a humanitarian retreat of the defeated Palestinian forces.

On August 25, 1982, 800 US Marines came ashore to safeguard the retreat of Arafat's 15,000 Palestine Liberation

Organization fighters. The evacuation was completed by September 10, 1982. Four days later, Bashir Gemayel, the newly elected president of Lebanon and leader of the Christian Phalange Party, was assassinated. The Lebanese forces avenged the death by killing more than 1,000 Palestinians in refugee camps.

Through October, the presence of "Christian" US forces helping to rebuild the Lebanese National Army polarized the Islamic Moslems and the Lebanese Christian militias. The Lebanese forces received tanks, ammunition, and training from the United States. The diplomatic mission seemed to be working. Beirut was quiet, the Lebanese army was reorganized, and Israel was planning their withdrawal.

In December of 1982, the Israeli forces suffered from hit-and-run guerrilla ambushes, resulting in six dead and 30 wounded. The result was a stepped-up campaign with patrols near the US forces positioned at the Beirut airport. The Israelis pursued aggressive patrols south of the Beirut airport and their actions produced a series of confrontations between Israeli forces and the US Marines at multiple security checkpoints. The incidents continued through a deadly winter and into March of 1983. The calm retreat had deteriorated into chaos and sporadic violence.

On April 18, 1983, a generally calm day was marked with disaster when a light truck entered the embassy compound and detonated a gas-enhanced bomb that destroyed one-third of the embassy building and killed more than 60 people, including 17 Americans. In the months that followed, the US troops and other multinational forces were regarded as the enemy and not as neutral peacekeepers. The civil war fighting continued between the Lebanese forces and the Druze militia. Beirut was again under assault from indiscriminate artillery fire from the Druze and the Palestinian forces. In September, four Marines and 16 French troops died in the shelling.

On September 10, the Druze and Palestinians rained 1,600 shells into the village of Suq al Gharb, and five waves of attacking infantry stormed the city. The Lebanese Army held the city, but pleaded to the US forces for assistance. The US Navy responded with 350 rounds fired from the cruisers positioned offshore. Four days later the battleship *Virginia* fired 72 more rounds into the city. The deadly exchange emboldened and polarized the Druze and other Moslem factions. The locals viewed the US forces as bad and Khomeini as good.

In October of 1983, the US Marines were bombarded with daily rocket fire and sniper fire. The following phrase was coined by the Marines: "In the States every Marine wants to get over to Lebanon, and every Marine in Lebanon wants to get back to the States." On the morning of October 23, a 19-ton yellow Mercedes stake body truck was initially mistaken for a scheduled water delivery. The truck drove up the access road and into the parking lot. Revving its engines, the large truck accelerated through a concertina wire fence and passed through an open chain-link gate, plowed through a bunkered guard shack, and crashed into the lobby of the US Battalion Landing Team barracks. The blast battered a 50-foot building into a collapsed 10-foot-high pile of rubble. Three hundred dead and wounded marines were crushed in the collapse. The gas-enhanced bomb was the equivalent of 21,000 pounds of TNT.

Ten minutes later, the nine-story barracks of the French 1st Parachute Chasseur Regiment was destroyed by another truck bomb. The driver was shot as he approached the building and the truck coasted to a stop before exploding and killing 58 French paratroopers. The bomb blasted the building off its foundation and moved it 20 feet to the west before it collapsed. The explosions killed 234 people and injured more than 100. The blast broke every window in the surrounding neighborhood. The Islamic Jihad took credit for the bombings. The Jihad was a front for Hezbollah, which is a proxy for Iran and the spearhead for the Muslim struggle against foreign occupation of Lebanon. On November 4, a third suicide truck bombed the Israeli military headquarters in Tyre, Lebanon, one of the oldest continually inhabited cities in the world. Forty-six Israelis were killed.

A multinational force was sent to Beirut to bring an end to the violence there. While at first the forces were viewed as neutral peacekeepers, the role was obscured by the attacks and ambushes by factional elements in Lebanon that opposed the central government. American, Italian, and French troops sustained injuries and 350 deaths as a result of suicidal terrorist attacks. Back in the States, families of the 241 US peacekeepers ultimately prevailed in civil suits filed against Iran and collected $3.4 billion from the frozen assets of Iran's Central Bank.

The first two months of 1984 brought further deterioration of the Lebanese Army's positions. Shiite Amal and Druze militias gained control of West Beirut. The US Marines were ordered to redeploy to their ships, and the US naval ship *New Jersey* unleashed the heaviest bombardment since the Korean War, firing 290 16-inch rounds into artillery and command positions in the Shuf District of Lebanon. (Located southeast of Beirut, the historic city also known as Chouf, was the home of the emirs of Lebanon.)

As the Israeli forces pulled back from Lebanon and the US Marines departed Beirut, good intentions were followed by negative consequences: the Khomeini-backed regime in Iran sent 1,000 elite Revolutionary Guards to Southern Lebanon. The Iranians created and trained the newest radical faction of Islamists, now revealed as Hezbollah. This radicalized group would continue supporting the fighting in Syria, and place America and Israel as targets for terrorism.

Before leaving the Syrian timeline and the ongoing civil war, we must recognize the evil presented by the Iranian-backed Hezbollah and Iran's Islamic Revolutionary Guard. The Shiite group, inspired by the ideology of Iran's Ayatollah Khomeini, claims responsibility for countless atrocities committed by the "Party of God." The terrorist activities included the kidnapping of American University President David S. Dodge, US Embassy bombings in Beirut, the kidnapping and murder of CIA operative William Buckley, the hijacking of a Kuwait Airlines plane and TWA Flight 847, the murder of three Americans, and numerous other bombings and murders over the last two decades of the millennium.

Thousands of Americans have perished in the service to the United States of America. Every year we mourn the loss of soldiers and other first responders who sacrificed their safety for the protection of others. They are each worthy of our recognition of their life, their history, and their sacrifice. Their stories are filled with all that life brings to us; happiness, sorrow, success, and jubilation intertwine to create their life stories. Their lives meant something special to those close to them. That they lost their lives in service to others brings greater sadness and empathy for their loved ones suffering the absence of their husband, wife, father, brother, or sister.

I am compelled to commemorate the life of an American warrior. William Francis Buckley was born in Medford, Massachusetts, on May 30, 1928. He graduated from a Stoneham, Massachusetts, high school, and joined the United States Army. Buckley served two years in the army and then attended officer candidate school, and was commissioned as a second lieutenant. During the Korean War he served as a company commander in the 1st Cavalry. He then graduated from Boston University with a degree in political science and began his career with the Central Intelligence Agency. He left the CIA and joined the 11th Special Forces Group and attended Special Forces Airborne and Officers courses. In 1965 Buckley rejoined the CIA in the Special Activities Division. He served in Mexico in 1963, and then as a lieutenant colonel in Vietnam from 1965 to 1970. Following his service in Vietnam, he served in Zaire, Cambodia, Egypt, Pakistan, and, finally, Syria. He became the Beirut station chief in 1983 after the Marine Corps barracks' bombing.

At the age of 57, William Buckley perished in captivity while being tortured by Hezbollah in 1984. He was held in captivity in chains and blindfolded in a coffin-sized cell. At the hands of deranged psychiatrist Aziz al-Abub, Buckley was reduced to an incoherent gibbering and terrorized shell of a man. His shaking body screamed out in terror. Contrary to claims made in October of 1985 by the Islamic Jihad that they had executed Buckley, it is now known that he died of a heart attack earlier that year on June 3. Buckley's remains were recovered by the Royal Danish Army in December of 1991, after his body was dumped on a road to the Beirut airport. He is buried in Arlington National Cemetery.

There is a small park in the main square of Stoneham, Massachusetts, commemorating the life and service of James Francis Buckley. A list of James Buckley's awards and decorations is excerpted from the records and relisted here:

> Among Buckley's decorations and awards are the Silver Star, Soldier's Medal, Bronze Star Medal with "V" Device, two Purple Hearts, the Meritorious Service Medal, the Combat Infantryman's Badge, and the Parachutist Badge. He also received the Vietnam Cross of Gallantry with bronze star from the Army of the Republic of Vietnam. Among his CIA awards are the Intelligence Star, Exceptional Service Medallion

and Distinguished Intelligence Cross. Among Buckley's civilian awards are the Freedom Foundation Award for Lexington Green Diorama, Collegium and Academy of Distinguished Alumni Boston University. The William F. Buckley Memorial Park in Stoneham, Massachusetts, is dedicated to his memory. The 51st star on the CIA Memorial Wall represents him, surrounded by about 132 other stars (as of January 2021) representing CIA officers killed in the line of duty. Approximately 35 of the stars are for unnamed agents whose identities have not been revealed for national security reasons. His name and year of death are recorded in the "Book of Honor" at the wall. The CIA awarded him the Distinguished Intelligence Cross, an Intelligence Star, and an Exceptional Service Medal .... https://en.wikipedia.org

In what can now be seen as an amazing confluence of continuous global destruction, just two days after the 1983 bombing of the US Marine barracks in Beirut and upon receipt of a request for help from the Organization of Caribbean States, the United States invaded the island of Grenada. The fighting started with the detention of the country's Communist leader Maurice Bishop. Grenadian Deputy Prime Minister Bernard Coard gained the support of Grenadian soldiers loyal to his quest for shared power. Shooting between civilians supporting Bishop and the renegade Grenadian soldiers started the conflict.

On the morning of October 25, 1983, the United States invaded with an overwhelming coalition of armed forces. The assemblage looked more like a massive military exercise, consisting of the US Army's 1st and 2nd Battalions of the 75th Ranger Regiment, the 82nd Airborne, Marines, Army Delta Force, Navy SEALs, and the clandestine paramilitary Special Operations Group of the SAD (Special Activities Division).

The mission of the combined 7,600 troops was in part to ensure the safety and evacuation of 600 US medical students from the island. The outcome lists 19 US soldiers killed, 116 wounded, and nine helicopters destroyed. Ninety-three lives from Grenada, Cuba, and the Soviet Union were also lost.

In a 108 to 9 vote, the United Nations General Assembly adopted a resolution condemning the US invasion and overthrow of the Communist government as a deplorable return to barbarism. It was judged as a flagrant violation of international law and the independence and sovereignty of Grenada. The outcome of the short war included the death by firing squad of the Communist leader Maurice Bishop, and the installation of Queen Elizabeth's representative, Nicholas Brathwaite, as chairman of the interim government. Elections were held and a new government was formed and led by Grenadian Prime Minister Herbert Blaize.

What could be worse than genocide and civil war? Ethiopia is 1,700 air miles away from Beirut. The answer to the question is civil war simultaneously mixed with failed government policies and widespread famine. Ethiopia is familiar with drought and famine. In 1973, famine in the Wollo Province in northern Ethiopia killed more than 50,000 people. Wollo was the home of the Solomonic Dynasty of the Ethiopian empire. The 13th-century citizenry believed themselves to be descendants of King Solomon and the Queen of Sheba. The economy of modern-day Ethiopia is based on agriculture, with 80 percent of all employment and half of the GDP coming from agrarian production. The long and colorful history of the country did not protect them from two decades of war, beginning in the 1960s and continuing into the '80s.

Even though the grain and food production from 1980–1982 was the largest ever, widespread famine from 1983–1985 left 1.2 million people dead (UN estimates). Millions more were left destitute, with 5.8 million people dependent on relief food supplies. The human rights abuses in the war, coupled with the famine, displaced 2.5 million citizens from their homes and orphaned 200,000 children. Agricultural policies that extracted food from the rural peasant farmers to feed the urban population exacerbated the impact of the drought and famine. Farmers were also prohibited from traveling to seek other work and food sources. The ultimate collapse of the system of state-controlled farms further reduced the sources of income to 500,000 farmers in northern Ethiopia.

In 2021, drought-stricken Ethiopia was again at war with itself. A year of fighting between the rebels (Tigray People's Liberation Front / TPLF) in the northern region of Tigray, and Ethiopian government forces displaced more than 2 million people and left hundreds of thousands without food and other life-sustaining supplies. Drought in southern Ethiopia impacted the entire country of 111 million people. About 60 percent of the population was in need of humanitarian aid. Al Jazeera news reported that the United Nations estimated that 100 truckloads of food were needed every day to feed 5 million people. One-fifth of the children in northern Ethiopia were severely undernourished. Caregivers were also severely affected and were literally starving on the job.

The early '80s brought violence to the streets of India. Ongoing civil unrest sparked chaos in the state of Punjab. Repressive policing created anger and resentment in the Sikh population, against authorities. Demands for more autonomy for Punjab were dismissed by the central government. Violence erupted and continued throughout 1981–1984. The combined death toll from violent incidents for civilians, police, and militants reached 410 deaths and more than 1,000 injured.

On June 1 of 1984, India's central government launched an attack to remove the armed militants from the Golden

Temple complex in the city of Amritsar in Punjab, India. Eighty-three army soldiers were killed and 249 were injured in the operation. An estimated 1,600 militants were arrested, and 493 civilians and militants were killed. Four months later, Prime Minister Indira Gandhi was assassinated by bodyguards. After the assassination on October 31, 1984, riots erupted and continued for several days. Congress MP Sajjan Kumar handed out weapons, money, and liquor to the assailants. He offered 5,000 rupees to anyone who killed the Sikh revolutionary Roshan Singh, and 1,000 rupees for any others killed. This resulted in 17,000 Sikhs killed in 40 cities across India, and 50,000 more were displaced by the mayhem. Rioters carried iron rods, clubs, kerosene, and knives. They killed Sikhs indiscriminately and burned businesses and buildings. Gang rapes and acid burnings added to the barbaric chaos. The police sided with the rioters and did little to stop the murders. India's Congress Party officials distributed voter lists to identify the names and locations of Sikh houses. It would take more than three decades before the perpetrators of the genocidal riots would be identified and arrested.

That we can individually and collectively insulate our daily life and thoughts from the atrocities of war and death around the globe is truly a human phenomenon. The global cycle of death and destruction has become an annual and daily struggle for survival for hundreds of thousands of people year after year, decade after decade. The quest for power and control and the imposition of ideologies by barbarous forces have become an accepted norm in modern society. We intellectually and politically condemn the acts of war and the perpetrating forces, while simultaneously going about our normal lives.

The millions of lives lost, the death and genocide of innocent children and families, do not deter the insulated activities of modern life. "The play must go on!" Our children go to school while Mom and Dad are off to work. We play on our beaches and hustle to sporting events and concerts. History will look back on the past millenniums and adjudicate us not by our respective countries or religions, but collectively by a distillation of what is clearly a battle between good and evil.

In 1963, The Reverend Martin Luther King Jr. wrote: "The richer we have become materially, the poorer we become morally and spiritually. We have learned to fly in the air like birds and swim in the sea like fish, but we have not learned the simple art of living together as brothers." From another speech, he added, "He who passively accepts evil is as much involved in it as he who helps to perpetrate it. He who accepts evil without protesting against it is really cooperating with it."

The cycle of man-made self-destruction continues across the globe and into the new millennium. Catastrophic conditions are prevalent in many other countries not mentioned here. Politicians are far too keenly and falsely focused on topics like CO2 emissions and global warming, and the controversial impact of climate change.

Many of the topics and events recorded in the decades between 1950 and 1990 became prescient actions and movements that laid the groundwork for various aspects of life in the 2nd millennium. Advances in space travel, computer science, medicine, and communications technology can find their foundations in the earlier decades. Students lacking knowledge of this history will have a skewed understanding of the importance of the continuum of research and development for the advancement and potentially the destruction of mankind.

"What if free people could live secure in the knowledge that their security did not rest upon the threat of instant retaliation to deter a Soviet attack, that we could intercept and destroy strategic ballistic missiles before they reached our own soil or that of our allies? I call on the scientific community in our country, those who gave us nuclear weapons, to turn their great talents now to the cause of mankind and world peace, to give us the means of rendering these nuclear weapons impotent and obsolete." (President Ronald Reagan, Star Wars Speech, March 23, 1983)

In 1967, physicist Edward Teller inspired California Governor Ronald Reagan with a briefing on directed-energy weapons (DEWs). Twelve years later, after a tour of the underground NORAD facilities deep inside the Cheyenne Mountain Complex near Colorado Springs, Reagan had a revelation. During the tour, General James Hill explained to Reagan that while we had the technology to track incoming nuclear missiles to their targets, we had no capability to stop the ultimate and total destruction from the nuclear detonation.

The defense strategy employed by the United States and the Soviet Union was one of Mutual Assured Destruction, or mutually assured deterrence (MAD). Ballistic missiles could eliminate land-based missile sites and obliterate population centers. However, they could not destroy the nuclear-armed submarines. This mutual second-strike capability was the deterrent to the potential destruction of both countries. The introduction of a space-based capability to neutralize the Soviet threat was seen as escalating an arms race and was met with concern and resistance by the Soviets and our allies. President Reagan's Strategic Defense Initiative (SDI) was misunderstood by his own Cabinet and legislative leaders. His motivation is best explained by remarks made at the unveiling of the Strategic Defense Initiative—nicknamed the "Star Wars program"—in 1983: "I've become more and more deeply convinced that the human spirit must be capable of rising above dealing with other nations and human beings by threatening their existence." (President Ronald Reagan)

President Reagan's vision for a defense against nuclear attack was more than just a desire to fulfill his presidential duty to defend and protect the citizens. It was the advent of a new scientific era. The Strategic Defense Initiative was launched and supported, but was *based on science and technology that had not yet been invented.*

Scientists and inventors of all sorts can now employ Dr. Norman Vincent Peale's power of positive thinking. "Believe you can, and you can. Belief is one of the most powerful of all problem dissolvers. When you believe that a difficulty can be overcome, you are more than halfway to victory over it already. … Change your thoughts and you change your world." (Norman Vincent Peale)

Sadly consistent with past decades, 1985 scrolled through 12 months of continuing human tragedies. Thousands perished in wars, earthquakes, train and plane crashes, and man's inhumanity to man. A chronicle of all the devastating events through the year would fill volumes of history books. As a link to current weather events, a tragic weather phenomenon worth mentioning is the devastating series of 44 tornados ripping through Ohio, Pennsylvania, New York, and Ontario, Canada. Ninety people lost their lives in the storms. Tornadic events of this magnitude would not be seen again until December 10, 2021, when 11 tornadoes ripped through western Kentucky, killing at least 76.

A First Time for Everything

In this 1980s segment, we explore an era of firsts. The evolution of scientific breakthroughs often requires many years of development and experimentation. Some discoveries happen by accident, while others are made coincidentally with other related and unrelated exploratory efforts. The same may be said of sociologically significant events and announcements. Like running water in a stream reshaping a stone, positive and negative changes in the lives of humans can take millenniums. Other, more rapid sociological changes have precipitated from remarkable human interactions, and from wars and other conflicts.

History shows that religious and political leaders and masses of people following one man or woman can bring about rapid changes. Presidents and other iconic leaders have influenced history and shaped society in various ways. In a tragically short lifetime, Dr. Martin Luther King Jr. advanced the remediation and understanding of racism and civil rights in America. His influence is as fresh and meaningful today as it was when he was assassinated in 1968. Eighty-eight-year-old Gloria Steinem is a feminist, journalist, and author. One of her books, titled *The Truth Will Set You Free, But First It Will Piss You Off!: Thoughts on Life, Love, and Rebellion*, depicts the power of her presence and the unparalleled effect she has had on the advancement of women's rights and the battle against child abuse that spans six decades. The list of her awards and accomplishments would fill dozens of pages.

In the world of computing and communications, MIT internet pioneer Paul Mockapetris created the first internet Domain Name System (DNS). Alpha characters and common names replaced the numeric internet protocol addresses used to find machines and services on the internet. This one seemingly mechanical alteration to the way we use the internet has ongoing benefits that we enjoy 36 years later.

Young people today do not know of a world without mobile phones. The first analog cellular network was established in 1983. The United Kingdom saw its first mobile phone network deployed by Vodaphone and Cellnet in 1985. It would be needlessly redundant to describe the benefits of mobile telephony here. Suffice it to say that the firsts of great things are usually followed by continued improvement and development of related applications and technology for the many years that follow.

While not the first artificial heart recipient, in 1984, 54-year-old William J. Schroeder was the first to survive long enough to leave the hospital and resume a limited but normal life. He was the first to use an 11-pound portable support unit for the Jarvik 7 artificial heart. He survived with it for 620 days. Efforts continue today to create a permanent replacement for the human heart.

The decade of the 1980s was the platform for amazing medical discoveries and the implementation of newly developed advanced medical procedures. In 1980, the first child conceived by in vitro fertilization (IVF), Louise Brown, had her second birthday. Numerous advances followed in the next 10 years. The first human heart-lung transplant kicked off the decade.

Dozens of phenomenal advances followed. A list of a few of the more notable developments include: artificial skin, human insulin use, automated DNA sequencing and fingerprinting, robotic surgery, intervascular stents, laser cataract surgery, and Merck & Co. statin drugs.

Taking a stroll through the '80s, we find technology in the news at every turn. The introduction of computer games made the world stage with Nintendo video games. Pac Man and Space Invaders captured the time and interests of children and adults alike. The gaming industry would eventually become a $174 billion market, with nearly a billion players. The sociological consequences on family life and childhood education and development are ongoing areas of concern and study. The current trend in the number of users is strongly upward, with numbers expected to double by 2026. On the positive side, the industry also developed digital video simulators and other online training tools. The first Microsoft Windows operating system was released in 1985. In that same year, the first top-level dot-com domain was registered by a computer systems company as symbolics.com.

On September 1, 1985, explorer-scientist Robert Duane Ballard led a joint French-American expedition to the discovery of the wreck of the RMS *Titanic*. The ship was located south of Newfoundland in 12,500 feet of water. Robert Ballard has participated in over 150 expeditions. In my conversations with the iconic explorer during a visit to Jacksonville University, he explained that a significant number of his undersea explorations were in search of sunken nuclear-powered submarines—ours and the Soviets'. The development and utilization of side-searching sonar and deep-sea submersibles was motivated by more than the quests to find and salvage the *Titanic*.

Tragically, in 1986, NASA's Space Shuttle *Challenger* exploded during launch, killing all seven astronauts. Only a month later, the Soviets successfully launched the *Mir* space station. Plans for the International Space Station, a first, were launched and would be completed 12 years later, in 1998. In July of 1986, Northrup Grumman introduced the first B-2 Stealth Bomber. The reign of the Stealth Bomber continues today, but may see obsolescence with the advent of hypersonic intercontinental rockets traveling at five times the speed of sound.

Other events in the human realm that changed life for the decades that followed included the first legal interracial marriage in South Africa. The '80s brought continued turmoil to the country of South Africa's more than 60 million people. The most notable figure of that era was Nelson Rolihlahla Mandela. Nelson Mandela was imprisoned for 27 years in a tiny cell on Robben Island, off Cape Town. Even though he wasn't released until February of 1990, his voice for change was heard throughout the '80s. In 1964, before beginning what was to be a life sentence, he was transported from his island cell to the courtroom. He spoke from a makeshift dockside lectern for four hours. He ended his speech with the following remarks: "During my lifetime I have dedicated myself to this struggle of the African people. I have fought against white domination, and I have fought against black domination. I have cherished the ideal of a democratic and free society in which all persons live together in harmony and with equal opportunities. It is an ideal which I hope to live for and to achieve. But if needs be, it is an ideal for which I am prepared to die." Mandela became the first Black president of South Africa. He served from 1994 to 1999.

In the United States on May 11, 1985, the FBI arrested and brought charges against five Mafia families in New York City. Members of the Bonanno, Colombo, Gambino, Genovese, and Lucchese crime organizations were charged with murder, drug crimes, illegal gambling, loan sharking, extortion, racketeering, and arson. Five hundred FBI agents and 200 other law enforcement officers brought in more than 110 suspected criminals, including at least 30 of the highest-ranking members of the La Cosa Nostra crime families. While not as colorful and movie-like as in the earlier years, organized crime continues today in the form of offshore online gambling, money laundering, and extortion.

Some firsts in 1987 included the Dow Jones Industrial Average closing above 2,000 for the first time. By April it had cleared 2,500 points. As of this writing, in 2021, it is over 36,000. The year also included "Black Monday." On October 19 the Dow fell 508 points, for a 22.6 percent correction. The largest attendance at a sporting event was recorded in March of 1987: 93,173 sports fans attended the World Wrestling Federation's WrestleMania. While not a sporting event, the record was eclipsed on May 27 when a crowd of 800,000 people stood, shoulder to shoulder, on the Golden Gate Bridge, celebrating the 50th anniversary of the bridge's opening. The phenomenon represented by the gathering of large masses of people is intriguing. We gather for sporting events, speeches, celebrations, and protests. Some events are scheduled and ticketed, and others are spontaneous assemblies of singularly-minded people coming together for a common cause.

Black history was shored up in 1987 by Teddy Seymour when he completed the first solo circumnavigation of the world, sailing safely into the harbor at St. Croix in the US Virgin Islands. Earlier in the year, the iconic singer Aretha Franklin became the first woman to be inducted into the Rock and Roll Hall of Fame.

Modern Protests and Revolutions

Death and destruction never skip a year. In December of 1987, Iraqi planes dropped mustard gas bombs on the civilian population of the Iranian town of Sardasht. The deadly violence continued in Ireland when the Provisional Irish Republican Army (IRA) attacked the barracks of the Royal Ulster Constabulary (RUC). The IRA forces were counterattacked in an ambush by the British Special Air Service (SAS) and all the IRA members were killed. More violent acts made the calendar when Iraq killed 37 American sailors onboard the naval ship USS *Stark*, with two French-made Exocet AM39 missiles.

In 1987, the calendar of destruction is filled in month to month. The country of Chad destroyed a brigade of Libyan soldiers. In Lieyu, in Kinmen County in coastal China, the Republic of China army executed unarmed Vietnamese refugees. Basque terrorists killed 21 and injured 45 when they car-bombed the Hipercor shopping center in Barcelona, Spain. In Mecca, the holiest city of Islam, 400 Iranian pilgrims were killed in clashes with Saudi Arabian security forces. In a genocidal insurgency ordered by Iraqi President Saddam Hussein, Ba'athist Iraqi forces kicked off 1988 by killing more than 150,000 Iranian Kurds. The viral plague of human violence continued throughout the entire 20th century.

On the upside of 1988, the eight-year Soviet-Afghan War came to an end with the withdrawal of Soviet troops in May. By August of that same year, the Iran-Iraq War ended. One million lives were lost in the Iranian-Iraqi conflict. Iran's evil and oppressive intolerance was internationally illustrated in 1989. Ayatollah Ruhollah Khomeini ended diplomatic relations with the United Kingdom and issued a fatwa against the British author Salman Rushdie. The Indian-born author's 1988 novel, *The Satanic Verses*, was the basis for the condemnation and it angered Muslim communities in several countries. The Quranic verses are believed to be Muhammad speaking the voice of the devil and not the Islamic God Allah. The modern re-creation of the ancient stories was considered blasphemous by the offended Iranians and other Muslims. Iran offered a $3,000,000 bounty for the death of Rushdie. After a decade of hiding, Rushdie is now an award-winning author and Distinguished Writer in Residence at New York University. The fatwa was never rescinded, and he lives daily with the Iranian death threat. In August of 2022, Rushdie began to think his life was normal again, but as he was preparing to speak in Chautauqua, New York, he was attacked and stabbed multiple times. His injuries were severe and he lost his vision in one eye. Nerves severed in the attack caused him to lose the use of one hand. The assailant was an Islamic extremist attempting to complete the fatwa against Rushdie.

Across the globe, misery continued to be the predominant theme. Argentina declared a nationwide state of siege in May of 1989 as rioters broke into stores and businesses. Riots and looting were the result of inflation, and that had reached triple digits. The protests were not about a political ideology. They were the result of hunger and the prospect of things becoming worse. A picture of the rioters included working-class people who were experiencing real poverty and hunger. The prices in stores changed hourly. People were looting and demanding that supermarkets give away the food for free. The police were present, but did little to stem the street violence and protests. The riots paused in June when domestic and international food assistance was provided. Hundreds of food stands were opened to distribute the food. The Argentine economy was overwhelmed by government debt, and living standards had been steadily declining for years.

Outgoing President Raul Alfonsin blamed the leftist parties for the collapse. In the prior year Alfonsin had implemented price controls and wage freezes to try and stem the inflation. The plan failed and inflation soared. Interest rates rose sharply, and banks saw their deposits withdrawn or transferred abroad. Businesses lost confidence in the government and refused to pay their taxes. Schools and businesses were closed, and public transportation ceased to operate. The people wanted President-elect Carlos Saul Menem to assume office immediately. Menem opposed the early inauguration and argued that he needed time to prepare for a new government and allow the rioting to subside. In 1990, businesses slowly began to open, but with protective barriers and enhanced security. The rioting continued, but less frequently and in smaller groups that were more easily contained by police.

This brief but tumultuous interlude of desperation and violence was prefaced by decades of governmental failings. It began 30 years earlier when Argentine President Juan Perón and his wife Eva began implementing their plans to create a better life for the poor working class. Their "Social Justice and Love" policies ignored economic reality. They bought the loyalty of the people with massive social spending programs and other union-driven policies. Argentina became the most unionized country in Latin America. The Peróns depleted all income from agricultural exports and shored up failing, inefficient government-directed enterprises. The bureaucracy grew larger, and the governmental mismanagement and high taxes began making a tangible impact on the economy.

The 10 years of rule by President Carlos Menem did not substantially change the inflationary path toward collapse. His programs privatized state-owned utilities and the state-owned oil company, post office, and electric and water companies. The effort initially attracted international investments that temporarily helped to lower inflation, but as the money dried up and government spending continued to exceed income, the economic death spiral continued. The International Monetary Fund (IMF) was partly to blame since their lending and payment postponements hid the underlying economic policy failures.

In the new millennium years that followed under the presidency of Fernando de la Rua, large government spending cuts spurred a new wave of protests. The IMF continued its lending in a financial aid package that created new optimism, but the fiscal deficits and reduced exports income continued to negatively affect the value of Argentina's currency. On December 1, 2000, unemployment was up to 18.3 percent. Labor unions were in a nationwide strike, and the government placed restrictive limits on personal and business cash withdrawals and foreign transfers of money. Unrest and rioting ultimately forced President de la Rua to escape his besieged residence by helicopter. He later resigned and was followed by three more presidents in the next year. The saga of Argentina's economic and social challenges continues today with 40 percent of its 43 million people living in poverty. The IMF is still monitoring Argentina's economy as they restructure the country's $43 billion of debts.

The social and governmental problems presented in 1989 were represented in a historic way when 1 million Chinese protesters marched through Beijing, demanding more economic freedom and democratic rule. The protests began on the evening of April 17, 1989, when 4,000 students marched to the square and joined others already encamped there. Reports of police brutality angered more students, prompting them to join the crowd of protesters. The students were demanding an open dialogue with their government. They wanted increased funding for education and transparency regarding the excessive income of state leaders and their family members. The students wanted to privatize the news media and end laws against freedom of speech and peaceful protesting.

Chinese General Secretary Hu Yaobang was initially sympathetic and tolerant of the student protests. His party blamed him and his lenient policies for the student protests and forced him to resign. When he died on April 15, 1989, the student population blamed the party for his death and the protesters began more aggressively organizing. The student organizations consisted of members from 21 universities. By April 22, the protests took a different turn, and stores were ransacked by rioters. Houses and cars were damaged or destroyed. On April 27, 100,000 students marched to Tiananmen Square. On April 29, Chinese government officials appointed representatives to meet with the students.

Like many organizations formed for change, there were conservative factions that wanted to escalate the protests and more moderate components that wanted to extend the open dialogue with the government. The students began a widely publicized hunger strike. As the news spread in the country, more residents were mobilized in solidarity with the students. Labor unions and other non-Communist political parties joined in the demonstrations. Protests were now staged in over 400 Chinese cities. In Hong Kong, 300,000 gathered in a Concert for Democracy. The next day 1.5 million people paraded and sang their way through Hong Kong in support of the protesting students.

Western countries urged China to show restraint, but the Chinese government declared martial law on May 20 and sent 30 divisions of soldiers to the capital city, where they were met by tens of thousands of demonstrators that surrounded the military vehicles. The army forces retreated to the outskirts of the city and planned for an assault on the square. After failed efforts by moderate student groups and government officials to de-escalate the conflicts and retreat from the square, the Chinese army was ordered to clear the square.

After seven weeks of protests, a force of 300,000 soldiers and 180 military vehicles began the assault on 150,000 student protesters. The actual death and injury reports show conflicting numbers. The Chinese government downplayed the death toll and placed it at 200 students and residents. Press articles published in the United Kingdom put the number at more than 10,000. We know at least 23 soldiers and 218 students were killed, and 7,000 students injured along with 5,000 soldiers. The actual numbers are still not available. The days in the first week of June are chronicled and inscribed in world history with battle scenes that mirror the atrocities of warfare. Mention or discussion of the incident is still discouraged and restricted in China today. Parents avoid sharing knowledge of the massacre with children to protect them from governmental persecution.

Regardless of early governmental efforts to appease the student protesters and avoid violence, Chinese Premier Li Peng will be forever remembered as the leader who oversaw the Tiananmen Square massacre. In the two decades that followed, the Chinese people remained under Communist rule, without freedom of speech or press, and without the right to vote. Reforms would come slowly to the Chinese Communist Republic. Talk of the incident or press editorials were banned. The government refers to the incident as a successful bloodless defeat of revolutionaries seeking to overthrow the Chinese government.

Meanwhile, around the world, life continued its day-to-day exploration into the future of mankind. In America, calming forces prevailed as the FDA approved the drug Prozac as an antidepressant treatment. A UFO landed in Voronezh, Soviet Union, never to be heard from again. Iceland ended a 74-year prohibition on beer and celebrated the first ever Bjordagur, known as Beer Day. As we approached the 1990s, commercial internet providers ramped up their services, and PC manufacturers exponentially pushed their processing speeds into a revolutionary new realm of interpersonal communication. The world was changing at a faster pace than ever seen before.

Death by Electrocution

In the mid-'80s, my career in the electrical contracting business was in full swing. I was a licensed electrical contractor working for Miller Electric Company. My dad was president of the company, and I was a senior project manager. I managed multiple construction and maintenance projects for dozens of customers. My duties required me to visit factories and office buildings to design and plan projects, and investigate problems in existing electrical systems. While I did not actually work with tools and install materials, I did utilize measuring and testing instruments to analyze electrical systems and troubleshoot problems and performance anomalies.

One day in 1987, I visited a large industrial site owned by the Buffalo Steel Company. They manufactured large steel tanks for bulk fuel storage. Bending and cutting large sheets of thick steel required correspondingly large electrical components. Buffalo's incoming power service was delivered at 13,200 volts of electricity. The high-voltage circuit was routed across the site on overhead power lines that dropped down to a fenced-in transformer and switching yards. The high-voltage service was transformed to 5,000 volts for distribution to the buildings and ultimately to 480 volts to serve the plant's manufacturing processes.

I was charged with measuring and evaluating the capacity of the electrical service to determine if it could adequately support an expansion of the manufacturing facility. I planned to place recording meters on the 480-volt lines at the secondary, or output, side of the three large transformers in an outdoor fenced-in yard. The meters had jawlike clamps that encircled the large, 480-volt insulated cables and recorded the amperage flowing through the conductors. The high-voltage 5,000-volt side of each transformer was connected with bare single copper wires in free air, without insulation or protective conduits.

Because the current levels fluctuated through any given day, I needed to install the instruments and record multiple days of plant operation to collect the data and calculate the available capacity for additional loads. The fenced-in transformer yard was a secured area and only qualified personnel were allowed access. I removed the locks and entered the yard with my case containing the recording instruments. The floor of the outdoor yard was covered in white gravel stones. Weeds grew through the rocks in the yard. This one had not been maintained in a while. I carefully moved through the gate, toward the transformers and the bundle of insulated 480-volt conductors. I could touch and manipulate the insulated wires as needed to place the recording clamps around them. I set up the instruments and as I moved toward the transformers, a thorny briar bush snagged my pants leg and caused me to lose my balance. Striking the transformer or the insulated 480-volt cables would not have caused much harm, but coming into contact with the exposed terminals on the transformer would be lethal. The uninsulated 5,000-volt terminals were on the left side and the 480-volt terminals were on the right side of each of the three transformers. My fall placed me in very close proximity to both sides. If I had reached my hand out to stop my fall, I would have been electrocuted. I completed the task and never told anyone about my near-death experience.

Still, the subject of death by electrocution is permanently preserved in my memory. I can clearly recall and see the faces of a dead apprentice electrician, along with his devastated fiancée and his parents with their painfully blank stares. I was managing an electrical expansion project for AT&T in St. Augustine, Florida. It was not a complex project and required the use of only one electrician, assisted by an apprentice, named John Herbert "Jack" Wilson. Jack and his foreman were installing a power circuit to a new insulating stripping machine. The AT&T facility used machines to strip the thermoplastic insulation from telephone cables that were no longer in use. The bare copper conductors were then salvaged and melted into stock for the manufacture of new, higher-performance communications cabling.

The 480-volt, 30-ampere circuit being installed consisted of five 10-gauge copper conductors in a one-inch diameter steel conduit. While the wires were relatively small and similar to the circuit supplying power to a dryer or water heater in a home, the voltage applied to the circuit was much higher. Jack and his journeyman had nearly completed the installation of the wiring, and the electrician was on an elevated scaffold 20 feet above the concrete floor below. He fed the flexible one-inch conduit down to Jack and the location of the new stripping machine.

Jack sat cross-legged on the floor and worked to remove the plastic tape and pulling eye attached to the bundle of cables in the flexible steel conduit. He grabbed the wires and attempted to cut them loose from the pulling eye. At the panelboard on the other end of the circuit, the conductors were terminated on a circuit breaker in the panel. The breaker had been turned off and secured with tape and a sign that read: DO NOT TURN ON. The panelboard also served other actively used machines. Occasionally the active machines would jam and trip the circuit breaker serving the machine. AT&T workers would clear the jammed machine and attempt to reset the tripped breaker at the panelboard.

The workforce employed by AT&T at the stripping facility was mostly Hispanic. Apparently, most of the workers did not understand or read the English language. One such worker had removed the warning sign and unintentionally turned on the wrong breaker. Jack and his supervisor were several hundred feet away and did not know that the circuit had been inadvertently energized. When Jack cut into the bundle of wires, his uninsulated metal cutting and stripping tool short-circuited the conductors. The 480-volt fault current surged through his body in search of "ground." His sitting position on the bare concrete provided the electrical connection to earth. The duration of the short circuit and the extremely high fault current was extended because the neutral and grounding conductors were not involved in the wire cutting. The circuit breaker would not trip until the current exceeded the designed time and current levels.

The electrician on the scaffold 20 feet above Jack screamed for someone to turn the breaker off. By the time the electrician reached Jack, he was unconscious and did not have a pulse. The electrician started CPR and continued for 20 minutes, until the emergency response team arrived. The chest compressions kept Jack alive, but he perished 10 hours later. Electric shock damages the heart and nervous system and other major organs. The lungs are particularly susceptible to electric shock. Jack's lungs filled with fluids, and he was unable to breathe. He never regained consciousness.

Jack's death, along with hundreds of other deaths and thousands of injuries in the electrical construction industry, brought about a wave of changes to codes and regulations at local, state, and federal levels. The insulation of tools used in electrical construction is now an industry standard. Working on or in close proximity to energized electrical systems and components is prohibited in our company. Exceptions are highly documented, with multiple layers of approval required. Highly specialized protective gear and clothing are required to be worn.

The National Electrical Codes, the Occupational Safety and Health Administration (OSHA) guidelines and laws, the national Life Safety Code, and state and county laws and ordinances now more comprehensively address electrical construction safety, and require strict adherence to the safety procedures mandated by law. Changes in electrical safety requirements have created a major market for manufacturers of safety products. Circuit breakers have been redesigned with ground fault–interrupting features. Mandated electrical safety training programs are prevalent in every state. OSHA requires recurring training and certification for workers and supervisors. Insurance providers are also major players in the efforts to prevent jobsite injuries. Death and injury in the construction industry is no longer an accepted hazard. The prevention of death and injury is the first priority on every construction site. Jack's death was a tragic loss, yet it brought about major change in the construction industry. His name is immortalized in the naming of an annual award given to electrical workers for demonstrating excellence in electrical safety. Rest in peace, Jack Herbert Wilson.

Ten Years before the Millennium

The 1990s continued the juxtaposition of the modern world and extraordinary advances in modern technology, with the irony of the ongoing medieval atrocities of war around the globe. The dot-com frenzy surged in the '90s amidst the sounds from the rave, hip-hop, grunge scene. The youth culture brought about a regression to the retro countercultural styles of the '60s and '70s. The Millennials, born in the '90s, embraced surreal individualism with tattoos, body-piercing jewelry, and attention-seeking extreme sports. Meanwhile, regional and civil wars and assassinations plagued the earth in more than a dozen countries around the globe.

The Congo War, Gulf War, Chechen Wars, Ethiopian, Pakistan-Indian, Yugoslavian, Croatian, and Bosnian Wars all filled the months and years of the 1990s. The questions and answers pertaining to the causes and reasoning in each war will fill many textbooks and biographies. The just and unjust causes included: economic and social pressures in Iraq, ethnic cleansing in Bosnia and Yugoslavia, fighting for independence in Chechnya, Hutus killing Rwandan Tutsis (800,000 in 100 days), and the quest for political power in a dozen more civil wars.

The word "civil" and its five different and unrelated definitions has no meaningful place as an adjective to war. The atrocities in all the conflicts mentioned were horrendous. One could attempt justification of the horrors of war with quips like "Fight to win" or "Right must prevail."

The truth that will hopefully be adjudicated by a truly "civil" society in a future millennium is that man is bifurcated with equal contents of good and evil. If he feeds the good wolf with a passion for godliness and loving compassion, the evil wolf will starve and remain at bay.

Two very significant changes occurred in the time between 1988 and 1991 that literally changed the landscape in Europe: the unification of East and West Germany and the dissolution of the Soviet Union into 15 independent, self-governing republics. It is remarkable and historic when the will of the people is conjoined with the actions and persistence of a great leader. Mikhail Gorbachev was in the right job at the right time to bring about changes that reshaped the geopolitical world. Millions of people came to experience newfound freedoms and prosperity.

Mikhail Gorbachev was named *Time* magazine's "Man of the Year" in 1988 and "Man of the Decade" the following year. In 1990 he won the Nobel Peace Prize recognizing the radical reforms he had implemented as leader of the USSR. Despite his progressive political successes, he was disappointed when the Soviet Union was dismantled in 1991. Members of the Communist Party were also disappointed and removed him from office in August of 1991. Regardless of his feelings, his actions brought about a peaceful end to a long and bloody reign of Stalinism.

Gorbachev's *glasnost* policy brought about a new and open atmosphere of governance. Political prisoners were released. The policy of controlling the press and book banning ended. The secret police were no longer omnipresent. He brought an end to the arms race and ended the war in Afghanistan.

Additionally, Gorbachev released the government's grip on the economy and allowed individuals and companies to form and run their own businesses. His policy of *perestroika* shifted the government-controlled economy to a free market economy. Such a drastic change did not immediately bring relief to the Soviet State. The economy was headed in the right direction, but collapsed under the weight of the enormous transformation and the lingering remnants of a militarized government.

A remarkable step forward for human advancement was made in 1987 by Soviet Premier Mikhail Gorbachev, when he responded positively to a challenge by President Ronald Reagan to tear down the Berlin Wall and allow the reunification of East and West Germany. The wall was originally built to stop the enormous flow of East Germans fleeing to the West. In the 12-year span between 1949 and 1961, the departure of 3.5 million East Germans destroyed the economy and productivity of East Germany. What started as a barbed-wire barrier ended up as an 830-mile-long concrete-and-steel fence obstruction with land mines and armed guard stations. The wall represented a line between Western-style freedoms and militarized Communist rule.

The news spread quickly after a series of missteps and confusing televised communications announcing that East Germans could legally and permanently emigrate to West Germany. On October 9, 1989, 70,000 people assembled at the St. Nicholas Church in the East German city of Leipzig. Despite the presence of armed police forces and without a shot being fired, many in the group began to march to the border and crossed into West Germany. This was the beginning of the fall of the Berlin Wall.

A convergence of new and freer governance policies and the effects of a struggling economy inspired Soviet satellite states to seek independence. Like dominos falling, the Baltic states of

Estonia, Lithuania, and Latvia declared their independence from the Soviet Union. In December of 1991, Gorbachev prompted a peaceful separation for Belarus and Ukraine and eight more republics. Newly found freedoms quickly prompted revolutions against Communist rule that swept through the Eastern Bloc countries. Europe, Poland, Hungary, Czechoslovakia, and Romania revolted and turned away from Communist rule. On August 23, 2 million people in Estonia, Latvia, and Lithuania joined hands and demanded freedom and independence from Soviet occupation. The continuous 600 km chain was called the Baltic Way and marked what was known as the Singing Revolution. Earlier, in 1989, 35 European nations had met in Vienna and vowed to strengthen human rights and promote East-West trade. The year was a turning point for humanity in the Eastern Hemisphere.

On Christmas Day, Soviet Premier Mikhail Gorbachev resigned from office and shared this sentiment: "We're now living in a new world. An end has been put to the Cold War and to the arms race, as well as to the mad militarization of the country, which has crippled our economy, public attitudes and morals." That was the end of the Soviet Empire.

The '90s were packed with so many things, good and bad. Some things brought both attributes. The introduction of the 24-hour news cycle emanated from CNN's 24 x 7 coverage of the Gulf War. Initially, the continuous availability of current news was a welcome advancement. Today the economic pressure to produce meaningful information for news broadcasts has morphed into a ratings game that often yields incorrect information and even "fake news." Narratives and graphic summaries are posted and re-posted without journalistic research and verification. Phone cameras, email, YouTube, and Twitter became amateur news broadcasting tools. Mass media outlets coalesced and created common agenda–driven dialogues with key words and phrases being simulcast to an unsuspecting public audience. Buying decisions, social and moral judgments, and even elections are now influenced by organized social media and televised for-profit newscasts.

Overarching events such as Monica Lewinsky's affair with President Bill Clinton, Anne Heche's firing for dating Ellen DeGeneres, and the birth of Justin Bieber are only a few of the impactful occurrences recorded in the decade of the '90s. The movie *Pretty Woman* and the first push-up Wonder Bras were introduced. As interesting as those two occurrences may have been, the real pronouncement was about "power and money" as a theme for the decade. Those in power gained wealth, those with wealth gained power, and those with disparate computer skills changed the world.

To the topic of money, in 1994 Amazon changed the world of business commerce forever. Two Princeton graduates—an engineer and a novelist—were in a bar, and one says to the other, "Let's get married and become the richest people in the world." In July of 1994, Jeff and MacKenzie Bezos started Amazon as an online seller of magazines and music videos. After going public in 1997, Amazon added consumer electronics, games, toys, home improvement items, and software to its product list. In 2018, the company added the nostalgic brick-and-mortar business of selling books in small stores around the world.

Jeff continued his reign as CEO until 2021. Today Amazon provides a multilevel e-commerce platform that allows anyone to sell almost anything to anyone. E-commerce businesses use their own websites for sales, as well as placing products on Amazon's sites. Third-party individuals can also post Amazon sales links and earn commissions from click-through sales. In 1998 Amazon's annual revenue was $610 million. By

2010, revenue grew to $34 billion. In 2020, with total assets exceeding $320 billion, 1.3 million employees saw total annual revenue grow to just under $400 billion.

In 1994, 24-year-old MacKenzie Scott and 28-year-old Jeff Bezos did actually get married and moved to Seattle and lived happily ever after. Well, not quite. They were divorced in 2019 and she took her 4 percent stake in Amazon and became the third-wealthiest woman in the US. In 2020, she donated almost $6 billion of her $60 billion net worth to charity. Jeff went on to become the second-wealthiest man in the world, with a net worth of more than $200 billion. *Forbes* magazine titled him as "The richest man in modern history."

In January of 1996, Stanford University graduate students Larry Page and Sergey Brin, assisted by Scott Hassan and Alan Steremberg, developed a search engine algorithm called "BackRub." The creation ultimately became the software application known today as Google. The book of all knowledge was now at the fingertips of internet users around the world.

Page and Brin formed a company and registered the domain name www.google.com on September 15, 1997. They began work in a garage owned by Susan Wojcicki. Susan became Google's first marketing manager. Today, along with many other accomplishments, she is the CEO of YouTube. Susan was listed in *Time* magazine's "100 Most Influential People in 2015." She was also on the *Forbes* and *Fortune* magazines' lists of the "World's 100 Most Powerful Women."

In the fall of 1998, the successful convergence of higher education and entrepreneurial will produced the fulfilment of "the American Dream" for two young men. It ultimately brought enormous wealth to them and to thousands more. The company provides gainful employment to well over 135,000 employees. The world's real-time access to current events, historical knowledge, and learning opportunities in every academic and scientific discipline is now available at the touch of a keyboard or a query from a voice command. With an initial investment of $100,000 from German immigrant and electrical engineer Andy Bechtolsheim, and another $200,000 from Canadian computer scientist David Cheriton, Google was incorporated on September 7, 1998.

Andy Bechtolsheim was the founder of Sun Microsystems. He and David Cheriton founded Granite Systems and developed Gigabit Ethernet products. Granite was acquired by Cisco Systems for $220 million in 1996. Today more than two-thirds of the US population and 2.3 billion users worldwide enjoy the benefits of Google's online services, Google's search engine, and Google internet advertising products. Google's annual revenue in 2021 will exceed $240 billion, with $65 billion in earnings.

Regarding "power" as an asset, the resignation of Russian President Boris Yeltsin, in December of 1999, gave rise to Prime Minister Vladimir Putin stepping into the role. Thirty-two years later, his presidency continues its impact and relevance on the world stage. An overlook of Putin's life finds a man beguiling and resourceful in his youth. His government service was apparently well regarded; he was regularly promoted and supported with greater influence in his appointed political positions. After becoming Russia's president in the year 2000, he was seen as a savior by the citizens that had become weary with Boris Yeltsin's economic and geopolitical failures.

Vladimir Putin was born October 7, 1952, in Leningrad, Russia, the second-largest city in the country. The original name, in 1703, was Saint Petersburg. In the beginning of World War I, the name was changed to Petrograd to reflect a more Russian-sounding heritage. In the Russian Revolution of 1924, Vladimir Lenin and the Bolsheviks took control and renamed the city Leningrad. When the USSR collapsed in 1991, the city voted to return to the original name of Saint Petersburg.

Putin grew up in a very cramped and dilapidated communal apartment with no bathtub. Their toilet was located next to an unstable, rat-infested stairwell. Putin's father was a disabled factory worker who had lost the use of his legs in World War II. Putin's mother, who lost a child during the war, did odd jobs cleaning and sweeping the street. Starvation was an ongoing threat in the war years. Putin and his friends spent time chasing rats in the apartment stairwell. In his own words, he described how he once cornered a large rat. "It had nowhere to run. Suddenly it lashed around and threw itself at me ... now the rat was chasing me." This was a lesson in his life and the memory stayed with him.

Vladimir Vladimirovich Putin attended the local grammar school and high school. He graduated from Leningrad State University with a law degree. His education and other forces obscured in his history launched him into East Germany as an intelligence officer in the Committee for State Security known as the KGB. The KGB was established by Nikita Khrushchev and had the role of state security and foreign affairs, as well as its notorious history as the secret police. The precursor was the NKGB, established before World War II by Joseph Stalin, as the People's Commissariat for State Security.

In 1990 Vladimir Putin retired from the KGB with the rank of lieutenant colonel. The next year, he was taken in as an advisor and quickly promoted to head of External Relations by the mayor of Leningrad, Anatoly Sobchak. Three years later Putin was named to a new position created by Sobchak, as deputy mayor. In 1996 Putin moved to Moscow and within two years he was appointed by Russian President Boris Yeltsin to the position of Deputy Head of Management. Less than one year later, Putin was appointed to be Yeltsin's Head of the Security Council and the Federal Security Service. Within months, in August of 1999, Yeltsin replaced Prime Minister

Sergei Stepashin and his cabinet and named Vladimir Putin as prime minister. In December of that same year, Russian President Yeltsin resigned and appointed Putin as interim president. Elections were held in March of 2000 and Putin was elected to his first term as president of Russia.

Prior to and parallel to the tumultuous changes in Yeltsin's administration, Russia was in an extended war in the Muslim Republic of Chechnya in southern Russia. While they were part of the Soviet Union prior to 1991, for two centuries the Chechen people resisted Russian rule and, following the collapse of the USSR, they sought independence. Russia bombed the towns in Chechnya and destroyed the buildings, killing thousands of soldiers and tens of thousands more civilians. After two years of battling rebel soldiers, Boris Yeltsin's government lost the war and signed a peace treaty with Chechnya.

By the end of the same month that Vladimir Putin was named prime minister in 1999, he began a new bombing campaign in Chechnya. The country was devastated and under Russian control again. Four years later, in 2004, Chechen President Akhmad Kadyrov was assassinated. He was succeeded by his 30-year-old son Ramzan Kadyrov, who remains president today. Ramzan was ironically a Chechen rebel, but after taking office he descended into despotism. New York–based Human Rights Watch has called out his crimes against humanity. His restrictions on the public lives of women and his anti-gay positions and gay-purging disappearances of Chechen citizens, along with incidents of kidnapping and torture of activists and critics, have defined him as a tyrannical Muslim ruler. Chechen soldiers are assisting Vladimir Putin in the war in Ukraine today (2022).

Putin's enigmatic stronghold on political power was demonstrated again in 2008 when he was prevented from running for reelection by constitutional term limits. His protégé,

Dmitry Medvedev, was elected president and immediately named Putin as prime minister. In 2012 Putin was reelected to a third presidential term and appointed Medvedev as prime minister. This phenomenal manipulation of political power was met with protests and allegations of election fraud.

Pulling away from US diplomacy at the end of 2012, Putin banned the adoption of Russian children by US citizens. He banned adoptions of children by gay Russian couples. He also spiked US criticism when he provided asylum to the National Security Agency (NSA) spy Edward Snowden. US President Barack Obama's reaction was to cancel planned meetings with Russian President Putin.

The years 2013 and 2014 brought more turmoil to the region as Putin aligned with Syrian President Bashar al-Assad regarding challenges by the US over the use of chemical weapons in Syria. A three-party agreement ultimately averted a crisis, and a deal was made to destroy the weapons. In the buildup to the conflicted Winter Olympics in Russia, Putin welcomed open dialogue to avoid escalation of Middle East unrest and conflict. Following the Winter Olympics and the political removal of Ukrainian President Victor Yanukovych, Putin dispatched 16,000 Russian troops to the northeast coast of the Black Sea and into Crimea. The country was previously part of Russia before it was given to Ukraine in 1954. Avoiding violence and warfare, the Crimean populace voted to secede from Ukraine and reunite with Russia. While the international community contested the referendum of reunification, Putin's efforts to achieve a nonmilitary resolution placed him on the list of nominees for the 2014 Nobel Peace Prize. As the opening paragraph suggested, Vladimir Vladimirovich Putin is both beguiling and contemptible.

Expanding My Medical Vocabulary

In 1994 my wife went in for her usual annual physical with our friend and obstetrician, Dr. Bill Long. He referred Hilah to St. Vincent's Hospital for a routine mammogram. The results were not routine. The low-dose X-ray showed ductal microcalcifications, which potentially indicate a cancerous condition. A needle biopsy confirmed the cancer diagnosis. In 1994, the five-year survivability rate was approximately 60–80 percent, and 50,000 women in the US would die that year from breast cancer. In a world where Powerball lottery ticket buyers demonstrate confidence in winning despite the one in 300 million odds, the prospect of mortality for more than 20 out of 100 cancer patients was very upsetting for my wife and me. We dealt with the negative outlook by focusing on researching the disease and the best treatment plans. With early detection, breast cancer today has a survivability rate of 99 percent in women ages 15–49 years old. My wife was only 44 years old.

We were presented with treatment options that included a lumpectomy, which would have been significantly invasive because the cancer was diffusely distributed in the mammary ducts. A close friend had recently elected to preserve her breast and chose the lumpectomy procedure, but died six months later when the cancer metastasized to other parts of her body. The treatment we selected was a modified radical mastectomy and removal of the right breast. Due to the early detection and the localized nature of the disease, radiation and chemotherapy were not required.

For women aged 44 or so, it was a common procedure to follow up breast mastectomies with reconstructive surgery. We consulted with a couple of surgeons at St. Vincent's Hospital and the Cancer Institute at Emory University. We selected Dr. John Harris, a renowned plastic surgeon at the Mayo Clinic in Jacksonville, Florida. He performed a complicated reconstruction surgery involving the relocation of muscle tissue from her back to form a breast with natural appearance and density. Twenty-eight years later, Hilah remains cancer free and lives a healthy, normal life.

In the fall of 1994 my wife and I sold our home in the Ortega Forest development in the West Side area of Jacksonville, Florida. We moved to a rented home on the Atlantic Ocean in Jacksonville Beach. My wife was in the hospital for a couple of days after her reconstructive surgery. The day before I was scheduled to pick her up from Mayo Hospital's temporary facilities at St. Luke's Hospital in Jacksonville, I developed an unusual headache in the occipital lobe of my brain, at the back of my head. The pain was intense and unlike any headache I had ever experienced. I attributed it to stress, or, more accurately, the consumption of unusually large amounts of Scotch liquor to counter my anxiety and stress. That night I slept in a near upright position to relieve the pressure building in my skull. The next morning, after a sleepless night, the pain was still intense.

I dressed and began the drive to the hospital to retrieve my wife. After she was discharged from her hospital room, she developed some dizziness and nausea. Dr. Harris conveniently managed to place her in an emergency room bed to stabilize her for the trip home. I called her and spoke to her as I drove toward the hospital. When I was within a mile of the highway off-ramp to the hospital, my speech became slurred and unintelligible. Hilah was alarmed and handed the phone to Dr. Harris. He immediately recognized the signs of a stroke and told me to pull over and wait for an emergency vehicle.

I could see the highway exit, and the ER was located very close to the exit. I kept driving. My left arm was now in a cyclical spasm and shaking about in a Parkinson's-like tremor. I was still on the phone with my wife and Dr. Harris, but I could not speak. I approached the entrance to the emergency room, and for some politely delusionary reason I parked in the parking lot and walked to the entrance. The triage nurse was aware of my impending arrival and took one look at me and my purple head and took me by the arm and said, "Come with me." She took my blood pressure and recorded it at a record high level of 225 over 128. I was about to hemorrhage my life's spirit into an already troubled brain.

A double dose of the miracle drug clonidine was administered, along with other lifesaving intravenous fluids and medications. Within two hours, I was stable and coherent and moved to a hospital room set up for patient monitoring. After an extensive cardiac workup and an evaluation by a physician who specialized in my condition, he surmised that due to my age and the lack of any findings of heart-related anomalies, my condition was likely caused by stenosis of a renal artery. He was correct, and I was scheduled for angioplasty of the right renal artery.

The news of my near demise spread to family members and friends. The day after the angioplasty, my two sisters visited me in the hospital room. I was stable and feeling generally okay. I was connected to a blood pressure and heart monitor. My sisters sat on the edge of the bed and offered encouragement and consoling thoughts for my recovery. I was watching my blood pressure readings and they were not normal. They continued to rise. I told my younger sister that when the lower, diastolic, number exceeded 110, significant things would begin to happen.

The blood pressure level did rise, and I reacted in a distorted poltergeist-like manner. My voice wavered and my legs began to shake uncontrollably. My older sister Susan stepped to the doorway and screamed, "Somebody get in here now!" It could have been real or just an overactive imagination, but I was hovering at the ceiling above the bed. I was surrounded by a very bright light, and I could hear my sisters talking below as they tried to calm me down. A young nurse's aide came in and exclaimed that it must be an anxiety attack. She was of course wrong, and I was quickly transported to an intensive care unit on a different floor, where I was treated and electronically monitored. Following a repeat angioplasty procedure, I remained in intensive care for four more nights and days. Sleeping alone in a dark hospital room illuminated by small blinking red lights and kept awake by an automatic blood pressure cuff pumping up every 20 minutes is not an experience I care to repeat.

Life returned to normal in the first months of 1995. Living on the beach was pleasant except for the nearly continuous Northeaster winter storms that blasted the sand against the beachside windows of the house. We went about living a normal life and shopped for a new home in Ponte Vedra Beach. One evening in February, while visiting friends at their oceanside condominium in St. Augustine, I developed a case of shivering chills and a feeling of dread that I was having another ischemic attack. When your blood pressure goes up and the brain is not receiving enough oxygenated blood, it impedes the blood to the rest of your body and you feel very cold. My wife could see what was happening and she said, "Let's go now." She drove me to the hospital in St. Augustine. After a couple of hours of my not getting the proper attention and treatment, Hilah drove me to the Mayo Hospital in Jacksonville. They repeated the angioplasty and cleared the renal artery stenosis with a catheter that pumped up the tiny balloon in my collapsed artery. A few more days in a hospital bed and I was as good as new. Today I travel with a clonidine pill bottle in my dop kit for emergency use. It's been 27 years now, without a repeat performance.

The Y2K Millennium Bug

The year 2000 branded a generation of young men and women coming of age as Gen Y Millennials. Young people ages 24–34, born after 1980, brought significant sociological changes: some good and many not so good. It was the year that many computer scientists believed would crash all electronic devices that used integrated circuit chips with a clock and calendar that ended at midnight on December 31, 1999.

The first generation born into a world with easy access and use of the internet, cell phones, and social media platforms brought a shift in attitudes toward major categories of human behavior. Institutional research in the years beginning in 1990 and into the first two decades of the new millennium confirms a great number of significant trends pertaining to attitudes and activities of the Gen Y group of young people.

The importance of wealth surged upward from 40 percent for baby boomers, to 75 percent for Millennials. The importance and knowledge of political affairs dropped from 50 percent to 35 percent. Contrary to common perceptions of the younger generation, the desire to participate in environmental cleanup projects dropped from 33 percent to 21 percent. While the trend was to prepare for careers in medicine, law, and jobs requiring STEM-based education curriculums, the unemployment rates increased significantly for Millennials.

The continued trend away from the use of tobacco products did not improve the quality of health for this population. Alcohol use trended slightly downward but coincided with increased use of marijuana and cocaine. Seventy percent of Millennials are or will be overweight by the age of 35. Diabetes, heart disease, high blood pressure, and strokes are on the rise for this segment of the population. There was a 40 percent increase in strokes among 20- to 30-year-olds in the years between 2010 and 2020. A 50-year trend in increasing cases of nearsighted vision turned upward as mobile device viewing screens were reduced in size.

For the world in general, the year 2000 continued to see the tragedies of war and natural disasters. Planes crashed, trains collided, tornadoes and storms took a steady toll of lives in the first years of the new millennium. Rwanda, Bosnia, Chechnya, Yemen, and the Philippines all made headlines with violent acts of war and terrorist bombings.

In what is known as the Great War of Africa, between 1998 and 2003, 6,000 fighters were killed, but 350,000 others died in the violence across nine African countries. More than 5 million more died from starvation and disease as a result of the fighting. A Second Chechen War erupted in 1999–2000, killing more than 7,500 Russian soldiers and 25,000 Chechens, mostly civilians. In February of 2002, Russians massacred 60 Chechen civilians in Grozny, and later in August, Chechens shot down an Mi-26 Russian helicopter, killing 118 soldiers.

The capstone of the year 2000 may be the Six-Day War in Kisangani, located in the Democratic Republic of the Congo. The Rwandan Patriotic Army (RPA) and Ugandan forces battled and destroyed the city, leaving 1,000 dead. For decades the Hutu farmers and Tutsi cattlemen laid the groundwork for ongoing conflicts. Initially they were fighting over class divisions and discrimination. The more contemporary conflicts in the Congo are over taxation and distribution rights for uranium, silver, gold, zinc, copper, and other precious metals. The mining of more than 1,100 minerals, including cassiterite, cobalt, and coltan, has devastated entire forests. Columbite-tantalite, known as coltan, is used in the production materials essential to the manufacturing of electronic components. Economists place the value of the mineral wealth in the Congo at $24 trillion. Congo is also home to nearly 200 million acres of arable land. The Rwandans control the sale of minerals to enrich and arm their army. At least 10 flights daily land and load, and continue on to European cities for the illicit trade of the country's natural resources.

Tragic death is brought by other heinous acts other than warfare. The new millennium brought forward old human ills to the Congo. "Heaven's Gate," a Ugandan cult promoting Armageddon and the "Restoration of the Ten Commandments of God," assembled thousands of followers in their church for a mass suicide. They nailed shut the windows and doors of their "Boat of Noah" before dousing themselves and others with gasoline. The death count of 924 people in the church included 395 men, women, and children reluctant to take their own life by fire. They were murdered by strangulation and other forceful means. Like many twisted cults, the elite members in leadership were also guilty of other crimes such as rape, kidnapping of children, and unlawful containment.

The first year of the millennium closed with an Austrian cable car fire killing 155 skiers and snowboarders. A Baku (Azerbaijan) earthquake took the lives of 26, and another in Gujarat, India, left 20,000 dead.

Death comes to us frequently, with widely varied impact and responses. We read about the casualties of war and think sad thoughts and wish that wars would end. We send our "thoughts and prayers" from an endless supply. We express our frustrations with brutal dictators and the political statespeople who facilitate the acts of war with equal disdain. When a death is more personal or close to our insular well-being, we weep with sorrow over the loss. Wars are often protested when the news of tragic losses manifest into organized revolts. More personal losses leave behind devastated families to suffer with unending grief.

September 11, 2001, marks an indelible turning point in American history. More than 20 years after the fallen World Trade Center Towers were destroyed by Islamic terrorists, the heinous act remains a fresh wound in the psyche of the American people. Though the Islamic Caliphate in Afghanistan was obliterated, the battle continued around the world with soldiers of radical Islam bombing and killing innocent people in New York, London, Madrid, Paris, Philippines, Indonesia, and Moscow. Militant followers of radical Islam have killed more than 200,000 innocent people in 48,000 attacks since 2001.

The World Trade Center was built on a 16-acre site in the borough of Manhattan, New York. The complex included seven buildings and a large plaza over an underground shopping mall. The two largest structures contained 110 floors in each building. From the top floors, elevated to 1,300 feet, you could see for 45 miles on a clear day. The 99 elevators in each tower moved 70,000 workers and tourists daily.

Osama bin Laden was the emir and criminal mastermind behind the terrorist acts carried out by al-Qaeda henchmen dispatched around the world in clandestine cells. Ayman al-Zawahiri was the devil's partner in the uncountable crimes perpetrated against humanity. Nineteen al-Qaeda extremists from Saudi Arabia, United Emirates, Lebanon, and Egypt were activated, received the directives and training, including the flight training required for the 9/11 attacks.

At 8:46 a.m. on September 11, 2001, American Airlines

Flight 11 with 92 people onboard, was flown into the North Tower of the World Trade Center. Seventeen minutes later, a second plane, United Airlines Flight 175 with 65 people onboard, crashed into the South Tower. The resulting fire was immediate and intensified by the burning jet fuel. Floors 93 through 99 in the North Tower and 77 through 85 in the South Tower were severely impacted by the crashes. First responders had no ability to reach the people above the impact zones, and the rooftop antennae farms prevented an airborne rescue.

Four hundred police officers and firefighters were killed when the molten steel beams in the Twin Towers collapsed and the buildings cascaded into a pile of smoldering rubble. A total of 2,753 innocent citizens died in this unthinkable tragedy at the World Trade Center. Survivors and first responders continue to die and suffer from health problems associated with their presence in the burning and toxic air, both in the buildings and in the aftermath and cleanup of the destruction.

During the mayhem in Manhattan, and with no less deadly impact, at 9:37 a.m., a third plane flew into the Pentagon in Arlington County, Virginia. American Airlines Flight 77 crashed into the west side of the building, killing 59 people onboard and 184 others in the building.

A fourth plane, San Francisco–bound United Airlines Flight 93 was the final leg of the terrorists' strike. The intended target was the US Capitol Building. While the four al-Qaeda terrorists seized control of the aircraft, flight attendants and passengers became aware of the other suicide attacks in New York and the Pentagon. Passengers heroically struggled with the hijackers, and the plane crashed into a field in Stonycreek Township, 65 miles southeast of Pittsburgh and 130 miles from Washington, DC. Forty people lost their lives in the crash.

Islamic extremists believe that violence is an acceptable

means to their goal of imposing strict adherence to the cultural and religious practices emanating from the revelations from God and the prophet Muhammad contained in the Quran and the Hadith. The al-Qaeda network of extremists was founded in 1988 by Osama bin Laden. It is one of many Islamist extremist groups. Their main goal is to punish and overthrow governments in the Middle East who do not strictly adhere to the political and social codes sanctioned by their religion. Attacks against the United States were designed to be a punishing deterrent to our assistance to the Middle Eastern countries evolving toward a more Western-style culture.

The 1998 US Embassy bombings in Kenya and Tanzania, the 2000 attack on the USS *Cole*, and the 9/11 attacks all represent the stated goals of al-Qaeda in the fatwas issued by bin Laden in 1996 and 1998. As President George W. Bush said following the 9/11 attacks, "Their leaders are self-appointed. They hate our freedoms, our freedom of religion, our freedom of speech, our freedom to vote and assemble and disagree with each other."

Osama bin Laden sent a "Letter to America" in 2002. In it he described our support of Israel as a great crime which must be erased. "The second thing we call you to do, is to stop your oppression, lies, immorality and debauchery that has spread among you. (a) We call you to be a people of manners, principles, honor, and purity; to reject the immoral acts of fornication, homosexuality, intoxicants, gambling, and trading with interest." (www.Aljazeera.com/archive) Osama bin Laden and al-Qaeda resorted to terrorism as their only alternative to influence their enemies. They could not defeat Middle Eastern or Western countries on the battlefield. But as we witnessed, they could turn the symbol of the World Trade Center and freedom to the ground in a pile of 500,000 pounds of steel and concrete—strewn over

2,753 human bodies.

The subsequent American wars in Iraq and Afghanistan brought more death to American families. We removed the dictator Saddam Hussein from power and witnessed his execution by the Iraqi people. Our attempts to create and maintain a democratic city for the Iraqis ultimately failed as quickly as it was created. Operation Enduring Freedom, in Afghanistan, drove the Taliban from power and tyranny over the people, only to return the same oppressive Taliban to power with our poorly planned and executed exit 20 years later.

On March 13, 2003, the 350,000-year-old footprints of an upright walking human being were found in Italy. To know that mankind has had that many years and more to define and resolve the conflicts of good and evil is either an indication of our lack of resolve, or the failings prescribed by a genetically predisposed condition that prevents the maintenance of peace in our souls.

In February of 2004, 1 million Taiwanese people held hands, creating a 310-mile-long human chain. They were commemorating the 2/28 massacre that occurred in 1947 when Chiang Kai-shek's National Revolutionary Army killed 28,000 citizens to end civil protests and unrest. The ensuing martial law known as the White Terror was maintained for 38 years. Public mention of the incident was prohibited until 1985. The amazing display of collective sorrow was obscured internationally by current events and other tragedies. The memory of the tragic loss of lives will lie dormant until the Taiwanese again reassemble to remind the world of the human cost of despotism.

In April of 2005, 4 million people assembled for the funeral of Pope John Paul II. What was the collective thinking of that mass of people? Was it mourning, or more of a plea for God to open a gateway to a higher plane of existence? Can man achieve a state of equilibrium that will allow the human body and mind to create a world without violence?

In 2004 we sent an unmanned vehicle to Mars. What were we looking for? More minerals, signs of life, a new world? The following year we tuned up a 70-meter satellite communications dish and aimed it toward the stars. We sent extraterrestrial messages to unknown recipients. What did we ask? What did we share? Was it a message that we were a civilized and advanced society? Any intelligent foreign beings looking toward Earth would surely question the veracity of that message. Perhaps we will receive a return message. Perhaps that text will read: "You are in our thoughts and prayers."

The Silver Slipper

In 2001 I was completing the final year of service on the Florida Electrical Contractor's Licensing Board. As chairman of the board, I was required to attend many meetings in the state's capital city of Tallahassee, Florida. On one overnight trip I asked Jack Eller, my friend and avid FSU fan and graduate, to join me for a visit to his favorite town. He eagerly accepted the invitation and suggested we have dinner at one of his old favorites, the iconic Silver Slipper. The restaurant was built in 1938 on South Adams Street. It changed locations over the years and ended up just south of the Capitol, on Silver Slipper Lane. Its proximity to the state Capitol made it a famous place for politicians, lobbyists, and crooks to meet and make their deals. It was a legendary steakhouse and even more well known as the meeting place for Florida legislators, lobbyists, and other dealmakers. It closed permanently in 2009.

My memories of the Slipper are legendary but not pleasant. A single evening there left me scarred with a badly bruised ego and a sense of unfinished personal business. Jack and I were seated for what should have been a steak dinner with plenty of wine and Jack's customary Miller Lite beer. We were halfway finished with our meal. I watched four oversized fellows approach a young couple seated in the middle of the restaurant and several tables away from ours. The young Black girl and her White companion looked terrified as they were surrounded by the sloppy-looking men.

The four thugs looked to be in their late twenties, with the leader of the pack clocking in at closer to 30 years of age. They were unattractive and clearly trained in the mannerisms and posture of full-bred Tallahassee rednecks. After a few tormenting minutes, they left the couple and returned to their table. I rose to visit the restroom and had to pass their table along the way. Jack had joined me and continued to the restroom as I approached the table of rednecks. I was smiling and friendly, and leaned over their table and politely suggested that they "should leave the poor young couple alone. They are not harming anyone and should be free to dine in peace."

The leader of the pack rose from his seat and stood very close to me and asked, "Who the f— do you think you are?" This cleared the path for the others to rise and circle my position. The chief redneck grabbed my necktie and, before I could react, he cinched the tie tightly around my neck and pulled me forward and away from the table. I followed and stumbled as he dragged me between tables. The situation was desperate. As we passed the second table I grabbed a steak knife from the empty setting and pushed the thug away from me. One of the other gang members reached into his pocket and, with a flick of his wrist, flipped open a five-inch blade.

Another patron who was watching the scene unfold called 911 and reported the disturbance. Within seconds the restaurant's owner came rushing over, yelling to the chief redneck and his accomplices to leave immediately. "Leave now, the police are on the way!" They looked at me and said something like "This ain't over." The owner turned to me and said, "It would be best if you leave too." I commented that we had not paid our bill, and he replied, "Please leave now. I don't need trouble with the police."

Jack returned to our table as I was preparing to exit. I explained that there had been some trouble, and we were leaving. He looked confused. From my appearance and expression, he knew better than to question me. We left the Silver Slipper, and I never returned. The evening could have ended horrifically with bleeding stab wounds for both sides and severe legal consequences for all parties. I hope this is my last recollection of that troubling night.

Iraq, 2005

In 2005 the country of Iraq held the first parliamentary election since 1958. This was gauged to be the result of a successful US invasion and war in Iraq. The cost of the tenuous Iraqi freedom was paid with the lives of 1,500 US soldiers. The total number of civilian deaths has not been accurately established or agreed upon. It is safe to say that the total is somewhere between the low estimate of 185,000 and maybe as high as 207,000. The annual price tag was measured in billions of dollars, and by 2008 exceeded $3 trillion.

Prior to the first parliamentary elections in 2005, Iraqi President Saddam Hussein was elected by a national referendum in 1995 and again in 2002. The authoritarian government was a Unitary Ba'athist one-party Socialist republic. At present, Iraq is a parliamentary representative democratic republic with multiple parties. A National Assembly and Council of Representatives is elected, and they select the prime minister as head of the government. They also select the president. Legislative power is held by the Council of Representatives.

At the conclusion of the Iraq War in 2011, a Transitional Administrative Law was created that selected a president and two vice presidents. This three-person Presidential Council appointed a prime minister and drafted a constitution. The document provided freedom of religion, speech, and rights of assembly. Under the new electoral system that was later used in the 2005 parliamentary election, 25 percent of all candidates elected to the National Assembly were required to be women. The system was ultimately divided into 18 governorates and 83 multi-member electoral districts. The 329 parliamentary seats are allocated proportionately to the districts, based on the size of the district. The three to six seats in each district go to the candidates receiving the most votes.

In the first general election in 2005, 12 political parties gained representation in the Assembly. The other 99 political groups did not have seats. Out of well over 14.5 million registered voters, 8,456,263 votes were cast in the election. The Assembly appointed the popular Kurdish leader Jalal Talabani as president. He served until 2014 and worked hard to soothe the tempers of the Sunni's Shiites and Kurds, and to avoid being seen as only a pro-Kurdish leader. While Talabani was seen as an elder statesman, in his youth he was a classical Kurdish guerrilla fighter.

The electoral process has been maintained in Iraq. Except for the deadly violence brought by the losers that mistrust the final outcomes, their political struggles look a lot like those we face in the United States. Government corruption and crimes against the people perpetrated by the Iraqi Security Forces in 2019 and 2020, including unlawful arrests, killing of demonstrators, and forceful detainment and disappearances, prompted a call for a regime change. Mustafa Al-Kadhimi, a British-Iraqi lawyer and politician, was nominated in May of 2020 to serve as the new prime minister.

On October 10, 2021, 83 electoral districts in 18 governorates produced a relatively low 44 percent voter turnout to fill 329 Parliament seats. The Sadrist Movement led by Muqtada al-Sadr increased representation from 54 seats to 73, while the Shiite Fateh Alliance representing the al-Hash'd al-Shaabi paramilitary groups lost seats, falling from 48 in 2008, to 17 in the 2021 election. Fateh also lost 10 seats to former prime minister Nouri al-Maliki's State of the Law Coalition.

In keeping with examples found in US elections, the losing Shiite parties reacted with shock and dismay. They formed a united protest claiming election fraud and insisted on legal remedies and a full national manual recount. The Independent High Electoral Commission, consisting primarily of judges, conducted a partial recount and determined that only a small number of seats would be suspect.

November 5, 2021, marked the beginning of violent protests when al-Hash'd factions with links to Iran staged a sit-in at the government buildings campus. In the mostly peaceful protest, two protesters were killed and 100 security forces were injured. The next evening, pro-Iranian groups launched three bomb-laden drones in an assassination attempt on Prime Minister Kadhimi. The attack received international condemnation, and the failed effort was walked back and labeled only a warning. Iranian Commander Esmail Qaani met with Prime Minister Kadhimi and in an effort to bring unity to the Shiite factions, he asked the Fateh block to stand down and accept the election results. The attack resulted in increased tension and division in the Shiite camp, with the majority seeking peaceful assembly and the creation of a Shiite-led government, and a diminishing group of those wanting violent escalation of the protests.

In American style and procedure, the election was ratified by the Iraqi Supreme Court, and the new Parliament convened its first session in December of 2021. In keeping with the shared governance model adopted in the 2003 Transitional Administrative Law, the premiership is owed to a Shiite, the presidency to a Kurd, and the Speaker of the Parliament to a Sunni. Aside from the complexities of Iraqi elections and governance, the economy is more easily understood. Seventy percent of the country's economic sustenance comes from the sale of crude oil. More than 90 percent of the national budget is funded by the sale of oil through the Iraq National Oil Company based in London in the United Kingdom. In addition to National Oil, other domestic oil companies in Iraq also contribute up to 90 percent of all earnings to the government.

Back in 2005, good news was hard to find. Headlines included the death of Johnny Carson at age 79, Tiger Woods winning his fourth Masters, and oil topped $160 per barrel, placing gas prices at $3.07 per gallon. Natural disasters never miss a year. Hurricane Katrina landed in Louisiana, bringing death and destruction, and flooding 80 percent of New Orleans. The storm claimed 1,800 lives and caused $125 billion in damage. To further broaden the perspective of senseless death, an earthquake on the Pakistan-India border killed 86,000 people and left 3.5 million homeless.

2006

The last four years of the decade continued an ongoing and worldwide transformation of sociological mores and human behavior. Google's 2006 acquisition and development of YouTube and the 2007 release of the first Apple iPhone sharply ramped up the rapidly changing way we communicated with each other. One million iPhones were sold in the first 90 days. The impact of mobile technology will go down in history as having changed the way we do business, how we raise a family, and the way we learn of and store information and news of world events.

The World Wide Web opened new mediums of network access in 2008 when the US government auctioned off the next generation of wireless broadband airways. In 2021, 250 million iPhones were sold and only represented one-fourth of the total number of mobile phones sold that year. The immeasurable distortion that new technology brings to our way of life is not yet definable.

The speed at which we communicate has shaped society for thousands of years. The crude boats crafted in the Neolithic period, or New Stone Age, before 3500 BC, and the invention of the wheel in the Bronze Age that followed, advanced mobility beyond the capacity of the upright walking human. Two-wheeled chariots were replaced by carriages with four wheels. Horse-drawn covered wagons evolved over the centuries, as did the roads on which they traveled. The purpose of most vehicles was to move people or materials.

As recently as 1899, the first motorized mail car was introduced and could reach more than 100 mailboxes in less than three hours. A man on horseback could do the same, but it took most of the day. The evolution of horse-drawn mobility in Europe allowed messages and mail to reach nearby villages and towns as far away as 70 miles in a single day. The availability of information avoided many needless conflicts over territory. The need to attack before being attacked was mitigated by the ability to send current information across long distances. Communication yields knowledge and power over the unknown. Today the United States Postal Service has 190,000 mail vehicles and delivers over 600 million pieces of mail daily.

Before the invention of the telegraph, news and articles from foreign correspondents working for US newspapers would take as long as six weeks to reach the desks of the *New York Times* or the *Washington Post*. A paradigm shift occurred in 1844 when Samuel Morse sent a telegraph message across the country. His famous words were "What hath God wrought?"

In another quantum leap forward, transcontinental wireless voice communication was introduced to the world on September 29, 1915, when a radio telephone transmitted a voice message sent from Virginia to Honolulu—5,000 miles away. The first wireless transcontinental voice call was completed the following month in Virginia, when an engineer at an Arlington radio station said "Hello" and "Goodbye" to another engineer in Paris, France. The call was received by an antenna installed on the top of the Eiffel Tower. Fast-forward to April of 1973, when a Motorola engineer called his rival at Bell Labs on a two-pound mobile cellular phone that cost $4,000.

The rapid disbursement of information is both beneficial and sometimes detrimental to society. Quick access to current information frequently has proven to lead to accelerated judgment of people and events. The advent of social media has yielded "social justice" as having an erroneous yet often accepted place in our daily existence. The phrase "innocent until proven guilty" has been largely discarded by our highly informed generation of screen viewers.

So far, television has maintained its first-chair position as the platform of choice for comprehensive news coverage. However, television programming is often and unduly influenced by the onslaught of information produced in the world of electronic social media. In other words, sometimes they get it wrong. Print media also falls prey to the attraction of readily available fodder in the minute-to-minute news blasts.

The advertising world made giant leaps forward with the advent of electronic media delivered to desktops and handheld devices. The corporate world has developed many uses for the technological advances produced in the first decade of the third millennium. Like most new applications of technology, some will also come with unintended consequences. Many companies have suffered from the crushing consequences that negative information can bring. While some circumstances of corporate mischief or product failures may warrant the quick and positive responses of instantaneous broadcasts, dishonest and fraudulent accusations can be harmful and even devastating. Viewers sometimes depersonalize "corporations" as inert and inorganic entities. It has been said, and I agree, that "Corporations are people"!

One example of the damage that false information can bring transpired in March of 2005. Anna Ayala charged the fast-food chain giant Wendy's with serving her a bowl of chili that contained the end section of a human finger. She hired attorneys and filed charges, and appeared on ABC's *Good Morning America* to share her story. The Wendy's store in San Jose, where the event occurred, suffered immediate lost sales of $2.5 million. Several employees were fired as the story reverberated across the nation.

The truth revealed that the finger actually came from a friend of Anna's husband. He had lost the digit in a construction accident. Anna's husband became complicit in the crime when he paid $100 for the fingertip. Mrs. Ayala had a history that included other cases of fraudulent claims. The Wendy's case provided her with a nine-year prison sentence and an order to repay $170,000 in lost wages. The total losses suffered by the Wendy's corporation exceeded $21 million. The list of companies caught up in the world of fraudulent claims is long and ever increasing.

In a close race with communications technology, US energy policies and oil production dominated the news in 2006. The United States' dependence on foreign oil has presented a national security risk that extends from the 1970s to the present day. This perplexing dilemma is contrasted by the fact that the shale oil reserves in the Green River Basin in Colorado, Utah, and Wyoming hold 1 trillion barrels of shale oil equaling or exceeding the reserves found in all the rest of the world. Seventy percent of the basin is on government-owned land. Alaskan oil reserves on 23 million acres of public land hold a proven total of more than 2.4 billion barrels.

As a result of government rulemaking and legislation, the oil industry in the United States has spent billions of dollars enhancing the oil refineries with pollution reduction measures to reduce the release of harmful pollutants into the atmosphere. Importing oil from other countries that employ less rigorous controls is counterproductive to these efforts. Looking at just the raw material, US oil from the Midwest is inherently cleaner than that from other countries. Even before the refining process, the sulfur content of crude oil exceeds 2 percent in products from Saudi Arabia and Venezuela, while US Midwest oil averages 0.4 percent in sulfur content.

Government controls and regulations applied to major refineries in the United States have reduced the release of greenhouse gases by 60 percent, and lowered sulfur dioxide and nitrous oxide emissions by 2 million tons each year. Rules promulgated from 1995 to 2013 reduced emissions of carcinogens like benzene by 59 percent and 53,000 tons annually. The premise that China is leading the world in environmental advances is false. In 2021 China announced the addition of 43 new coal-fired power plants. These plants will add 150 million tons of annual CO_2 emissions, representing an equivalent of more than half of the emissions from the entire United Kingdom. To add perspective, the total CO_2 emissions produced by China exceeds 10 billion tons, compared to the US at 5 billion and Russia at less than 2 billion tons. A closer analysis reveals the per capita CO_2 emissions in each country to be 7.41 tons per person in China, 14.24 tons in the US, and 10.81 tons in Russia. (ourworldindata.org)

An argument can be easily made that CO_2 emissions are not as important as we often report. Humans and animals breathe in oxygen and exhale carbon dioxide. Plants and trees take in carbon dioxide and produce oxygen. This intelligent design provided balance in our environment for several thousand years, and perhaps many hundreds of thousands of years. The climate change and environmental debate will be explored later in the timeline of this personal treatise.

Putting aside the enormous amount of data and comparative analyses of all the parameters of pollution and its sources, the importation of fossil fuels by the US from foreign sources, in lieu of our own domestic production, computes to a net increase in all forms of pollution. It is also pseudoscience and just bad policy. A bifurcated effort by the United States and other countries to simultaneously pursue pollution-eliminating initiatives, in parallel with the continued use and further refinement of our own natural resources, is the best answer for the sustenance of our future as an economic world leader. Hypercharged liberal "green" agendas lacking scientifically and economically based logic is not only a threat to our national security, but also a guarantee for the ultimate failure of our country's infrastructure and future prosperity.

The midterm 2006 national elections returned power to the Democrats in both the House of Representatives and the Senate. The new Speaker, Nancy Pelosi, called the victories a rebuke to President George W. Bush for the war in Iraq. Everyone promised to come together to improve the lives of Americans and to rise above the restraints of partisanship. History shows that the decade to follow would galvanize the parties into nonnegotiable forces seeking polarly opposite positions on all major problems and issues. The next presidential administration accelerated the liberals' agenda and set the country in a sociological spiral. The traditional values of most Americans were obstructed and ridiculed by fringe minority groups as they systematically dismantled our form of government and the course of our daily existence.

In 2005, 1,283,000 homes were built and sold. The largest homebuilders saw record sales and profits. D.R. Horton's stock soared from $3 per share in 1997 to $42.82 in July of 2005. Pulte Homes' revenue grew from $2.33 billion in 1996 to nearly $15 billion. The demand for land and housing soared to peak levels before plummeting in 2007 and 2008. The new recession had begun.

The not-so-hidden disaster that America would face next came from the most basic level of Maslow's hierarchy of needs.

Physiological needs are at the bottom of Maslow's pyramid and include the basic need for food, water, and warmth: in other words, a home to live in that provides protection from the outside forces of man and nature. Housing prices were on the rise in the beginning of the decade and peaked in 2006. Prices began rapidly declining and by 2008 we witnessed the largest price drop in American history.

As a reaction to the dot-com bubble in the previous year, in 2001, Federal Reserve Chairman Alan Greenspan dropped interest rates to an unnatural level of 1 percent. This led to relaxed lending standards and rampant home buying. The mortgage industry was caught up in a synthetic trading arena of subprime mortgages. They wheeled the bad debt from one institution to another as the true underlying asset value and the ability for consumers to pay back the loans spiraled downward. The loss of equity in homes that owners experienced led to a record number of home foreclosures and bankruptcies. By 2011 the savings and spendable income of American families had turned red, leaving one-fourth of America's households with no liquid assets.

Shares of Fannie Mae and Freddie Mac plummeted in 2008, and they were removed from the New York Stock Exchange. New Century Financial was one of the largest subprime lenders. Their stock fell 84 percent while clouded by a Justice Department investigation. They filed for bankruptcy in 2007, with more than $100 million in liabilities.

The country passed through the low point of the housing crisis sometime during 2012. The prospect of normal housing and lending conditions would take another two to three years. The strength of this metric is shored up by the overlay of population growth in the United States. The country's population increased from 281 million in the year 2000 to more than 309 million by 2010. Despite the demographics of an aging boomer population and a decreasing number of those between 20 and 64, the need for new homes in 2012 was measured at 1.2 million per year. Estimates for the number of excess housing units was somewhere between 2 and 4 million. The number of vacant homes (adjusted for second homes and uninhabitable housing) was placed at 1.2 million in 2012. In general, 2012 presented a good opportunity for home purchases. Low interest rates, reduced housing prices, and an upward trend for family incomes boded well for the prospect of a continued recovery.

Piracy of the *Maersk Alabama*

International incidents and notable tragedies are often the basis for novels and movies. Directors and actors enhance the scenes and add drama and intrigue to attract and hold the attention of viewers. Off the Horn of Africa in the Indian Ocean and 300 miles from the Federal Republic of Somalia, the US-flagged cargo ship MV *Maersk Alabama* provided a real-life drama that the movie industry would find hard to embellish beyond the actual reality of the event. The hijacking of the *Maersk Alabama* in April of 2008 took center stage around the world.

The east coast of the African continent has been a home for pirates for centuries. In the years 2005 to 2008, the frequency of ship hijackings doubled. Young enterprising Somalians came to recognize that hijacking and piracy was a quick way out of their impoverished existence. Cargo ship captains understood this and plotted their routes far offshore and beyond the reach of the small fast boats used by hijackers. The hijackers responded with the use of previously stolen mother ships to carry the pirate skiffs to the new shipping lanes hundreds of miles offshore.

The seizure of an American ship by pirates had not occurred since the Second Barbary War in 1815. That changed in April of 2008, when four young pirates in a small fast boat attacked and boarded the 508-foot-long, 19-ton cargo ship, MV *Maersk Alabama*. The pirates were between the ages of 15 and 18 years old. Two days earlier, the ship had been approached by other pirate boats that eventually turned away without incident. The *Maersk Alabama* could run at a top speed of 18 knots. Small skiffs, while speedy, can have difficulty when the seas are rough.

On the dead calm morning of April 8, while most of the crew was still sleeping, the pirates approached within one mile of the ship. Having spotted pirates at midnight the previous evening, Captain Richard Phillips had stayed up most of the night with the bridge watch officer. As the pirates approached the ship, the captain sounded the general alarm and reported the pending attack over the ship's intercom to all stations. They were jolted awake by the startling report. Having been recently trained in the procedures for such an event, they quickly responded.

The deck crew was limited to fire hoses and flares as a defense against pirates armed with AK-47 rifles. The crew's best plan for survival was to retreat to a secured safe room that had been recently constructed for this purpose. While 14 of the ship's 20-man crew were safely separated from the armed young men, the room had poor lighting, no toilet, and no air conditioning or ventilation. This would prove to be a critical disadvantage as events unfolded under the hot midday sun.

The four barefooted armed pirates tossed a gang hook and rope over the side of the ship and climbed up and onto the main deck. They shot the lock off a security gate and approached the stairs to the ship's command and control bridge. As the first pirate entered the wheelhouse, the captain announced over the intercom, "The bridge has been compromised."

Chief Engineer Mike Perry was stationed in the engine control room. He knew from practiced procedure that command of the ship's steering and engine control would be transferred and disabled on the bridge by Captain Phillips. Chief Perry would take control of the ship. The ship was still running at top speed, and Perry, not knowing that the pirates had already boarded the ship, ordered the first assistant engineer to begin swinging the ship's steering rudder hard to port and back to starboard. This repeated action eventually swamped the pirates' skiff that was dragging alongside the *Maersk Alabama*. The pirates were now stranded onboard the ship and had no contingency plan for this situation.

Captain Phillips and Third Mate Colin Wright, along with Seaman "ATM" Reza and his relief, Clifford Lacon, were guarded prisoners on the command bridge. The pirates discovered that they could not control the ship and ordered the captain to summon his crew. Captain Phillips used the intercom and took advantage of the hijackers' poor understanding of English as he called for the crew to surrender to the bridge. The crewmembers knew of the ruse and did not respond. The pirates had no backup plan.

A savvy navy veteran, Chief Perry knew to deny the pirates access to the ship's assets. He began shutting down the ship. He shut down the engines and their controls and monitoring stations. Second Engineer Dick Mathews shut down the ship's air conditioning, ventilation, plumbing, and lighting systems. Except for the sparse emergency battery lighting, the ship was dead in the water. Chief Perry knew that after killing the ship's main power source, the emergency generators would eventually start and resume partial power to the ship's systems. He bravely exited the engine room and climbed through the emergency escape hatch to the side deck of the ship. He was exposed to the pirates and their gunfire, but successfully disabled the emergency generator. The ship's batteries were left on to provide power to the automatic distress signals being broadcast to the rescue ships en route to the *Maersk Alabama*.

Down below, in the makeshift safe room, the conditions were getting worse. It was dark and hot, with no ventilation. They managed to open a portlight that provided a discharge point for urination and human waste. The seawater temperature surrounding the steel hull of the ship was 90 degrees Fahrenheit and the safe room temperature reached a high of 125 degrees.

Chief Perry summoned First Assistant Engineer Matt Fisher, and the two collected a case of bottled water and made their way back to the safe room. After the water was delivered and Matt was safely inside, the door was closed and locked. Perry returned blindly to the dark engine room. He searched for zip ties that could be used to subdue any pirates he might capture. He knew they would be looking for the crew so they could get the ship underway. Two darkened silhouettes appeared at the engine room door. Perry recognized the voice of one of the men as Seaman ATM Reza. The pirate had a gun and a flashlight. He commanded Reza to take him to the other crewmen. When the light was directed away from Perry's position, Perry exited the room and moved down a passageway and right into the pirate's beam of light.

The pirate ran screaming after Perry. As they turned a corner Perry pulled out his utility knife and lunged at the pirate's neck. The pirate blocked the knife blade and was cut badly on his left hand. The chief pushed the small man down and secured him with the zip ties. ATM, who had retreated when the pirate began his pursuit, had now returned and he helped Chief Perry secure the pirate. Perry yelled to the crew in the safe room. Second Mate Ken Quinn and Bosun William Rios opened the secure door and grabbed Abduwali Abdukhadir Muse and dragged him into the safe room. Abduwali was terrified and mumbling something about meeting Allah. Assistant Engineer John Cronan attended to the prisoner's wounded hand to stop the bleeding. Ken Quinn looked down and saw that the pirate was wearing Quinn's shoes that had been taken during a search of his sleeping quarters. He could sense how desperate these young men must have been. Once the scene was secure, Chief Perry announced over his radio, "One down!"

After conversations in broken English, John Cronan announced that Abduwali was the man in charge. While it was good that they had taken out the ringleader, they also came to understand that the remaining pirates would become frustrated and confused. Their reaction could be devastating to the crew on the *Maersk Alabama*. The pirates had no leader, no plan that would return them to safety, and no hope of ever seeing their share of the $3 million ransom they had been promised. What they did still have was the captain of the ship. They also had First Mate Shane Murphy, who had repeatedly suggested that the pirates leave the ship on the man overboard rescue boat. Captain Phillips convinced the three remaining pirates that they could escape following an exchange of their leader with the safe release of Captain Phillips and his crew.

Chief Perry and his engineers began bringing the ship back online. Lighting and control systems were restarted and the engines were made ready for starting. The plan was to launch the rescue boat with the pirates and Captain Phillips onboard. The MOB was launched as planned, but 200 yards from the ship the boat's engines failed. Phillips instructed the pilot to row the boat back to the ship. The ship's crew were instructed to lower a lifeboat as an alternate craft for the pirates.

As Phillips and the pirates boarded the semi-enclosed lifeboat alongside the ship, the prisoner Abduwali was brought to deck in full view of the pirates, and he descended the rope ladder to the lifeboat. Now the tired and angry pirates were back to full force and still armed with automatic weapons. They had their leader and Captain Phillips in the lifeboat. Cronan and Rios were in the nonfunctioning rescue boat, armed with nothing but plastic paddles. The prisoner exchange plan had failed.

At midnight that evening the ship was in communication with a US Navy search plane, the guided-missile destroyer USS *Bainbridge*, and the guided-missile frigate USS *Halyburton*. Early the next morning an 18-man team was put on the *Maersk Alabama*, and the ship's crew was ordered to stand down. The next day, the crew of the *Maersk Alabama* was instructed to continue their original course to the port of Mombasa in Kenya. They reluctantly complied and sailed to Mombasa with the 18-man security detail onboard. Captain Phillips remained a prisoner on the lifeboat with the four tired, scared, and angry armed pirates.

On the second day, the two naval ships remained a few hundred yards away from the lifeboat. The lifeboat lacked good ventilation and had no toilet or other amenities. A P-3C Orion provided aerial surveillance and fed live video to the ships. Radio communications alerted the *Bainbridge* and *Halyburton* that four foreign ships commanded by pirates were headed to their location. The four ships commandeered by pirates also held an additional 54 hostages from seven different countries.

Day three: Captain Phillips escaped from the lifeboat. The pirates fired their weapons, compelling Phillips to return to the lifeboat. The pirates broke off communication with the naval ships and tossed the boat's portable radio into the sea. Negotiations continued with satellite phone communications connecting the captain of the *Bainbridge* to the pirates and with FBI hostage negotiators. On the morning of the fourth day of the hijacking, one of the pirates fired his weapon indiscriminately from the front opening of the lifeboat. A satellite phone message was sent to Reuters international news agency and the other pirate vessels, with the message: "We are safe, and we are not afraid of the Americans. We will defend ourselves if attacked." The *Bainbridge* did not return fire, and no one was injured by the gunfire from the lifeboat.

The sea became rough, and the pirates were losing control of the lifeboat. They were severely ill from seasickness and dehydration. The captain of the *Bainbridge* convinced them to allow the ship to tow the lifeboat to stabilize it and allow for medical treatment of one of the pirates who had been injured in the initial hijacking of the *Maersk Alabama*. The lifeboat was secured and under tow 30 yards behind the 9,200-ton, 509-foot-long nuclear-powered cruiser. The *Bainbridge* had enough firepower to instantaneously take down 100 hostile targets with the flip of a switch.

Two days earlier, on Friday, April 10, United States Navy SEAL Team Six parachuted into the waters next to the naval ship *Halyburton*. The 4,100-ton ship joined the *Bainbridge*. Another US assault ship, the USS *Boxer*, also was holding nearby, ready to intercept any other approaching vessels commanded by pirates.

On Sunday morning, April 12, Ali Aden Elmi, another pirate known as Hamac, and one other unknown captor remained onboard the lifeboat. The SEAL team snipers were on the stern of the *Bainbridge*, with orders to take lethal actions if Captain Phillips' life was in danger. Using their high-resolution rifle scopes, the SEAL team saw one of the pirates pointing a rifle at Captain Phillips' head. Targeting the heads of the pirates, the SEAL team fired multiple shots, instantly killing all three.

After bouncing around in a small covered lifeboat for four days in 100-degree temperatures, 53-year-old Captain Phillips safely boarded the USS *Bainbridge*. After a shower and a brief medical evaluation, Richard Phillips telephoned his wife and family waiting anxiously at their home in Vermont. Captain Phillips was okay and in good health. The crew of the *Maersk*

Alabama was also elated by the news and celebrated with great joy as they waved American flags and fired flares into the night sky.

Captain Phillips was regarded as a national hero by the crew of the *Maersk Alabama* and the citizens back home in America. As you have learned in my summary of the harrowing events occurring on the high seas in April of 2009, there were many heroes in this larger-than-life drama. The power of the United States Navy, the courage of the ships' commanders, the steady resolve of highly trained sniper-warriors, and sweat-level daring and courage of the crew onboard the *Maersk Alabama* saved their own lives and that of the now famous Captain Richard Phillips.

We know who the winners are, but what of the losers in this ongoing battle of piracy and commerce? The young teenagers who lost their lives off the coast of Somalia were not hardened criminals. They were perhaps desperate young men who wanted a way out of their impoverished way of living. They were taken in and convinced by older men, who fill the ranks in the hierarchy of the piracy kingdom of Somalia. The 25- to 30-year-old men had somehow survived their earlier battles to work as recruiters and trainers of younger, more susceptible minds that were desperate for a step up in life. They were promised the freedom that only money could buy in a land where opportunity was scarce and unreachable.

Is the motivation of young men in Somalia any different than that of challenged young men in metropolitan cities? Poor young men want to move out of poverty and often skirt the law to survive on the streets. Young men and women around the world want a way up and into the wealth they see in America and other developed countries. Certainly, the means and methods of advancement vary, but they generally do not carry guns or hijack ships at sea. The young pirates saw the promise of shared bounty as a way out of their impoverished way of life. We struggle to define the roles of world leaders when looking at the root causes of poverty and desperation around the globe. The rich diversity and histories of every country on multiple continents defy a simple solution or mantra for overcoming the constraints of economic and social development.

Maine Republican William Cohen was the Secretary of Defense under President Bill Clinton, from 1997 to 2001. Mr. Cohen told me in a private conference of business leaders, "America is playing 300 chess games every day, and we are expected to win every one of them." Despite the complexity involved in our role as a world leader, it remains in our best interest to promote the economic and social development of all poor and developing countries. Whether we are addressing the severity of starvation and droughts or the calamities of natural disasters, we should fulfill our role as compassionate human beings to extend help to those suffering.

In the case described in Somalia, we should look through the violence manifested by poverty, and create and support policies that mitigate the misfortunes that struggling countries are facing. The acclamations made by some pompous and aspiring politicians that we cannot be the "world's keeper" is myopic and only ignores the problems that perpetuate human misery. Yes, we must win our chess games, but we must also share our wealth and technology to make the world a better, more peaceful place for the generations that follow us.

Gun Control

Some topics and incidents establish and maintain relevance for only a day, or weeks, or an entire year. The subject of gun control has been with us for three centuries. Like many subjects emanating from situations that result in senseless death, the manufacture, sale, and ownership of firearms has become politically polarizing in America. Like many topics in political discourse, the conversational balance is not influenced by predominant statistical data or proportional logic. Contrary to the common themes promulgated by gun control proponents, it is true that more than 75 percent of gun owners support the notions of background checks and the prohibition of sales to felons and mentally disturbed people. Still, the minority voice fills the stage with unsupported bombastic claims that focus on the hardware and not the fingers on the triggers.

Significant regulations and licensure requirements are imposed on physicians and other healthcare workers. Nevertheless, thousands of people die in botched medical procedures each year. The logic applied in gun control should be presented as a call for the banning of the scalpel, or at least making it less sharp. Cars kill nearly 100,000 people each year. The manufacturers' design limits and safety features are prescribed by governmental authority, and drivers are trained and regulated. Despite the restrictions, deaths continue in many regulated activities.

Guns kill people! Gun violence is in the news every week throughout each year in America. The debate divides our country with people on each side standing with great resolve and not yielding to the other. Well-founded statistics dissect the problem but fail to provide a cure to the senseless killing. The tragic memory of the Columbine High School shooting spree in 1999, and a gunman killing 12 and injuring hundreds more in an Aurora, Colorado, theater in 2012 are just two of dozens of examples of the misuse of firearms in that same timespan. In 2016 a follower of the terrorist Abu Bakr al-Bagdadi killed 49 people and wounded 53 more in a gay nightclub in Orlando. A year later a disgruntled 64-year-old man fired 1,000 bullets into a crowded music festival in the streets of Las Vegas. Sixty people died and hundreds more were wounded or injured in the panic to escape the field of fire. The headlines did not focus on the victims. The terrorist was not condemned for terrorism. It was the gun that perpetrated the heinous acts of murder. The capacity of a metal clip holding the bullets was to blame. The spring-loaded butt stock that kinetically converted the weapon to one having automatic firing capability was the culprit.

The constant reference to the AR-15 as a military assault weapon is incorrect. The US Armed Forces do not have or use the term "assault weapon." The term came from the movie industry and the news media. The *A* in AR stands for Armalite, the manufacturer's name. The term semiautomatic means that each time you pull the trigger, the gun fires the .223 caliber bullet. The most common size or capacity of the detachable magazine for an AR-15 rifle is 20 rounds of ammunition. It takes approximately 15 to 20 seconds to fire all 20 rounds in a semiautomatic AR-15 with a 20-round magazine.

Banning high-capacity magazines sounds virtuous, but it will not affect the ability of a shooter to fire a dozen, or as many as 100 rounds, in a shooting spree. The common deer rifle with a 5-round capacity, a 12-shot Glock pistol, a pump-action 3-shot shotgun, and even a single-shot rifle or shotgun can fire the same number of rounds that a so-called assault rifle with a high-capacity magazine can in a relatively short time period. Whether it takes two minutes for a single-shot weapon to reload and fire 20 rounds, or the 40 seconds for a hunting rifle to do the same, the carnage is the same. Murder by any means is already against the law! Assault and battery are already against the law. Laws define the behavior of good people. Criminals and some mentally deranged people break laws. They do not check the state statutes or the *Federal Register* before committing crimes.

Guns are not the only instruments of death used by deranged killers. In 2013, 64 people were killed in the Boston Marathon bombing. Automobiles have been intentionally driven into crowds of bystanders in multiple incidents around the world. Deranged killers and gang members wielding baseball bats, knives, and machetes brought horror to the streets of London in 2019. But the legislative debates continue to focus on the *gun* as the primary target for stemming violence in the United States. The highest per-capita murder rates can be found in countries and cities that have commanding restrictions or outright bans on the ownership and display of firearms. Anti-gun supporters argue that simple pro-gun rights slogans like "Guns don't kill people, people kill people" are just cultish pro-gun slogans. The facts show that taking guns away from law-abiding citizens does nothing to deter gun possession and use by criminals. The truth is that many dynamic and complex evaluations can be adequately reduced to certain indisputable corollaries.

In 1792, the law required men to own guns "suitable for military service" or be subject to citations and fines. Physicians, lawyers, and schoolmasters were exempted from this requirement. The Jim Crow laws in 1865 prohibited gun ownership by freed slaves. Any slave caught with a firearm was subject to "39 lashes" in the state of Georgia. Following the killing of seven notorious Chicago gangsters on St. Valentine's Day in 1929, the federal government decreed a ban on all "machine gun" ownership by private citizens. In 1938, gun dealers were required to possess a Federal Firearms License and to maintain records of gun purchases. Following the assassinations of President John Kennedy in 1963, Malcolm X in 1965, Dr. Martin Luther King Jr. and Senator Robert Kennedy in 1968, the Gun Control Act of 1968 prohibited the transfer of firearms across state lines by anyone other than a federally licensed gun dealer.

Nearly one in four people in America owns a firearm. The number of guns in the US is estimated to be 400 million, or 120 firearms per 100 people. The weapons are not all in the hands of men. Twelve percent of American women own at least one gun. An excerpt from the 2nd Amendment to the Constitution of the United States reads: "the right of the people to keep and bear Arms, shall not be infringed." Unlike most other constitutional rights, the right to bear arms has been restricted by local legislation and federal laws that are rewritten in the aftermath of every new firearms tragedy in America.

One-third of households in Delaware own guns. About 50 percent of adults in Vermont and Maine own guns. Same for North Dakota. Montana has the highest rate of gun ownership at 66 percent. Even the liberal-leaning state of Massachusetts has 15 percent of their adult population armed with a gun. More than 1 million guns in Texas are already registered with the government. All of the other states have registered guns in quantities ranging from 5,000 to 500,000 in each state.

Fast-forward to 2022 when a mass shooting in Sacramento, California, that killed six and wounded 12, prompted this response from President Joe Biden: "We must do more than mourn, we must act!" Prominent legislators asserted that we must pass "smart gun laws," "commonsense gun laws." Contrary to inflammatory rhetoric from anti-gun activists, polls show that 80 percent of the US population are in favor of prerequisite background checks and waiting periods for retail and gun show purchases of firearms. Seventy percent of the population believe it is more important to protect the right of gun ownership than to control gun ownership. In April of 2020 the FBI completed over 3.9 million background checks, and 10.6 million more in May, June, and July. The total for the year approached 40 million background checks.

According to the Bureau of Alcohol, Tobacco, and Firearms, there are more than 20 million privately owned AR-15 rifles in the country today. There are over 650,000 fully automatic weapons (machine guns) in the US that are permitted and owned by US citizens. These numbers are only the guns that the Bureau has recognized as being sold, or for sale, or registered and permitted. The number of illegally purchased and possessed guns will increase these numbers. If the existence and quantity of guns was truly the problem, the statistics do not support that assertion.

Compare the data from private gun purchases and gun control regulations with the sharp upturn in crime in major metropolitan cities, and one might correlate the increase in gun ownership with increased crime. This would be an erroneous assumption. A closer look into cities like Chicago, Portland, Seattle, and New York, where the strictest gun laws have been enacted, reveals an alarming lack of criminal prosecution, low and no-bail arrests, and leniency in sentencing for repeat violent offenders. The increase in violent crime is likely to continue and may be indexed to the increased drug trafficking through the southern border of the United States. In 2021, Chinese and Mexican drug cartels brought in 4,000 times more fentanyl to the US; 79,000 young people between the ages of 18 and 45 died from fentanyl overdoses that year. There are approximately 11,000 homicide deaths each year in America, along with 21,000 gun deaths by suicide. The increase in gun sales in the US is a direct result of an increased desire of the people to provide self-protection from crime. Restricting the rights of private citizens to own guns does nothing to the criminals that use guns and other weapons to perpetuate their crimes.

The quest for survival is a genetically prescribed characteristic of human behavior—morality and good behavior are not. Parents and neighbors, churches, and teachers write and implement the programming for young people to learn the proper societal mores for good behavior. "Thou shalt not kill" and "Thou shalt not steal" are the supreme laws of the land. How you teach or learn these commandments is not the point. Lost souls that miss these lessons are the problem. Not the guns. The ancient Mayans of the Yucatan prophesied that the end of the world would coincide with the end of the Mayan calendar on December 21 in 2012. The world did not end, and the debate over guns and who should own firearms continues today.

Street Crossing #2

I left active employment in 2012. While I remained chairman of the Board of Directors of Miller Electric, my day-to-day duties were set aside, and the new management team assumed the leadership and management functions of the company. This left me with plenty of time for endless thought on long-ignored projects and other activities. Daydreaming became a frequent respite and I was prone to drift away in thought at brief interludes like red traffic lights and stop signs.

One afternoon when returning to my Ponte Vedra home in the Sawgrass Country Club, I was waiting for a green light and turn signal to enter the gated community. Florida A1A is a divided four-lane highway running north and south along the East Coast of Florida. As a major highway it supports both local residential traffic and large commercial vehicles.

Most coordinated traffic light systems use an elementary level of logic that controls the timing and sequencing of red and green lights and turn arrows. Depending on the car's arrival point in relation to the system's programmed sequencing, you may see a turn arrow or you may simply have a green light for the two-way traffic. Most of the time, there is always a turn arrow to allow me to turn right and into the roadway to the security gate for my community.

One fall morning in 2012, I was lazily daydreaming at
the traffic stop and thinking mindlessly about my day. The
light changed and the cars to my right proceeded forward in
a southerly direction. I accelerated into the northbound lanes
as I almost always do, but there was no turn signal—only a
green light for both directions of traffic. As I entered the first
northbound traffic lane, I saw the front of an approaching
cement truck. The image was increasing in size at a rate of 50
miles per hour, or more appropriately expressed in this incidence
as 73 feet per second.

It was immediately apparent that I would be broadsided
by the large 30,000-pound truck loaded with another 40,000
pounds of revolving concrete. It was too late to simply apply
brakes and hope that the truck would swerve around me. The
decision was nearly instantaneous, and I pressed the accelerator
to the floor and sped across the lane with only a few feet left
between silence and the crushing blow of the massive truck.
Thankfully, there was not a car or pedestrian in front of my car
as I leaped across the roadway and into the private road toward
the security gate. In these few seconds, my inattentiveness
could have ended my life and severely changed the lives of
my wife and children, and grandchildren, and other family
members and friends. I knew then that I had to address a new
set of challenges.

My wife presented me with a book titled *I'm Dead, Now
What?* I am working through the hundreds of questions that
must be answered after my demise. The complexity of financial
obligations and providing for the future security and comfort of
my family is foremost in my mind. My thoughts while waiting
for traffic lights will be forever scripted by this near-death
experience. In my doddering years you may find me waiting
endlessly at a post-mounted metal stop sign, waiting for it to
turn green.

A Search for Justice

When we think of protests and marches today, we tend to associate them with violence and rioting. The group Black Lives Matter protested the 2012 killing of Trayvon Martin by George Zimmerman. Their group was initially formed with nonviolent intentions, but morphed into a noncentralized movement that violently demanded equality and justice for Black people. Millions of people rioted and looted after the death of George Floyd at the hands of police. In the name of social justice and equality, buildings were looted and burned, police cars were overturned and burned, and high-end shopping districts were looted.

History shows us that significant change can also be made with nonviolent protests. Perhaps the most notable example was the assembly of 200,000 peaceful protesters on the National Mall in Washington, DC, where Dr. Martin Luther King Jr. delivered his famous "I Have A Dream" speech. He was also seeking equality and justice for Black people.

The Salt March

In 1930, Gandhi and 78 of his volunteers participated in a 24-day-long Salt March and walked 239 miles through India, protesting the oppressive exploitation of the Indian people. British rulers imposed property taxes and prohibited the Indian people from making, selling, or buying sea salt. Even though the salt is easily made from the distillation of seawater, they were required to purchase salt from the British government.

Gandhi and his followers drew crowds of up to 50,000 people as they passed through 48 villages along their route. Sixty thousand people gathered on the bank of a river in Sabarmati, India. Another 100,000 people lined the roadway between Sabarmati and Ahmadabad. The march drew international attention. Dozens of European and American media and film companies covered the march and Gandhi's speeches at each stop. The *New York Times* provided daily coverage of the 24-day protest march. *Time* magazine covered the march and the April 6 public display of the making of salt by Gandhi. *Time* named Mohandas Gandhi *Time* magazine's "Man of the Year."

Mohandas Gandhi's movement generated continued protests. Ghaffar Khan, a Muslim disciple of Gandhi, trained 50,000 nonviolent activists. Seventeen days after the Salt

March, Khan was arrested. A crowd gathered in the Storytellers Bazaar in Peshawar. Soldiers from the Royal Garhwal Rifles battalion opened fire, with machine guns trained on the peaceful unarmed protesters. The nonviolent followers faced the firing soldiers as they were trained, and 250 people died from the gunfire. Some of the troops from the rifle platoon refused to fire into the assembled protesters and were arrested for their disobedience.

Next, Gandhi planned a peaceful assault on the Salt Works in Gujarat, India. He was arrested the evening before the event. A female poet and freedom fighter, Sarojini Naidu, assumed the leadership role and continued the approach to the Salt Works. Naidu instructed the protesters to strictly adhere to the code of nonviolence and to take the beatings without resistance. Bones and skulls were broken by the angry police and blood stained the white clothes of the sprawling agonized and unconscious marchers.

The story was printed in more than a thousand newspapers worldwide. The British government prevailed in the protests in 1930, but they lost the confidence of free nations around the world. They now knew that their continued rule would be dependent on the ongoing and future approval of the Indian people.

Vietnam War Protests

In 1965 a small number of peaceniks and leftist intellectuals on a few college campuses began protesting the Vietnam War. They staged sit-ins and small marches, carrying signs with peace symbols. By 1967 there were 500,000 American military troops stationed in Vietnam. In that same year, 100,000 war protesters assembled at the Lincoln Memorial in Washington, DC. The newly formed Students for a Democratic Society (SDS) added significant numbers to the activists' groups springing up around the country. About 30,000 war protesters marched from the memorial to the Pentagon, where they were met by US Marshals protecting the facility. Many of the protesters were arrested for unlawful assembly when they blocked entrances or sought to gain entrance to the building.

The Vietnam War was not popular among the younger generation. The rising death toll and lottery-based military draft were chief on the list of complaints. Notable names joined the ranks of people speaking out against the war. Dr. Martin Luther King Jr. joined the list in 1967. Musicians including John Lennon, Pete Seeger, Joan Baez, and Marvin Gaye produced iconic anti-war songs that remain on the airways today. The Tet Offensive in 1968 sent a message home that the end of the war was not in sight. The tumultuous confrontation between protesting students and the Ohio National Guard on Kent State University's campus solidified the positions for Americans opposing the war in Vietnam. Four students were killed when the soldiers fired into the crowd of chanting protestors. "Four Dead in Ohio" was a tune that many people would hear for years to come.

The war and the protests were both new chapters in my life in the early '70s. At the time, I did not see or understand the entrenched schools of thought on each side of the Vietnam War debate. It was to me, a simplistic, albeit ignorant, perspective. The spread of Communism was bad, and we should combat the perpetrators of that failed idealogue. I was not drafted into military service and continued my education in college, while other young men fought and died in a north-south war that had been going on for centuries. News of the Vietnam War came to me in the feature articles in *Life* magazine.

Occupy Wall Street

Forty years after the height of the Vietnam War, the country faced an economic crisis that rivaled the misery of the Great Depression. Working-class people revolted against the corporate establishments and government agencies that had created the crisis. The wealthiest top 1 percent of the economic ladder were targeted and called out for their greed and exploitation of the systems of commerce and banking. Matching the numbers from the Great Depression in 1928, the top 1 percent received nearly one-fourth of all income. Occupy Wall Street became the front-line organization opposing the status quo of inequality and corruption. Their slogan for the activist movement was "We are the 99%."

Unlike the historic European economic protests, these activists were not socialists seeking fair and distributed government support. They were not all anti-capitalists. They were in large part frustrated working people who had lost their livelihood and sense of well-being. The foreclosure rate for homes was at an all-time high. The American Dream had become a nightmare of unemployment and despair. They viewed the corrupt corporate ties in government as deceitful and criminal. The core movement was joined by other fringe groups seeking forgiveness of student loan debt and the redistribution of wealth and income.

Modeled after other recent protests in Britain, Spain, Portugal, and Greece, in mid-September of 2011 a group that grew to thousands of people occupied Wall Street and camped in Zuccotti Park in New York City's Financial District. The movement was covered live by social media, magazines, newspapers, radio, and film. The occupiers slept in sleeping bags and were provided food and restrooms by supportive vendors and nearby businesses. The protesters remained until November 15, when they were forced out by the New York Police Department for sanitary reasons. The campers moved into business buildings, banks, churches, and university campuses. They returned to Zuccotti Park on March 17, 2012, and blocked entrances to the New York Stock Exchange. They blocked street intersections and pedestrian traffic. The police arrested 185 protesters.

After being ousted from their Wall Street encampments, Occupy groups assembled in other public parks and spaces in New York and other cities such as Seattle and Cleveland. The unemployed 20- to 30-year-old activists were joined by older workers and professionals. Other left-wing radicals, along with AFL-CIO labor union members and Transportation Workers Union members, also joined the Occupy groups around the country.

The Occupy movement was not without its own internal problems. Their organizational philosophy was to be "leaderless." Their ranks suffered from internally manifested crimes like rape, theft, and other forms of violence. Except for the parasitic attachment of the followers of socialist presidential hopeful Bernie Sanders, they had no affiliated political voice. Through the course of the movement's lifespan, more than 7,000 people were arrested in more than 100 cities. The economic damage and expense borne by the Occupy cities that hosted the groups is measured in tens of millions of dollars. Despite the mostly failed efforts to create annual reunions to commemorate the Occupy Wall Street movement, the decentralized organization began to dissipate following the removal of the initial encampment at Zuccotti Park.

Black Lives Matter

The movement started with a hashtag #blacklivesmatter. It quickly attracted national attention after the death of Trayvon Martin on February 26, 2012. He was shot and killed in Sanford, Florida, in an altercation with a neighborhood watch person named George Zimmerman. The killing was perceived as unjust and triggered a nationwide protest. Trayvon's name was posted in over 2 million tweets in the 30 days following the shooting. From February onward, every Black person killed by police or any other non-Black person became the catalyst for protests in the form of rioting and looting and burning cars and businesses.

In Los Angeles in 2015, Patrisse Cullors, Alicia Garza, and Opal Tameti founded the organization called Black Lives Matter. The movement was embraced by a nation and grew into an international network of supporters. The initial strategy was to create local chapters with a central foundation to support the "Black Joy and Liberation." It became more widely known for violent rioting and looting anytime a Black person was killed by police. The "defund the police" movement evolved as the primary demand from the organization.

The BLM organization was both a success and a failure. It was successful because of the creation of an internationally-known brand. The group quantified their success with more than $90 million of donations in 2020. They continued operations into 2021 with $60 million in reserves. More than 20 million people joined in protests across the country. Their methods were not accepted by the balance of the population. The burning of businesses, looting in high-end stores, and violence against police severely diluted the nobility of their mission.

The death of Ahmaud Arbery in February and George Floyd in May of 2020 exacerbated the growing tension nationwide and prompted new rounds of violent protests. Arbery was killed in a confrontation with three White men who thought he was responsible for some neighborhood thefts. George Floyd died while in police custody, after being arrested for passing a forged 20-dollar bill. After Floyd's death, the three-night protests in Minneapolis-Saint Paul left two dead and $500 million in damage to 1,500 properties. Protesters occupied the intersection of East Thirty-Eighth Street and Chicago Avenue for 30 days.

On June 8, 2020, a six-city block autonomous zone was established in Seattle by a newly formed anarchist group, and dubbed the police-free zone CHAZ, for Capitol Hill Autonomous Zone. The name was later changed to CHOP, for Capitol Hill Occupied Protest. The protest group took on the moniker of BLM, Black Lives Matter. They established the social experiment as a community free from police intervention and governmental control. Instead of reacting with deadly force, the police precinct in the area was evacuated after repeated efforts by protesters to bomb and burn the building.

The BLM group demanded that the mayor and the Seattle City Council defund and abolish the police department. The group provided a long list of economic demands, including free college and free healthcare. They pushed for support for

Black businesses and the hiring of more Blacks in government agencies. While their motivations were noble, the tactics and organization were destined to fail. They fell ill to the very things they protested. Internal violence and bigotry prevailed in the futile anarchy. They established borders to keep undesirable people out. The local businesses boarded up and left. Those that stayed were subject to extortion as "reparations." A young Black 19-year-old man, Horace Lorenzo Anderson Jr., and another man, were shot multiple times by a CHOP zone occupier. Police and ambulances were blocked by protesters and were unable to reach the scene. Anderson died from his wounds. The failed social experiment yielded increased crime and violence and the CHAZ/CHOP occupiers were forced out of their enclave by police on July 1, 2020.

After the spectacular financial support in 2020, the IRS, along with BLM chapter leaders, began questioning both the sources of the funding and the plans for disbursement. There were no audited financial statements available. In 2022 BLM cofounder Patrisse Cullors called the demands for financial transparency "triggering." She asserted that disclosing the finances would put the activists' lives at risk. She believed that the system of filing federal 990 forms was being weaponized against her and the organization's larger-than-life goals. Cullors' image took a nosedive when it was revealed that she had spent over $6 million of the charity's money on a personal residence in California. She claims that the seven-bedroom house with the music studio, pool, and parking for 20 cars was purchased to "encourage Black creativity." Three other homes were also purchased with funds from the BLM charity.

Cullors stepped down from her position as the leader of the BLM parent organization and as the executive director of the Black Lives Matter Global Network Foundation (BLMGNF). Fundraising activities also ceased in 2021, after the pressure of state and federal investigations began pressing the organization for more financial details. Cullors apparently remains the head of the BLM PAC organization. Local BLM chapters still exist as BLM Grassroots, but their future is unclear. A $21.7 million grant was committed to the chapters by BLMGNF in 2021. This year the Grassroots organization has qualified to receive funding from a $12 million grant. Financial reporting and federal filings remain incomplete and obscured by a lack of details.

The Great African Safari

In 2016 my wife and I spent a month in Africa. We began our adventure in Cape Town, South Africa, and continued on to the Okavango Delta, Johannesburg, Nairobi, the Ngorongoro conservation area, the Serengeti National Park, the Maasai Mara game reserve, Amboseli National Park, and Mount Kenya. I would say it was a once-in-a-lifetime trip, but it was so amazing that we are compelled to visit Africa again very soon.

Our first stop included roaming the streets of Cape Town. In September of 2016 there were no security concerns for tourists on the streets of Cape Town. We did make note of the razor wire on high walls and the massive security gates at the entry to mansion-sized estates. Disparate wealth and social stratifications caused sporadic acts of theft if the houses of the wealthy went unguarded.

Cape Town is well known for its fabulous restaurants that offer exquisite food and award-winning wines. We visited scenic vineyards that were first established in the 18th century. The 400-year-old Dutch and Victorian architecture in the nearby village of Stellenbosch was stunning. A day trip took us to the Cape of Good Hope, where we met an entire colony of African penguins. From Cape Point and up to the vistas

on Table Mountain, the views are the most breathtaking in
the world.

Our most exciting adventure planned in Cape Town,
South Africa, was cage diving with great white sharks. I had
seen this adventure in movies, and the intrigue of seeing
these dangerous creatures up close was overpowering. While
studying the topic of cage diving online, I came across a recent
and horrifying cage diving incident that occurred in the same
waters we were planning to visit the next day. The graphic
details in the article and the detailed and colorful YouTube
video added significantly to our apprehension and anxiety.
A great white shark had attacked a diving cage and breached
the top of the cage, pinning the diver to the bottom of the
submerged enclosure.

The white shark incident occurred in False Bay, about
45 minutes by car from our hotel. The boat was a 35-foot
catamaran that was specifically designed for shark viewing and
cage diving. The divers wore full wetsuits with booties and
gloves. The cage is positioned alongside the boat and secured
with large ropes. The top of the cage is level with the water's
surface. Masks and air hoses are provided and attached to an
air compressor on the boat. The diver in the cage would never
be more than about one meter below the surface.

The water around the boat was chummed with chopped
pieces of fresh bloody fish. A large bleeding bonito was
suspended from an orange float drifting near the boat and the
shark cage. As soon as the cage entered the clear blue water,
sharks appeared and could be seen by the diver and other
observers. Makos and blue sharks circled the boat. Within
minutes, a 1,200-pound, 15-foot great white shark approached
the suspended bonito bait and clamped its huge mouth and
razor-sharp teeth around the bait. The crew onboard the boat
struggled with and excited the huge shark pulling on the end

of the rope. The great white blindly thrashed and rolled at the back of the boat and within 10 feet from the diver in the cage.

The great white shark suddenly charged the cage and its huge body rolled over the top of the cage, pulling against the taut ropes securing the cage to the boat. The shark's pectoral fin became lodged between the steel slats of the top of the cage. The clasp holding the top was forced open and the top of the cage was pushed violently open by the shark's fin. The huge shark was thrashing violently and rolled on the top of the open cage. There was very little the boat's crew could do to help the diver pinned to the bottom of the cage by the huge shark lodged headfirst, half in and half out of the cage. As the shark rolled out of and off the cage, one of the deckhands jumped into the open cage to assist the terrified diver.

The morning that we were supposed to be picked up for our cage diving experience, we received a call from the guide at the Cage Diving Experience. He explained that we would have to reschedule our dive. Offshore storms and strong winds had brought eight-foot-high waves that kept the boats at the dock. We were leaving the next day to begin our first safari and could not reschedule the cage dive. My wife Hilah was not at all disappointed by missing the cage diving experience, and it seems that I may have missed another near-death adventure.

The next leg of our safari took us to the Okavango Delta in Botswana, with stops in Johannesburg, South Africa, and Maun, Botswana. Our accommodations were in the classic glamping style you would expect on a luxury safari. We stayed in private tents with thatched roofs that were built on elevated wooden platforms. Our king-sized four-poster bed was in the center of the rustic air-conditioned tent next to a stocked mini bar and a full-sized bathroom with a tub and shower. The porch of our tent-suite was overlooking the wetlands and waterways of the Okavango Delta.

We had jeep safaris each morning and an exciting nighttime safari after dinner one evening. We moved through the waterways in dugout canoes and cruised by giant elephants, hippos, giraffes, and crocodiles. We herded antelope and Cape buffalo from a small helicopter based at the Four Seasons Safari Lodge. The area was well known for the opportunity to see the "big five" up close and within good camera distance. The lions, leopards, elephants, African buffalo, and black rhinoceros were all there.

Our next stop was in the fertile valley of Kenya's Maasai Mara, at Richard Branson's Mahali Mzuri Safari Camp. As you would expect, the 12 tented suites were in African luxury style, with serene privacy and en suite baths. The food, the bar, and elevated setting overlooking a large watering hole teeming with African wildlife was exquisite beyond description.

The Mara in the Serengeti was the home to the largest population of lions in Kenya. We also saw thousands of migrating wildebeests, gazelles, and zebras. After a morning safari, we had lunch on the banks of a Serengeti river and watched the migrating herds cautiously crossing the water. The scene was beautiful, but also tragic: we watched the timid gazelles approach the steadily running waters with a dozen large crocodiles waiting patiently along the riverbanks. The gazelles were devoured in Pac-Man–like progression. The larger animals were also subject to the attacking crocs. They would cross in tightly packed groups. Their immense size and weight provided an effective defense—they pressed the toothy crocs to the river bottom.

On the first of several afternoon safaris, we rode comfortably in an open-air, safari-designed Range Rover. There were no windows, and the roof was also open so we could stand and add to our range of vision. Zebras and giraffes were clustered around every stand of trees we passed on our route. Lion cubs and female lions walked lazily down the sides of the dirt trails we traveled on. The male lions were fewer in number and sat majestically alone as they watched over the fields of wandering animals.

We approached a large outcropping of rocks which extended 20 feet above the terrain. At the top of a large flat-topped rock, a pride of lions sat in a restful fashion. Two very large female lions and a half-dozen small playful cubs were sunning quietly on the exposed rock. After we engaged in a few minutes of rapid shutter-snapping photography, the largest female lion slowly turned her huge head and stared down and directly into my eyes. I could see it was thinking about the next move or possibly the next meal. The female lion has the role and responsibility for the evening kill to feed the male and her hungry cubs. The large males provide protection from other roving male lions.

The large female stared intently at me, and I was thinking only the worst thoughts about her intentions. Video loops of a lion attacking a jeep and its inhabitants flashed in my brain. The guide and driver were chirping away about the habits of lions, and I softly but sternly said, "You need to move this jeep." My wife looked quickly at me, and I repeated, "You need to move this jeep now!" As the jeep pulled away from the lions, the two large females rose to stand tall, as if to say, *We will get you next time.*

We flew in and out of Nairobi several times en route to the safari camps and game parks we visited. The capital city of Nairobi is the largest city in Kenya. It is located southwest of Somalia and east of Lake Victoria, at an elevation of 5,500 feet. The population of Nairobi in 1980 was 750,000. Today it is over 5 million people in a city the size of Charlotte, North Carolina. Crime was a concern in the city. We were warned to be vigilant and to take measures to avoid carjackings, robbery, and credit card fraud.

After leaving the Serengeti and Maasai Mara, we flew in a small plane to Nairobi to begin the next safari adventure at the Amboseli National Park. While in Nairobi, we had the opportunity to spend a few hours in the most impoverished areas of the city. Micato Safaris is the company we used for our African trip. They have been ranked more than 10 times by *Travel + Leisure* magazine as the #1 World's Best Safari Outfitter. The company owners arranged a visit to the Pinto Family Foundation's school and public assistance center in Nairobi. The center provides education and economic assistance to disadvantaged women and children.

While en route to the foundation school, we saw dozens of small stall-sized shops along the roadway. They sold food, basic hygienic necessities, and gift items. We also noticed several serious-looking, young dark-skinned males dressed in flowing Muslim-style thobe gowns/robes. The driver said they were religious Muslim men and were not from the area. In the heart of the district, the small bus we were riding in became stuck behind a large broken-down delivery truck. Before exiting the bus to speak to the other driver of the stalled truck, our driver instructed us to remain in the bus and to not speak to or make eye contact with the people outside of the bus. Within minutes, another truck approached from the rear of our bus. There was no cell phone signal and no one to call, even if there was. We were trapped.

Our anxiety increased as our driver continued an intense argument with the driver of the stalled truck. Finally, with hands in the air in exasperation, our driver put his head in the door and assured us we would be moving soon. A dozen or more men appeared and surrounded the rear of the stalled truck and began slowly pushing it to the next intersection of streets and out of our path. The scene was right out of a terrifying movie. I was very glad to be on our way. The visit to the school was amazing, and it was gratifying to know that these poor people were getting some desperately needed assistance.

After an evening at the Boma hotel in Nairobi, we moved to the Amboseli Elewana Tortilis Camp. Our rustic yet luxurious thatched-roof tent had a wonderful view of Mount Kilimanjaro and a large watering hole that was constantly surrounded by grazing herds of African wildlife. The next day we visited the Amboseli National Park, where Mount Kilimanjaro snow melts provide water to maintain the lush growth surrounding the marshes in the park. The constant source of water also provides for an abundance of wildlife in the park. We photographed elephants, wildebeests, zebras, eland, kongoni (African antelope), gazelles, until our batteries were exhausted. There were lions, tiny dik-diks, leopards, buffalo, and cheetahs. The list of beautiful and exotic birds in the parks is too long to describe, with over 600 species. We photographed the world's last male northern white rhino. He died two years later at the Ol Pejeta Conservancy in Kenya.

For the conclusion of our journey, we flew from Nairobi to the foothills of a magnificent snow-capped Mount Kenya. The beautiful Colonial design of the Mount Kenya Safari Club was a perfect way to conclude our African adventure. The club was a second home to the late actor William Holden for 25 years. Legendary names like Sir Winston Churchill, Clark Gable, John Wayne, and Lord Mountbatten filled the registry of guests. More recently, Robert Redford, Sean Connery, and Catherine Deneuve visited the Safari Club. Today you will also find the names of Ron and Hilah Autrey prominently listed in the book of 2016.

Our month-long excursion to South Africa, Botswana, the Serengeti, Nairobi, and southern Kenya provided me with a rich experience and an expanded global perspective. Certainly, seeing the numerous species of African wildlife was spectacular, and it yielded so many rewarding memories. I will never forget the people and their uniqueness.

The incredibly poor people and families—living in the squalor of shanties at the outskirts of metropolitan African cities—were juxtaposed with an unbelievable human spirit of optimism. The village streets in the safari towns were occupied by hundreds of very small shops selling food items, tools, and clothing. They were not like the strip-center architecture of modern cities. Each one was handcrafted from scrap materials and jammed in under a haphazardly constructed metal roof which extended along the street side. The roads were filled with local citizens busy moving in both directions as they went about their daily tasks. Young girls and boys, as well as old people, could be seen carrying water and fuel in a mixed assortment of repurposed containers. Drinking water was collected from the sparsely located wells and carried long distances to each family's home or, in many cases, a makeshift shanty.

I did not find young unemployed men and women on street corners pouting over their misery. I did not see children with their hands out begging for money. I saw enterprise and commerce, and people working to provide for their subsistence. I spoke with an enterprising young man in a Maasai Mara village. He offered to sell us handcrafted wooden and ceramic art, and purses made from animal hides. He proudly explained to me that his country was not a "third-world country." They were a "developing country." The young women in the villages we visited were elated beyond measure that we had brought them gifts. Not trinkets or jewelry—we gave them toothpaste, toothbrushes, and perfume. Shampoo and hair barrettes brought bright smiles to the faces of young girls and older women as well. To the young men, we shared a handful of the local currency. This was not an act of charity so much as it was our way of saying "Thank you for sharing your country with us."

Islamic Terrorism

A deadly development in the first 20 years of the new millennium has roots planted in the 7th century. I grew up in a world surrounded by people who lived and worked to make life better for themselves and their families. We studied in school and improved our knowledge of the world and developed our personal ability to not only cope with life and living, but to also expand and improve our existence. We were among the threads of the fabric that helped weave the American Dream. We also grew up in a world where violence became the primary tool for imposing ideologic beliefs on others.

Terrorist attacks were prevalent in Muslim countries in the two decades before 2001. Though peripheral to our daily lives and something we heard about from Fox News, CNN, the BBC, and other national news sources, the acts of murder and bombings eventually did find a home in the psyche of the American people. The 1983 bombings of the US Embassy in Beirut, Lebanon, somewhat narrowed our focus and introduced the American public to a new vocabulary that included words and phrases like Islamic Jihad, suicide car bombing, and Hezbollah. Our diplomatic presence in Beirut was supported by the CIA and 1,200 US Marines from the 8th

Marine Regimental Battalion Landing Team. Our purpose was to negotiate a cease-fire in the Lebanese Civil War and restore order and governance in the country. Sixty-three people were killed by the 2,000-pound car bomb, including 17 Americans. The president of Lebanon expressed his country's sympathy and asked President Reagan to double the size of the peacekeeping forces. The bombing marked the beginning of Islamic attacks on the United States.

Only six months later, on October 23, 1983, a building near the airport in Beirut was destroyed by a 2,000-pound truck bomb, killing 220 US Marines in the blast. The Islamic Jihad Organization claimed responsibility for the attacks. Their message to America was that the attacks were part of the Iranian Revolution's campaign against imperialist targets around the world. US troops were withdrawn from Lebanon in February of 1984.

Back at home, after our initial outrage and condemnation, we went back to our routines of daily living. Bombings and genocide continued in other countries around the world. The hateful agendas of the Islamic State tallied up thousands of dead warriors and innocent civilians in Egypt, Libya, Iraq, Pakistan, Somalia, and Syria. They were joined by al-Qaeda, the Taliban, and Boko Haram. Terrorism was being exported to other countries, including Russia, Australia, the Philippines, and Thailand. Israel continued to deal with random attacks from neighboring Palestine. India was home to more than 800 terrorist cells that brought random deaths to people across their country. From 2000 to 2019, there were more than 31,000 terrorist attacks around the world, with over 140,000 people killed in terrorist attacks in that 20-year time period.

The ideology of Muslim terrorism was summed up by a Pakistani academician, Dr. Javed Ahmad Ghamidi:

– Only Muslims have the right to rule.

– Modern Nation States are non-Islamic and constitute disbelief.

– The only truly Islamic form of state is a unified Muslim Caliphate.

– When Muslims obtain power, they will over-throw non-Muslim governments.

– The punishment of disbelief and apostasy is death and must be implemented.

The largest portion of those killed in Islamic terrorist attacks are Muslims. The radical extremist Islamic ideology provides that the killing of civilian bystanders is justified. Anyone who aids the disbelievers, buys or sells goods with them, or is merely standing by them, may also be killed. They argue that if the person is a good Muslim, they will find paradise in the afterlife. Bad Muslims will go to hell.

The extremist's view of death is posed as another justification for the horrific acts of terror and the loss of innocent Muslim lives. Islamic scriptures explain that our life in the temporal world has no value. Only life in the hereafter is worth living. A Pakistani author, Ali A. Rizvi, states that the 132 children killed in a 2014 massacre by the Taliban, were not really dead because they had been killed "in the way of God." Anyone killed fighting in the causes of Allah is also not dead, but alive and with their lord. Anyone grieving the deaths is not pure in their faith, and they should not be upset. Islamic extremists teach their youth to love death like their enemies love life. They preach that students have a religious obligation to spread the faith and bring war against the infidels.

As much as the Islamic extremists profess vows of "purity," their actions are inconsistent with anything defined as good and moral by the West. The al-Qaeda offshoot groups of Daesh ISIL fighters regularly persecute the Yazidi women and children in Iraq and Syria. Women and children are enslaved and shared with the Islamic fighters. They want to enslave all non-Muslims. The jihadist actions and beliefs of the ISIL are so horrific, they brought division to the international jihadi movement. The splintered and less violent ideologies are distancing themselves from the globally despised ISIL leadership. Even the Taliban, which was once the primary source of international disdain, is now pitted against the ISIL warlords that consider the Taliban to be too tolerant of the rival Shia.

The high cost of decades of war, in lives and treasure, has not stemmed the advance of Salafi jihadism. The manifesto of the Egyptian Islamist Sayyid Qutb sums up the current agenda for terrorism. His declaration imposes an absolute enforcement of sharia law and violent jihad. The extremists possess a belief that the West is a heap of filth and worthlessness, and that Islam is a construct of logic, beauty, humanity, and happiness. The proclamation that truth and falsehood cannot coexist on earth in peace is evidence of the likelihood of a continued exportation of violent conflicts around the world.

The manifesto of Qutbism calls out its own followers as not adhering to "pure Islam." Purity can only come from strict and literal adherence to the Quran and Hadith. The Hadith is a list of traditions and sayings from the prophet Muhammad. This cleansing of the impure will bring even more death and despair to the contiguous countries in the Muslim regions of the world.

The battle between Christianity and Islam has its roots in the religious Crusades dating back to the 11th and 12th centuries, when the Latin Church freed Jerusalem from Islamic rule. The Christian ideology was defended by kings, emperors, and scores of knights and warriors, in battle after battle that began in the year 1095 and continued for 175 years, into 1270. We no longer refer to the conflicts as crusades, but the underlying beliefs, motivations, and dedication to the causes remain as deadly today as they were 900 years ago.

The Twenty-Year War

The two decades spanning 2001 to 2021 were overlayed with a new American war against terrorism. Seven days after the tragic events of September 11, 2001, 420 United States congressmen and congresswomen joined 98 US senators to authorize the commencement of the war in Afghanistan. Only one person voted against the measure. Her name is Rep. Barbara Lee from California. Despite the broad support defined by the landslide outcome in the voting, it was thereafter and forever referred to as Bush's War.

Except for the open-ended Korean conflict, the war in Afghanistan would be the longest war in American history. The Vietnam War was officially declared in 1965 and ran until 1975. The conflict began in the 1950s, when American military advisors were dispatched to assist the French in the ongoing north-south conflict in Vietnam. The American war in Afghanistan provided 7,262 full days of military conflict that pitted US soldiers against the armed forces of Al-Qaeda and ISIS terrorists. The war on terror may have started in Iraq and Afghanistan, but over the course of 20 years, the United States had initiated and maintained counterterrorism activities in 85 other countries.

One-fourth of the US population today was born after the World Trade Center bombing on September 11, 2001. Couple that with the median age in Afghanistan today being 18 years old, and within one generation the Afghanistan War will most likely find the silence of obscurity in educational curriculums and world affairs. We went to war to take the country back from the evil forces of Al-Qaeda, only to hand the Taliban the keys to the capital city of Kabul, on August 15, 2021.

Summarizing wars is often presented as a simple tally of the lives lost and dollars spent in the conflicts, and in the aftermath of the wars. The cost of the war in Afghanistan exceeded $2 trillion. The cost of postwar care for the wounded will add another $2 trillion. The money did not come from tax revenues. The interest on $4 trillion of debt will add another $900 billion by 2030.

The Afghanistan War took the lives of 2,448 American soldiers. Over 20,000 US servicemen and women were wounded in battle. Nearly 4,000 US private military contractors and service providers also died in the conflict. Over 66,000 Afghan military and police forces lost their lives. More than 1,100 allied soldiers from 40 countries were also killed in action. Compare the deaths of the liberators with the 66,000 Afghan soldiers and 47,245 Afghan civilians who perished in the fighting. The body count for Taliban forces and other fighters was well over 50,000. The actual numbers seem so exact, but regardless of minor adjustments that may be made from one researcher to the next, the portrait of the tragedy of war depicts the same horrific image. (Statistics from Harvard University, Kennedy Public Policy School.)

History books and doctoral theses will ultimately bring the final metrics of the war back to the generations that follow. What of the hidden impact of lives lost in battle? In the United States alone, with over 10,000 American soldiers and noncombatants killed in Iraq and Afghanistan, there are tens of thousands more spouses, mothers and dads, children, betrothed, and friends that found instantaneous and immense grief upon learning the news of the deaths in a faraway land. They grieve and yearn to know when and where their loved one was killed. What were his or her last thoughts? Did they suffer intense pain before dying?

Was the revenge for 9/11 and the killing of Osama bin Laden and Saddam Hussein, and others in the top tiers of tyranny, worth the price? We could ask the 980,000 servicemen and women who served in the wars in Iraq and Afghanistan. We could ask the grieving mothers, dads, and lovers of dead warriors. Are we more free today as a result of the wars? These questions should be asked and answered. We stopped the exportation of terror to our homeland, but for how long? Was war the appropriate response to the 9/11 terrorist attacks? We know that economic sanctions do not work when imposed on a nation that is already starving. Certainly, changing the ideology of a people that has its roots planted in AD 610 is not possible. As a human species we also know that the Hitleresque extermination of a noncompliant faction of people would also be a crime against our human nature and spirituality. The ongoing battle of good versus evil will not be settled in our lifetime.

To add a painful overarching perspective to the death tolls of war, consider that beginning in 1939, World War II ultimately brought 70 million people into battle, and killed 17 million of those fighting in that global war. Before Germany surrendered in 1945, a total of 400,000 US servicemen and women lost their lives in World War II. The war left a scar on American history and humanity when American nuclear bombs fell on Hiroshima and Nagasaki, Japan. The bombs brought death to more than 150,000 Japanese people.

Good News Grizzlies

I visited Alaska several times in the years 2002 to 2012. Our trips were exclusively to the Good News River Lodge in the Eskimo village of Good News. The lodge is located on the Good News River, 400 miles northwest of Anchorage, Alaska. We flew charter flights from Anchorage to the village of Good News and were transported upriver on metal-hull jetboats to the lodge. Rustic elevated wood platforms support 11 sleeping huts, housing up to 22 anglers. The lodge owners and guides had similar sleeping quarters away from the anglers' huts. We fished for and caught several species of trout and salmon. The fly-fishing experience was phenomenal. Anglers who had never held a flyrod caught 50 or more large fish each day.

In 2004 my brother-in-law, Buz Livingston, put together a father-and-son expedition to the Good News River Lodge. My son Andrew and I joined Buz and his son Eric along with two other dads and sons. My father, Buck Autrey, also joined, making this an epic three-generation trip to Alaska. The boys were all around 10 years old and their excitement was audible and visible. The camp is situated in a remote uninhabited section of the larger Eskimo reservation, and the riverbanks regularly showed us large caribou, also known as reindeer. The beavers built dams along the river's tributaries, and hundreds of bird species also shared the setting in Northwest Alaska.

The North American grizzly bears were at the top of the food chain in Alaska. The bears grew much larger than those found in the Midwestern United States. Seeing 1,200-pound grizzlies, which stand 10 feet tall when erect, was common. They feed on salmon and trout, and the calves of elk and caribou. The grizzlies prowled the area looking for discarded food around the Good News Lodge at night while we slept. For very good reasons, food is not allowed to be kept in the sleeping huts. Upon arrival at the lodge, we circled around the owner Mike Gorton. He gave us a rundown on the camp rules, customs, and scheduling information. He emphatically warned the young boys that running in the camp was prohibited and could cause the nearby mountain lions and bears to see young boys as a food source or a threat. As soon as our camp conference concluded, five young boys took off running toward the river. Boys will be boys.

The fishing expedition was legendary, with our young sons catching large king salmon as big as 50 pounds, along with numerous 10- to 15-pound silver, chum, and sockeye salmon. The rainbow trout were 24 to 30 inches in length, and readily attacked our camp-made rabbit hair mouse flies. We made day-long hikes to a gold prospecting section of the river and panned the water for gold nuggets. We explored a pre–World War II barge outfitted with large diesel engines and a crane boom with a large chain of buckets that scooped the rocks from the riverbed. The rocks were sorted out and the gold was collected in mesh screens inside the equipment house on the barge. The barge was abandoned during World War II, when diesel fuel was no longer available. Over the years, the river took a different route and left the large wooden barge stranded in the landlocked tundra of Northwest Alaska.

The fishing was done from multiple guide boats that accommodated two anglers and one guide. The boats had outboard engines with jet drives in place of the usual lower unit with a propeller. We could jet upstream or down in the shallow-draft metal boats. The shallow streams and boulders banged the metal bottoms when we jetted across the rapids in the river. Steel and aluminum boat hulls were preferred over wood or fiberglass that would be destroyed by the rocks and boulders in the river.

One morning, in search of big rainbow trout, Artic char, and graylings, my son Andrew and I headed upriver and away from the salmon run. Once in position near a small island of dense underbrush, the guide secured the boat and we stepped into the shallow, cold running water. Our neoprene waders and wading boots kept our feet warm in the knee-deep stream. The setting was beautiful, and we began catching our targeted species. Andrew waded approximately 200 feet upstream from where I was fishing. The guide was situated between us and ready to assist with landing and unhooking the fish.

After about 45 minutes of catching trout, grayling, and char, we saw a large antlered caribou loping across a nearby clearing. That evening, the guide would share the location of the caribou spotting with the Eskimos in the village in exchange for other materials or services. The caribou would supplement the daily diet of salmon in the village. Winters in Alaska are brutally cold and the natives must collect and store food for the weeks and months that prevent hunting and fishing.

Humans have a sixth sense that collects information from the traditional five senses and produces a message of safety or of impending harm. As I looked at our fishing guide slowly moving toward me, I knew immediately that something was wrong. It was more than just an alert that we might see another loping caribou or some other animal. I saw fear and concern in his facial tension. He was whispering to me as he approached. I could not hear everything with the running water racing around my feet, but I could make out the word "grizzly."

The guide was trying to tell me that there was a large female grizzly bear in the underbrush, with a small cub. This poses a potential extremely dangerous situation. He said I needed to get Andrew back from upstream as quickly as possible, but with minimal noise and no running or panicked trudging as he moved in the stream. I called out to Andrew, and like any 10-year-old boy would do, he did not want to comply with my hand gestures to move toward the guide and me. I slowly moved toward him, and we could hear the bear grunting and pawing the dirt and rocks, looking for rodents and edible roots for her cub. I finally got the message across to Andrew that we were in danger. The three of us slowly and nervously exited the area and returned to the welcome but minimal safety of our boat. The experience opened a window into the harsh reality of what could have happened. Our guide carried a 12-gauge pump shotgun loaded with rubber slugs to deter an approaching bear, but an excited mother grizzly protecting her cub would not have been stopped by a bullet or a small metal boat. Alaska is a beautiful state, and I hope to return to the rivers of Good News one day soon.

Viva la Mexico

The United States started the "war on drugs" in 1971. The number of deaths from drug overdoses and drug poisoning has risen exponentially every year. It is safe to say that the war on drugs is ongoing. More than 100,000 Americans died from drug overdoses in 2021. Two-thirds of those deaths were from the use of a synthetic opioid known as fentanyl. It is a painkiller that is 100 percent stronger than morphine. Many of the victims did not even know they were taking it. The source: Mexico. The country is controlled by six or more drug cartels. The list includes the Jalisco New Generation Cartel, the Sinaloa Cartel, the Gulf Cartel, the Los Zetas, La Familia Michoacana, and the Knights Templar. The annual Mexican drug trade revenue is estimated to be nearly $30 billion. Mexico also started their war on drugs in 1971. In 2006 the crisis ramped up significantly when the government dispatched 6,500 soldiers to the federal state of Michoacan, on the west coast of the country.

Every year since the Michoacan Operation, thousands of people have died violently every month. In 2017, there were 29,168 homicides recorded. By 2021, the total death toll was more than 200,000 people, and over 61,000 people were missing. Bodies were found mutilated, decapitated, hanged, burned, and dissolved in acid. Drug lords were killed or captured each year, only to be replaced with new leaders that brought more violence and death. From 2006 to 2021, the United States spent billions of dollars on joint operations with Mexico. The mayhem continued.

In 2008, the Mexican government launched Joint Operation Nuevo León-Tamaulipas and captured drug lord Alfredo Leyva. The response: Federal Police Commissioner Edgar Gomez was killed in Mexico City. The commander of the investigative police force was also killed. The government launched Operation Sinaloa, and the cartel responded by killing seven Federal Police agents in Culiacán. The financial sanctions that were imposed on the drug cartels led to the death of another police commander in Mexico City.

To continue support of the war on drugs and violence, on October 22, 2007, the United States and Mexico announced the $1.6 billion agreement known as the Mérida (Yucatan) Initiative. The violence that followed was horrific. Two dozen tortured bodies were found in La Marquesa National Park. In Morelia, Mexico, hand grenades were thrown into a crowd, killing eight and wounding more than 100. Mexican criminal investigator Andres Dimitriades was shot and killed in his car on his way home. Seven soldiers and one police commander were kidnapped, tortured, and decapitated in Chilpancingo. Their heads were left at a shopping center with a warning note to the Mexican military. In 2009, police arrested Santiago Meza, who had dissolved 300 bodies from a rival drug trafficking group. Many more police officers, soldiers, and mayors were targeted and killed in the ongoing war.

In 2014, the Mexican government was no longer in a drug war; it had become an all-out war against the militant cartels. Dionisio Loya Plancarte from the Knights Templar Cartel was arrested. Joaquin "El Chapo" Guzman was arrested in

Mazatlán. Knights Templar leader Nazario Moreno Gonzalez was killed in a police shootout. Knights Templar's Enrique Solis was also killed in a shootout with Mexican naval forces. Los Zetas founder, Galindo Mellado Cruz, was killed in Reynosa, Tamaulipas.

The war reached an epic new high in 2015 with the killing of 20 Federal Police in March and April. In May 2015, the streets of Jalisco were blockaded by the New Generation Cartel. Fire stations were burned, and cartel gunmen dressed in military and police uniforms kidnapped and killed residents as they took over the town. They ambushed a police convoy and, using rocket-propelled grenades, they shot down a military helicopter that was dispatched to contain the violence. The heavily armed militant cartel was now a full-blown combatant enemy force in Mexico.

In 2020, a former Mexican Defense Secretary was arrested in Los Angeles for drug trafficking and money laundering. Mexican police departments were being steadily purged of corrupt officials and agents. The end of the year brought even more horror when the bodies of 59 young adults were found in a mass grave in Guanajuato. Former Jalisco mayor Aristoteles Sandoval died after being shot in a restaurant restroom. The horrific killings and kidnappings continued into 2021. Cartel leaders were arrested and some were extradited to the United States for prosecution. Mexican soldiers and Federal Police continued to die in gunfights with the militant cartel members.

Mexico's Public Security Secretary initiated a new strategy for the country's drug war. The government had detained or killed 120 of the top 122 cartel leadership targets. They were quickly replaced, and the violence continued. The new strategy was to combat the cartels by attacking their finances. Bank accounts of the most violent organizations were frozen. Money is what the cartels needed to maintain their drug trafficking operations. Weeding out police and government corruption is also an essential and ongoing effort.

The long-term solution to this war that spans both sides of the border is to bring about sustained improvements to the welfare and education of young people in Mexico, so that they can experience opportunities outside the tragic confines of the drug trafficking world. The same is true in the United States. Violence and drug use can only be overcome by raising the awareness and education level of our children and the generations that follow.

The Trump Presidency

On January 20, 2017, in the presence of more than 600,000 followers assembled at the US Capitol steps, Donald John Trump was inaugurated as the 45th president of the United States. His conservative plans included substantial immigration reform to stem the influx of people crossing at the southern border of the United States. Trump pledged to bring manufacturing companies back to the United States. On March 22, 2018, President Donald Trump rocked the unbalanced world trade market and imposed $60 billion of tariffs on Chinese imports. China had been stealing American intellectual property and using their impoverished labor force to create an unfair imbalance of trade. This was just a start, and the president also had plans for more sanctions in the technology sector. He reworked trade policies with other countries, and NAFTA was scrapped and redesigned to support American corporations more fairly.

In his pragmatic style, President Trump took North Korea head-on. The North Korean leader Kim Jong-un had been ramping up North Korea's nuclear weapons program. It started with the first underground nuclear detonation in 2006, followed by Kim Jong-un's first nuclear test in 2013. By 2017, North Korea had conducted at least six nuclear detonations. North

Korea also claimed to have a device that could be mounted on a ballistic missile. Kim's bombastic rhetoric prompted several verbal exchanges with President Trump.

In a historic development following the election of South Korean President Moon Jae-in, Kim and Moon began discussing the possibility of a unified Korea. The exchange led to a momentous display of North and South Korean athletes marching together into the 2018 Winter Olympics ceremony under a flag depicting the unified body. Kim's sister attended the ceremony and delivered a handwritten note to Moon, inviting the South Korean president to visit Kim Jong-un. The next month, Moon joined Kim at a dinner in Pyongyang, the capital of North Korea. Kim made it known that he was willing to give up the nuclear program if the United States would guarantee the security of North Korea and Kim's regime. On April 27, 2018, Kim and Moon met face-to-face at the "Truce Village" in P'anmunjom, where they discussed nuclear disarmament and an armistice to officially end the Korean War.

Communication was temporarily spoiled by harsh words between the North Koreans and National Security Advisor John Bolton. Vice President Mike Pence also contributed to the war of words by suggesting a parallel between Kim Jong-un and the fate of the deceased Libyan President Muammar al-Qaddafi. The exchange led to President Trump announcing that he was pulling out of the June meeting plans. Conciliatory tones prevailed and the historic meeting took place on June 12, 2018. Kim pledged to complete denuclearization, and President Trump committed to end US military exercises with the South Korean forces. With the election of US President Joe Biden in 2020, the talks with North Korea stalled and Kim Jong-un resumed missile testing.

Trump's presidency was marred in controversy and conspiracies from the very beginning. Claims of election fraud and foreign influence were charged by both sides. The probes and investigations eventually exonerated Trump, but not before being impeached twice. The first charges of obstruction of justice and abuse of power were lodged on December 18 in 2019, followed by a second impeachment on January 13, 2021. President Trump was acquitted in both cases by the Republican-controlled US Senate.

History will show that the Trump presidency was the catalyst that prompted a more robust and in-depth investigation into voter fraud. Electronic voting machine manipulation, ballot drop box fraud, and vote harvesting are in the forefront as potential crimes to investigate and prevent in future elections. At a more elevated level, the purposeful and designed influence of social media and large questionable expenditures by tech company billionaires are now recognized as improper and illegal influencing of voters. An inordinate amount of money was funneled to state attorney races in large US cities to elect a more woke cadre of liberal prosecutors. The subsequent no-bail and non-prosecution of violent crimes created an environment of tolerance for property theft crimes and gang-related assaults in major cities across the country. The meager Republican gains achieved in the 2022 midterm national elections will likely do very little to reshape the focus and direction of crime control in the country.

The year 2018 was an exciting period in the world of space exploration. It was also transformational because the missions were being funded and developed in the private sector. That is not to say that NASA is not essential to the ongoing private and governmental space programs, but the motivations and financing of new space missions are now also coming from businesses and individuals. The innovations in spacecraft design and function are also being privately developed and financed.

On February 6, 2018, a company founded by Elon Musk launched the most powerful operational rocket in the world. The company, SpaceX, launched the Falcon Heavy vehicle from the Kennedy Space Center in Florida. With 5 million pounds of thrust, Falcon Heavy blasted into space. Three minutes after takeoff, the large side boosters disengaged from the rocket, and with flawless design and performance, they navigated a route back to earth and safely landed upright on the launch pad. In the past, these boosters would have been jettisoned to the ocean.

The success of the SpaceX missions set the stage for the company to receive multiple government and military contracts for launching satellites into orbit. The Boeing Company is right on Musk's heels as they also pursue commercial space opportunities. In the most recent two years, both companies made amazing strides in spacecraft and mission development. In a historic moment on May 20, 2022, Boeing's Starliner capsule joined SpaceX's Crew Dragon when they were both docked at the International Space Station. Through open-ended contracts, the US military and NASA are now outsourcing manned and unmanned missions to both companies. The technology yielded from NASA's early missions contributed to an exponential wave of change in the 20th century. That exponential rate of technological change will itself become exponential as the private development of space exploration continues.

The phenomenal advances in private space expeditions recognized in the beginning of the year 2018 were appropriately bookmarked in August, by the 42-year-old Apple Company becoming the first public company to be valued at $1 trillion. Three years later, Apple surged to a valuation of $3 trillion. A company that started in a California garage in 1976 has shown the world that advances in technology and our quality of life are more effectively developed in the private business sector of our country's economy.

2019: Climate Change

Politically charged events and movements come with new catch phrases and frequently repeated mantras. Liberal politicians are repeatedly verbalizing climate change as the number one existential threat to Americans and the future of the planet. The coordinated broadcasts and speeches follow the common strategy that if you say something enough times and in enough places, it is declared by social consensus to be indisputably the truth. Like many topics taken up as front-page news, the news media showers the reader and viewing public with sensationalism. The raw data and honest interpretations by legitimate scientists are selectively edited or not shared in public news forums.

News anchors and politicians repeat false phrases until they believe what they are saying with such emotional strength that they must be true. Young adults hear the erroneous messages and act with outrage that the adult population is destroying the earth right before their helpless eyes. Students of science are also barraged with falsehoods and cherry-picked data by their instructors. They in turn continue the promulgation of the failing-earth narrative when they enter postgraduate employment and various positions of influence.

The outcome of the climate change–driven agenda in government is indeed one of failure. A failed US economy, a renewed dependence on foreign oil, and a breakdown in national security dangerously diminished our standing as the leading country in global affairs. President Biden's hasty and abrupt policies that restricted domestic energy production have contributed to a disruption of the supply chain for hundreds of essential goods and services. Most Americans have a malnourished understanding of the current uses of petroleum products. Thousands of household convenience products are crafted with components that are dependent on the use of petroleum derivatives. The cost of transporting products throughout the United States is economically impacted by the surging cost of fuel.

The newly created dependence on foreign oil and gas—in the US and abroad—has lasting and damaging ramifications in our relationships with European allies and our tenuous ties to Middle Eastern countries. The international instability caused by the implementation of President Biden's energy policies emboldened China and Russia. They now pursue policies and actions that threaten the freedom of the people in Taiwan and Ukraine.

"It is the carbon dioxide that is killing the planet," the climate warriors say. From a macro perspective, the increase in CO_2 gases in the earth's atmosphere is actually credited for the current increases in agricultural food production. Humans and other air-breathing creatures survive on the intake of oxygen and the exhalation of carbon dioxide. The survival of trees and plants of all types depends on the presence of carbon dioxide. This divine and balanced equation of the dynamic life support cycle is fluid and sometimes volatile, yet remains irrefutable.

Global-warming alarmists were somewhat quieted by the science compiled from historical warming and cooling trends.

First the polar caps were melting and then they were expanding the ice fields. The conversations brought new revelations pertaining to polar ice fields. The new narrative defined contrasting values between surface ice and submerged ice. Archimedes' principle that the volume of the melted ice will be the same as that of the water displaced by the ice seems to at least partially deflate the rising sea level debate. Record cold waves swept through the US Northeast, while searing heat and droughts plagued the West. In a more encompassing move, the green movement changed its wording from "global warming" to "climate change." This categoric nomenclature is at least the truth. Climates around the world are, and have been, changing for megaannums (one-million-year units).

Published climate records go back only 150 years. A carbon-dated study of stalagmites in caverns and deep fissures in the western US and the tropics of Central America gives researchers a valid timeline of changing wet and dry conditions going back 500,000 years. Scientific study of the stalagmites also revealed that what happened in the higher latitudes of the planet was not always consistent with the weather in subtropical zones. Periods of extreme dryness in the tropics yielded a corresponding period of heavy rainfall in the northern section of the continent. The science also reveals that historical trends of dryness, wetness, and cooler and warmer temperatures are displayed in cycles lasting as long as 1,500 years. Prolonged periods of steady climate trends would seem to be a normal characteristic of climate change. However, studies have documented that atmospheric cycles were uncharacteristically bumped up about 430,000 years ago when levels of carbon dioxide inexplicably surged by 30 percent. Current studies of carbon dioxide levels are showing the same recurring phenomenon regarding the earth's ozone layer. To claim and mandate that climate change is now solely a result of human inhabitation and use of the planet is not substantiated by proven scientific data.

It is true that effluents from the combustion of oil and natural gas can be considered toxic to both plants and animals. Power plants in the 1950s and '60s were notable for the odor of the visible sulfur dioxide gas rising from the smokestacks. Modern technology has identified other effluent harmful chemicals and compounds and applied electrostatic scrubbing technology to substantially reduce the output of harmful byproducts from manufacturing plants and power-generating stations. Oil and coal power plants in the United States now approach the pollution output levels of natural gas plants.

"Not good enough!" say the climate warriors. Solar, wind, and hydroelectric power are the only acceptable answers. There is much to say about all three of these natural green energy sources. The simple answer is that there are not enough sources of moving wind and water to meet the energy demands around the globe. Simultaneous with liberal mandates to prohibit the use of hydrocarbon-powered automobiles are the inevitable electric power consumption restrictions imposed by the limitations of our power grids. The state of California is a living example of the failed mathematics in the quest to convert to an all-electric transportation system.

Solar panels require the input of rare earth elements in the manufacturing process, as well as enormous repurposing of land area. The battery plants required to store the energy are also highly dependent on the mining of rare materials that are geographically confined and finite in quantity. The mining and manufacturing processes require the use of hydrocarbon-based energy at a level that significantly exceeds the environmental benefits of the end product.

The cleanest green answer to nonpolluting power production is in the use of nuclear fission reactors. Nuclear power generation has been around since the 1950s. Today in 2022, there are 92 nuclear reactors in 54 power plants in 28 US states, and over 443 reactors in 30 countries in the world. Collectively they generate only approximately 15 percent of the world's power capacity. The trend in construction of new plants is downward in the United States. The capital cost of construction for nuclear plants makes the electricity cost per kilowatt hour slightly higher than power from other sources. In contrast, China and Russia are not only building new nuclear plants in their own countries, but also exporting their government-subsidized nuclear expertise to surrounding countries.

While China has pledged to join the green movement and significantly reduce carbon emissions, they currently operate half of all the coal-fired power plants in the world. In 2022 they will add 8.63 gigawatts of electric power generation and commission 43 new coal-fired power plants and 17 new blast furnaces. Eighty percent of the coal power plants in the world are in China, India, Japan, Vietnam, and Indonesia. The United States could destroy the American economy trying to meet the unrealistic international climate standards proposed by the Paris Climate Agreement. The promise to limit the earth's long-term rising temperature to one or two degrees Celsius is unrealistic and unsupported by classical scientific research methods. That which we think, and what we wish for, are not scientific corollaries that should drive the economies around the world.

If restrictions on the exploration and production of petroleum in the United States continues, the attractiveness of nuclear fission power will undoubtedly rise. If we truly want to find new sources of clean energy, then ongoing nuclear fusion research and hydrogen-fueled power generation should also be heavily supported by policymakers and funding sources.

Nuclear fission power plants are expensive to build. The cost of the power for consumers is still slightly higher than power from other power sources. Putting the complexity of the underlying science aside, the nuclear power plant simply converts the heat energy produced by nuclear fission into electrical power. A large amount of electrical power can be produced from a small amount of nuclear fuel. Radioactive uranium weighing 2.2 pounds can produce the power output equal to the burning of 4,500 tons of coal (9 million pounds). Nuclear power plants require less fuel, thereby reducing transportation and handling costs. They require less physical space and far less water, allowing them to be located closer to the connected power users. Transmission capital and maintenance costs are also reduced.

Nuclear fuel is very expensive, and it produces radioactive byproducts and disposal issues. The long-term consequences of nuclear waste sites and deep disposal wells are an ongoing concern. The construction of nuclear power plants is relatively higher than other types of power plants. Power plant operators and engineers require more expertise and training and warrant higher salaries. While occurrences are rare, the public's fear of nuclear disasters is prevalent. Regardless of the disadvantages, from a green energy standpoint nuclear power plants remain the most efficient and economical solution to the world's energy demands.

A comprehensive discussion of nuclear fusion (not fission) is beyond the scope of this book and the competence of the writer. The analysis of a mixture of hydrogen isotopes like deuterium and tritium as a fuel source for nuclear power generation is a worthy endeavor that is best assigned to scientists who have dedicated their lives and talents to the research. Moving aluminum discs at a speed of 12 miles per second and generating fuel temperatures of 100 million degrees is beyond the quantitative capacity of most humans.

Nuclear power research began in the 1940s when scientists pondered the question of how stars were powered. At that time and in every succeeding decade, the generation of electricity from nuclear fusion was thought to be 30 to 50 years in the future. There were some significant successes recorded in the early '50s. This led to the creation of the Princeton Physics Laboratory and the first experimentally controlled product of thermonuclear fusion. Following the invention of the first laser in 1960, scientists made advances in laser fusion systems. Fast-forward to 1996 and 1997 for controlled releases of fusion power that generated a power flow of 1 million amperes for two minutes. A subsequent experiment produced 10 megawatts of power for 0.5 seconds. The possibilities of developing controlled electric power generation from fusion reactors was deemed to be possible.

Simply put, the practical use of nuclear fusion power systems is presently obviated by logical and economical constraints. It requires more input power to generate the output power produced by nuclear fusion. The development and operational costs of the facilities and the generation activity is also prohibitive. So as in past decades, we are closer, but the desired outcomes and benefits of nuclear fusion power is still three or more decades away.

The environment should be protected. The Industrial Revolution demonstrated that we have the capacity to significantly harm the environment. Deforestation by developers and manufacturers, oil spills, pesticides, leaded gasoline, and the use of coal for heating our homes, all produced visible and tangible polluting effects in major cities around the world. In 1968 when a NASA astronaut took a photograph of planet Earth, we saw firsthand how potentially fragile our existence could be. It was the beginning of a new global perspective on how we should manage and maintain Earth's natural resources.

Conservation of virgin forests and rivers was necessitated by the obvious destruction brought on by expanding industries. Perhaps we needed organizations like the Sierra Club to give the conservation movement a voice. Presidents Kennedy, Johnson, and Nixon made environmental protection a policy matter in their administrations. US Senator Gaylord Nelson established the first Earth Day in 1969. President Richard Nixon codified his 37-point plan to improve and protect the environment with the creation of the Environmental Protection Agency in 1974. In the years that followed we saw the enactment of the Clean Water Act, the Clean Air Act, the Endangered Species Act, and the Federal Pesticides Act.

Good science is possible and it does exist. If we peel away the fudge factors that are often used to support an agenda-driven, pre-crafted result, we can agree that climate predictions based on the fundamental application of physics and chemistry can be scientifically valid. The frequently discussed and debated atmospheric greenhouse effect is a good example. It is universally accepted that cloud movements, densities, and atmospheric opacity and chemical content will affect the temperatures of water and ice at the earth's surface. Some scientific models that have successfully re-created past temperature trends can, to some degree, predict future climate trends. The erroneousness arises when scientists collect and manipulate the data to calculate predefined results. If we want the answer to be number xyz, then we can accumulate and style the data to put out the number we desire.

A prudent energy strategy should be one of exploiting and benefitting from our capacity to be energy independent, while continuing to advance the science and applications of more environmentally friendly power-generating technologies. The relinquishment of our long-standing position as a premier world power is destabilizing to the entire world. Our interdependent economies may fail over time from a loss of productivity, and more abruptly from the wartime acts of Russia and China as they take advantage of our weakened role on the world stage. To the Greta Thunbergs in the world, I say yes, we should take action, but we should not succumb to the maniacal policies promoted by overemotional and uninformed stage players of the green movement.

Like any movement or amalgamation of thoughts and thought leaders, the spectrum of strategies and theories spans outward from a reasonable position of consensus to the extremes at each end of the platforms. The extremists take on a Machiavellian approach to the efforts to implement their agendas, losing the tools of logic and science in the process. The bombastic voices take the stage, and the media capitalizes on the noise. Meanwhile the stakeholders are clouded by misinformation, and the unprofitable and unpopular truths are buried. The mantras become the law, and the education of the public and future generations is flawed and misguided.

Healthcare

Humans are at the top of the food chain and arguably are the most evolved species on the planet. How we care for our health through our eight-decade lifespan has found the center of controversy in the 21st century. In Paleolithic times, the Neanderthals survived by following preventive care. So long as they avoided deadly attacks from other creatures and maintained access to food, water, and shelter, they lived out their expected lifespan. If a violation of those principles of existence occurred, then death, dismemberment, or disease was the likely outcome. Except for the practice of licking the wounds of another, the existence of cures or medical care did not exist.

The first medical practitioners appeared in the age of tribalism, in the millennium before Christ was born. The Hippocratic Oath came from Greece in the 5th century BC, and physicians were first trained in universities in the 13th century. Indian tribes in North America had a "medicine man" who administered herbal medicine and crude surgical procedures. Like many services needed for the sustenance of life, tribal specialists provided an optimum system with timely access and the application of available remedies. The leaders led, the warriors fought, the hunters hunted, and the women birthed and nurtured the children. No one was paid for their services. The socialistic model was one of survival and mutual assistance. The tribal leader provided the vision and direction required for the safety and well-being of the community.

One thousand years later, a push to return to a socialistic manner of providing community healthcare is politically dividing the populace. For the last 200 years, trained physicians worked both independently and within hospitals developed and supported by others. The cost of healthcare was paid for by the patient or their family members. Private insurance companies provided a product that collectively financed and prepaid the cost of healthcare.

The debate over who should pay for personal healthcare in the US goes back to President Teddy Roosevelt in 1912. He pushed for a government-sponsored system in his administration. The concept was not taken up again until President Truman attempted to create a national health insurance program in 1945. Truman's efforts failed, but 20 years later, in 1965, under President Lyndon Johnson, the US Social Security Administration created Medicare as an alternative to private insurance for Americans 65 years and older. At the time, more than half of Americans over 65 were uninsured. Today the number of people receiving health coverage from Medicare is approaching 65 million. For citizens under the age of 65 who are unable to pay for private insurance, the program of Medicaid was added in 1965. The cost of Medicare is now over $1 trillion annually. Mandated payroll deductions fund the Medicare program and the additional $600 billion cost of Medicaid is paid by other state and federal tax revenues.

With the amount of money spent annually on healthcare in the US exceeding $11,000 per person, the total annual expenditures are approaching $4 trillion. Half of the US population still receives health insurance coverage from their employers. That leaves another 75 million people currently enrolled in the Medicaid program, with children making up over 40 percent of the number of people enrolled in the program. While the number has decreased since the implementation of the Affordable Care Act, somewhere between 20 and 30 million people are still uninsured.

The debate on how to best pay for medical care continues. To say that the US does not have socialized medicine is not completely true. Our form of socialized care includes the Veterans Health Administration (VA), Medicare, Medicaid, and the heavily subsidized Affordable Care Act (ACA) also known as Obamacare. What we do not have is universal healthcare for all citizens. While the quality of the care provided by various countries can be debated, the average cost in the G7 countries of Canada, France, Germany, Italy, Japan, and the UK is less than half the cost of healthcare provided in the United States. Where we spend 20 percent of the nation's GDP on healthcare, the other countries spend far less, with the closest nation spending less than 12 percent.

Other nations pay for the government healthcare programs through varying levels of taxation and user fees. Most of the countries have privately employed physicians who are paid by government-provided insurance programs. In the French system, which is described by the World Health Organization (WHO) as the best in the world, households earning less than $9,600 per year pay nothing. College students pay about $200 per year. For other workers, the government taxes for premiums are paid in part by the employer and the employee. Private insurance is also available for those with higher incomes, to supplement their coverage.

Certainly, there is a relationship between the cost of healthcare and metrics like wait times for emergency care, surgical procedures, and elective surgeries. The values vary from country to country, but great disparities are generally not seen. If the United States shifts more toward a government-provided universal healthcare system, practicing physicians will likely be affected economically. Their options to relocate to other countries would be limited by the value of actually doing so. The most likely change would be a decline in the number of students electing the practice of medicine as a career. Our best hope is to continue a hybrid model of mixing privately funded care with government systems—much like we do now, except that the 20 million uninsured would need to be included in the cost burden of national healthcare programs.

The Immigration Crisis

The unlawful immigration at the southern border of the United States is a criminal tragedy for the American people. It is a humanitarian crisis for the people struggling to find a way out of poverty in their home countries. It is a national security concern for the United States. More than 900,000 "got aways" with unknown heritage and motives have entered the US since 2020. The estimated number of illegal entries and apprehensions in 2020–2022 now exceeds 2 million and is increasing every day.

The illegal immigrants are coming to the US from the Mexican border, but only half of the immigrants are Mexican. Tens of thousands more are from Asia, Europe, Canada, the Caribbean, Central America, and South America. We need only look at the widely distributed statistics of immigration in the US over the last 20 years to see that the system is politically and legislatively broken and mismanaged. Our failure to secure the border has created a crisis that will affect the way of life for millions of immigrants and a hundred times that number of existing legal residents. The illegal entry by drug dealers and other criminals has escalated the violence in our city streets across the nation. The number of deaths from opioid overdoses and fentanyl poisoning is soaring, with more than 100,000 deaths in the first seven months of 2022.

Our 46th president of the United States, Joe Biden, and his incompetent administration are speaking and acting on the issue without a complete understanding of the metrics and dynamics of the problem. The president and his staff are saying that the border is not open and that the illegal immigration problem is being well contained and managed. US senators, congressional members, and journalists who have visited the border and witnessed the flow of migrants know that the president and his team are either ignorant or simply lying to the American public. The videos being collected daily show the thousands of illegal border crossings every day and night. The statistics leading up to this crisis and the current data being collected daily clearly show that we have a serious problem. Over 2 million illegal immigrants entered the country from 2021 through 2022, and more than 1.5 million have remained and been released into various locations across our country. The Biden administration talks about and describes an immigration policy, but the narrative does not match the reality at the southern border.

Legal immigration is part of American history, with roots extending to the country's formation in 1776. In the year 1850 there were just over 2 million people that could be defined as immigrants living in the United States. By 2019 the immigrant population had grown to 45 million people, expanding to 48 million in 2022. The total number also includes over 16 million illegal or unauthorized immigrants distributed across the United States.

The US Customs and Border Protection (CBP) agency collects and publishes the number of southwest border encounters each month. In 2020, more than 400,000 unauthorized immigrants were expelled from the US and returned to Mexico and other countries of origin. Policy changes in the Biden administration sent a message to the world that the Trump policies were voided. The message was interpreted by the would-be immigrants that our southern border was open. Hundreds of thousands of migrants began assembling and marching toward the border. In 2021, 1.7 million people were caught trying to cross the border illegally. It is likely that hundreds of thousands more crossed undetected.

An analysis of the seven months leading up to April of 2022 saw a 68 percent increase over the previous year, with 1,216,173 encounters at the southern border. The majority of those apprehended were processed, given a future court date, and released in the United States. More than 300,000 single adults were apprehended in that seven-month period, along with 84,000 unaccompanied children. From 2017 to 2021, over 10,000 criminal arrests were made at the border each year, including arrests of people with criminal convictions in the US or other countries. Every month in the last four years, between 60,000 pounds and 128,000 pounds of illegal drugs were seized by the CBP, along with currency valued at more than US $200 million.

Aside from the political rhetoric proffered by politicians on both sides of the immigration issue, the policy and practice presented to the population of immigrants was to "keep coming." Drug traffickers and human smugglers also promulgated a message that border crossings were now *permitido* in the United States. The Yucatan government provided a guidebook to assist immigrants in the process of illegally crossing US borders. In 2005 the Mexican government produced a comic book guide advising immigrants on how to avoid detection after crossing into the United States.

Laws enacted in 1965 abolished the 40-year-old immigration quota system. The Civil Rights Act in 1964 also prohibited discrimination based on the race or country of origin of immigrants. In 1990 the annual immigrant limit was raised to 675,000. Joint guest worker programs established by Mexico and the United States addressed the need for an inexpensive and flexible labor supply. Many immigrants who did not qualify for the joint programs came into the country illegally. The demand for even more guest workers brought pressure on US immigration policies. In 1986 President Ronald Reagan enacted the Immigration Reform and Control Act that gave amnesty to 3 million illegal immigrants in the country. The relaxation of immigration laws had a measurable impact on US demographics. In 2012, over 14 million people in the US lived in a household where the mother or father or other relative was in the country without proper authorization.

Prior to recent surges in illegal border crossings by caravans of new immigrants, two-thirds of the illegal undocumented immigrants in the US were initially here with a legally-issued visa. Unlike illegal border crossings, a visa overstay is subject to civil penalties and is not a criminal prosecution. Determining the immigration status of workers presents several problems for law enforcement personnel. State jurisdiction in the matter of citizenship verification was challenged by the federal government and tested in the courts. The issue of profiling and targeting Latinos was also addressed in the United States District Court in Arizona and ultimately by the US Supreme Court. It is illegal for a US employer to hire illegal or undocumented workers. However, in 2012 the US Supreme Court issued rulings that were enabling to the immigrant population. It was no longer a crime for an illegal immigrant to work or seek work in the US. The court upheld the requirement for state law enforcement officers to determine the immigration status of any individual that they arrest and suspect may be in the country illegally. The legality of racial profiling of Latinos and other minorities remains a challenge and will be addressed by the courts in individual cases.

To add to the opacity and flux in the enforcement of immigration policies and laws, the state of California passed laws in 2013 that allow illegal immigrants to obtain professional licenses, including licenses to practice law. Large employers such as Walmart, Tyson Foods, and Swift & Company add to the challenge by hiring thousands of illegal immigrants. The US government prosecutes and fines the companies, but the demand for workers in the food and farming industries remains a challenge in the US.

In 2009 the US Supreme Court ruled that illegal immigrants who use a made-up Social Security Number to obtain employment cannot be prosecuted for identity theft. Illegal immigrants contribute $12 billion annually to Social Security, but do not receive any benefits. In the 10-year period from 2000 to 2011, illegal workers contributed more than $35 billion into the Medicare trust fund. Even after withdrawals by immigrants, there was a $3 billion excess remaining. The demographics of the millions of illegals crossing today will negatively change the balance of these trust fund numbers in the coming years.

Deportation of illegal immigrants remains in the forefront of the immigration crisis. When immigrants are found to be guilty of a crime or in violation of immigration laws, they are subject to removal or deportation. The federal government has a wide latitude regarding the reasons for deportation. Protection of national security is at the top of the list. In 2011, when 400,000 immigrants were deported, more than half were due to having been convicted of crimes including DUIs, sex crimes, drug convictions, and homicides. During President Obama's eight years, there were 2.5 million deportations.

Economic research indicates that immigration trends in the past have increased the size of the US economy. Lower-cost workers slowed the trend of manufacturers sending jobs offshore and importing lower-cost foreign goods. These days, legal and illegal immigrants are coming to America in search of better-paying jobs. Seasonal workers in agricultural jobs can earn as much as six times more in the United States. Other immigrants are fleeing oppressive governments and employers or excessive crime in their own countries. Famine and war also add to the numbers of people migrating to the US. A Gallup poll published in 2016 found that nearly 150 million people from 156 foreign countries would move to the United States if they could.

To say to the people in Mexico, Central America, and dozens of other countries that our border is closed is heard by the immigrant population as noise. The past practices and policies in the US shout no on the public stage and whisper yes in the night to the millions of people seeking a better life. A poor family in a crime-ridden city—with little or no opportunity to improve their quality of life—will, as a matter of human nature and a will to survive, grasp any opportunity to change their outcome. Couple that with the knowledge that many of them have relatives living in the US who have been there for an average time exceeding 10 years, and the desire to immigrate is all powerful. A very telling and amazing statistic in the metrics of immigration assessments is the total number of undocumented young people graduating from US high schools. A report based on US census data was issued in 2019 and indicates that 100,000 undocumented young students graduate from US high schools every year. Even reports from 20 years ago listed that number at 65,000. Illegal immigration is where incentives and opportunity overcome all obstacles.

As positive as the reports make illegal immigration appear, the act of crossing Mexico to enter the United States is very dangerous. Murders and human trafficking at the border are regular occurrences. Fatal confrontations with border agents and police are also frequent. Research by San Diego State University indicates that over 30 percent of the immigrants are trafficked by the smugglers and/or their sponsoring employers. As many as half of all Mexican immigrants were abused or exploited by their smugglers or employers.

Annually, over 50,000 women from India, Russia, Vietnam, and China are lured by smugglers, only to find themselves forced into prostitution or work as laborers and servants. Many Latina women are misled and forced into prostitution. They are also abused and assaulted by the illegal immigrants in the migration process. Thousands of immigrants are injured in the journey. Over a 10-year period, 120,000 have simply disappeared while traveling to the border.

The border crisis in the United States will receive more attention over the next three years than it has ever been subjected to. The topic is in the forefront of every political forum. Both houses of Congress, the Supreme Court, and the executive branch will drive new discussions and create new laws and executive orders pertaining to the immigration policies of the United States. The Department of Homeland Security, the US Border Patrol, US Immigration and Customs Enforcement (ICE), the US Commission on Civil Rights, and the Department of Labor have the border crisis at the top of their agendas. State and federal law enforcement at every level in every state is engaged in strategic planning for the issues of legal and illegal immigration. Even the entertainment and documentary movie industries are now active in the production of films covering the plight of immigrants in the United States and abroad.

This is not an issue that will be solved with the stroke of an executive pen or a speech on the White House lawn. We have been managing and mismanaging our southern border since 1845, when Texas became the 28th state. Arizona joined the conundrum as the 48th and last contiguous state in 1912. There is no turning back the clock. For good or bad or both, the population and mix of ethnicities and nationalities in the US has been changed forever.

The COVID-19 Pandemic

The year 2020 will forever be remembered as the start of the COVID-19 pandemic. The first diagnosis of the SARS coronavirus was reported by the World Health Organization (WHO) on January 5, 2020. The fumbled messaging in the United States, with its inaccuracies and missing information, built a perfect footing for the genuine and often misguided management of a worldwide pandemic through the three years that followed. After a later analysis of the data, it was reported that there were other early cases in Wuhan, China, in November and December of 2019. By the end of January 2020, Chinese officials reported that the virus had spread to all the provinces of mainland China. At that time, the World Health Organization declared that the spread of the virus was now a "public emergency concern." By the end of February there were more new coronavirus cases reported outside of China than from within the country.

A few of the early cases were alleged to be linked to the Huanan Seafood Wholesale Market in Wuhan. The connection to the wet market led to early claims that the initial transmission was from animal to human and not a human-to-human infection. This claim was later determined to be false. In 2022 it was widely accepted that the release of the virus came from the Wuhan Institute of Virology and the "gain of function" research being conducted there. The disease brought on symptoms ranging from no symptoms, to fevers, dry coughing, and fatigue. More serious cases required hospitalization for pulmonary failure and treatment with ventilators. On March 11, 2020, the WHO declared the coronavirus to be a pandemic. By June 6, 2022, the pandemic had infected 532 million people and claimed 6.29 million lives globally.

On May 17, 2020, I met a man named Jim Thomas. We were having a small gathering of friends onboard my yacht that was docked in the lagoon at the front of our home in Ponte Vedra Beach, Florida. I did not know much about Jim. I found him to be a very likeable and engaging fellow. At the age of 70, Jim was a year older than me. He was generally fit and pleasant, without any obvious signs of medical issues. We enjoyed our cocktails in the yacht's cockpit and jovially swapped stories about past events with the other guys, while the wives chatted in the salon of the boat. Forty-five days after our gathering onboard the yacht *Quality Time*, Jim was dead.

Prior to the 2020 COVID-19 pandemic, the acronyms of the CDC and WHO were not part of our daily vernacular. Before Jim's death, I was not personally aware of any one of my friends and family having contracted the COVID-19 virus. Like many people, I had my doubts about the severity of the pandemic. We have faced other pandemics in the past, and they were generally only vaguely known to most of us as something we heard on news broadcasts. US President Donald Trump and other politicians spouted off in press conferences that they had things under control and assumed credit for saving the country, if not the entire world. Jim had become another statistic for the insidious virus. But for me, and his family and friends, Jim Thomas became the face of the SARS-associated coronavirus.

The experience that Jim and his grieving wife Leslie were exposed to instantly changed my perspective of the COVID-19 virus. In June 2020, a symptomatic patient would be quickly isolated and insulated from exposure to others. Caregivers wore specially adapted gowns, gloves, masks, and face shields. Family members were not allowed to enter hospitals and could not visit their loved ones. In many cases, the last time they would see their spouse or family member would be on a Facetime phone screen. These hospital scenes were more akin to a movie set about some alien infectious contamination. In my friend Jim's case, he entered the hospital alone and the warmth of human touch was gone. His last days on a ventilator allowed only the mechanical sounds of moving air and the muffled voices of doctors and nurses.

In 2021, one year after Jim's death, my wife Hilah tested positive for COVID-19. She was in North Carolina at our home on Lake Toxaway. I flew up to meet her in Lake Toxaway, and she picked me up at a friend's home on the lake. She said she was not feeling well and asked if I would drive. She feebly moved around the car and into the passenger seat. She described her symptoms of muscle pain and headaches. Her skin felt warm. I told her that we should call the Mercy Clinic in the nearby town of Brevard and request an appointment for drive-through COVID testing.

That same afternoon, we were both tested and after only 20 minutes, the clinic called and told us that Hilah's specimen had tested positive for the virus. Though there were some reports of false negative results, the rapid antigen test is considered to be very accurate for positive results. We called our friend and primary physician at Mayo Clinic in Jacksonville, Florida. He emphatically directed us to drive home and receive immediate care at the clinic. We packed our luggage, drove through the night, and arrived around 2:00 a.m. the next morning. Hilah's symptoms progressed and she had difficulty walking and standing. She was very weak and had no sense of balance. Her temperature exceeded 101 degrees Fahrenheit.

When we arrived at the Mayo Clinic's newly created COVID treatment center, we were directed to a numbered outdoor parking spot where we were met by a nurse assigned to the COVID Clinic. I explained that Hilah could not walk, and a wheelchair was provided. She was so weak that I had to lift her from the car seat and place her in the wheelchair. With both of our faces covered by medical masks, we quickly said our goodbyes and she was wheeled away. I drove off in tears and, given the experience previously described in Jim Thomas' case, I did not know if I would ever see my wife again.

Hilah was taken to a specific area set up for the administration of monoclonal antibody infusions. Her condition was so poor that instead of administering the antibody infusion, the attending physicians referred her to the hospital's emergency clinic for treatment and stabilization. Later that evening she received the infusion, and the next day she was stable enough to be released from the hospital. I happily picked her up and returned to our home in Ponte Vedra for the 10-day quarantine. She steadily improved, but several months passed before the fatigue and balance issues subsided.

One year later, in 2022, I also contracted the COVID-19 virus. My infection was probably the latest, more prevalent and contagious Omicron mutation of the virus. My symptoms were mild and did not require any special treatments or medications. Due to my wife's weakened immune system which was compromised by rheumatoid arthritis, we slept in separate rooms and wore masks in our house for 14 days.

The pandemic rapidly developed in the spring of 2020. The Center for Disease Control (CDC) provided a platform for federal, state, and local political leaders to assume unlegislated power as they confronted the disease. Their actions altered the reality and perception of what it means to be a free citizen in our country. The threat of death from disease, coupled with ambiguous and sometimes disingenuous messaging from health officials and the news media, created a veil of frustrated distrust in our country. The pious centralized messaging from CDC Director Dr. Anthony Fauci created more harm than comfort. The agency will most likely not regain the trust of the American people for some time to come. To the public's benefit, the intense controversy surrounding the management of the pandemic has spawned new immunological research and heightened political discourse regionally and nationally. The past actions and failures will hopefully lead to a better outcome in the management of future disease outbreaks and international pandemics.

As the nation continued the struggle to return to normal in the first half of 2022, the news media and the CDC continued to promote the controversial merits of COVID vaccinations. Both sides of the disputed issue became consumed with controversy over the vaccination of children under the age of five. Multinational pharmaceutical companies raced in competition to develop a shot that could be safely distributed to children. The CDC recommended the vaccination of children as young as preschool ages, and was met with fervent opposition. The debate over the need, efficacy, and safety of the vaccines continues. Vax and anti-vax groups are still in the front lines of the argument. State governors were taking sides, along with major corporations, in the debate. Even as the science revealed that natural immunity and post-infection immunity surpass the benefits of COVID immunizations, some state and federal government agencies, military institutions, and branches of the armed forces were purging their ranks of those unwilling to be vaccinated. The talent and experience drain on these essential populations presents a national security concern with lasting ramifications.

Policy arguments today demand a more serious analysis of how we manage the uncertainty of contagious viral diseases. Dependence on a single voice in the US Center for Disease Control (CDC) did not prove to be our best strategy. We must somehow maintain an acceptable balance of the constitutional rights of individuals to the collective need for protecting large population centers from pandemic diseases. The pandemic and the lockdowns experienced in the United States and abroad placed the visions of leaders with one-world agendas in elevated conflict with those who want nothing more than to return to the country's founding values of individual freedom and state-level governance in a democratic national republic.

The War in Ukraine

Before the invasion of Ukraine by Russia on February 21, 2022, most Americans never gave much thought to the country of Ukraine. Despite being a country with a land mass the size of Texas (233,000 square miles) and having a population of 44 million people (about twice the population of New York), a substantial number of people, including students fresh from the study of world history, would find difficulty in describing exactly where the country is located. The history of Ukrayina (Ukraine) begins in the 9th century with the federation of the Kievan Rus' dynasty. The start of the Russian invasion coincided with the 1,540th anniversary of the founding of the capital city of Kyiv, now known as Kiev (founded in the year AD 482).

A brief look into the history of Ukraine reveals that the current Russian invasion is not the deadliest or most horrific event in the country's history. The first millennium BC saw continuous warfare over the territories in the region. Ukraine has at different times been subject to the oppressive ruling powers of Poland, Russia, and the USSR. During World War II, the Nazis invaded Ukraine, and were initially welcomed as a potential ally against the aggression from Poland and Russia. The Ukrainians quickly came to regret the initial acceptance of German advances into their country.

The southern Ukrainian peninsula of Crimea and its 2.4 million inhabitants are perilously and strategically located between Russia's Kuban region and Ukraine's mainland. The importance of the Crimean Peninsula extends back to the 9th century. The sea route between the Baltic and Byzantium was known as the Byzantium-Dnieper trade route. The ancient Greek city of Byzantium later became known as Constantinople. The geographic significance of the Crimean Peninsula made it the target of numerous conflicts in the centuries that followed.

Under Imperial Russian rule in the late 1700s, Ukrainian territories lost their boundaries and their sense of nationality. The Ukrainian nobility were subsequently accepted into Russian imperial service, where they achieved high rank and prominence. They lost their Ukrainian heritage. Seventy years later, in 1856, the Russians were defeated in the Crimean War by a coalition of the countries of France, the Ottoman Empire, the United Kingdom, and Sardinia. In 1861 the harsh imperial policy of serfdom was ended. Peasants were given more freedom to assemble and organize. Ukraine began to reestablish the country's national heritage.

In 1863 Russia was determined to fully integrate all of Ukraine as a Russian territory. Russian leaders banned all publications in the Ukrainian language. Educational systems were also prohibited from teaching in the Ukrainian native language. Stage performances and speeches in the Ukrainian language were banned. The literacy rate in Ukraine plummeted. Internal revolts spawned the formation of secret societies to salvage and promote Ukrainian culture and education.

Toward the end of the 19th century, student-led groups developed and formed the Revolutionary Ukrainian Party. Their published political objective in the year 1900 was for a "Single, Indivisible, Free, and Independent Ukraine." The revolution that followed, in 1905, was repressed by Russian Czar Nicholas

II. The czar killed hundreds of revolting peasants, students, and industrial workers marching in the streets. Continuing violence from worker strikes and sporadic guerrilla-style attacks ultimately forced the czar to stand down and promise reforms to appease the protestors.

After the Russian Revolution of 1905, Ukraine reinstated the Ukrainian language and the citizenry reestablished the historic culture of Ukraine. The theatrical and musical arts led the advances as the country redeveloped their national pride. The promising new order was short-lived as Russia entered World War I in support of the Serbs, French, and British allies. Russian forces were no match against the powerful and highly industrialized German forces. The Russian people suffered badly through the war with food and fuel shortages, and they lost their little remaining faith in the czar's promises.

The first Ukrainian Revolution, in February of 1917, started with 90,000 tired, hungry, and angry women marching in the streets of Petrograd, shouting "Bread, bread, bread," and "Stop the war." The following day, 150,000 male workers joined the march. Czar Nicholas II was not present, but knowing his inevitable fate, in March of 1917 Nicholas II abdicated his leadership role as monarch ruler of the Russian Empire. A provisional government was established that represented the workers and soldiers in the Soviet class and the middle and upper classes in a Petrograd Soviet group.

In a bloodless coup d'état in October of 1917, exiled Bolshevik Party leader Vladimir Lenin returned to Russia. He assumed the party leadership and formed a Soviet government led by a council of soldiers, workers, and peasants. Lenin became the first dictator of a Communist state. The unrest continued and civil war broke out after the October Revolution. The Bolsheviks battled the monarchists and the capitalist supporters of socialism. Czar Nicholas II, his wife

Alexandra Feodorovna, and their five children were executed, along with the footman, the physician, and the cook, in July of 1918. They were stripped, shot, bayoneted, and their bodies were blasted with hand grenades. The civil war ended in 1923, and in a historical move, Lenin and his Red Army established the Soviet Union.

Three months after Lenin and the Bolsheviks took over Russia, on January 26, 1918, Soviet Ukraine declared its independence, adopted Ukraine's first constitution, and formed the first Ukrainian Congress of Soviets. The country's large, mostly peasant population was 80 percent Ukrainian. It is puzzling that while the newly installed Ukrainian leaders assumed responsibility for domestic affairs, they left the essential roles of military defense, transportation, commerce, foreign relations, and foreign trade to Russia. Soviet Russia also maintained warships in Ukraine at the Crimean port city of Sevastopol. Despite efforts to build on Ukrainian nationalism, the country's independence remained subordinate to the power exercised by the Central Committee of the Communist Party of the Soviet Union.

The Russian Revolution of 1917, coupled with the devastation of the Russian economy following World War I, led to a civil war in 1923 which transitioned the failed Russian imperialism to a Communist form of government. This ultimately led to the creation of the Union of Soviet Socialist Republics, the USSR. The bloody civil war, with a death toll of millions of Russians, gave rise to a vicious extremist regime to rule the Soviet Union.

The aftermath of the war in the 1920s brought in a period of Ukrainization that advanced the culture of the country and promoted the use of the Ukrainian language in schools, in publishing, and in the workplace. The Ukrainian Autocephalous Orthodox Church gained a large following and played a role in the cultural shift in attitudes away from Moscow and toward Europe. The national revival raised serious concern in Moscow and encountered fierce resistance from the non-Ukrainian leaders in the Ukrainian Communist Party.

The first few years of the 1930s brought renewed pain and suffering to the Ukrainian people. Soviet leaders dispatched large groups of special agents to enforce the failing Russian agricultural production policy of collectivization. Below-average grain production, coupled with unrealistic government-issued quotas, left the Ukrainians and the Russians without enough food to survive. The unnecessary and preventable famine was an assault on the peasantry. To steal even a sack of grain was a criminal offense punishable by death by firing squad. Of the 5 million who died in the Holodomor Famine of 1932–1933, 4 million were Ukrainians. Throughout the Great Famine, the Soviet Union cruelly exported more than 1 million tons of wheat to Western countries. After the famine subsided in 1933 and in the years that followed, the Soviets publicly denied that there was a famine, and many of the devastated Ukrainian cities and villages were repopulated with Russian settlers.

Ukrainians suffered an onslaught of repressive moves by the Soviet Union. The Ukrainian Orthodox Church was closed. People who were supportive of an independent Ukraine were arrested and sent to labor camps or they were imprisoned and executed. The population of Ukrainian elites, writers, and artists was reduced by as much as 80 percent. Stalin loyalists continued the purging in 1936–1938, killing 99 of the 102 leadership members of the Ukrainian Communist Party. On Stalin's orders, the Ukrainian Communist Party was taken over by Nikita Khrushchev in 1938.

Relief for Ukraine was not in sight. On September 1, 1939, German Nazi forces invaded Poland and started World War II. In a reversal of their initial alignment with the Soviet

Union, German forces invaded the USSR on June 22 of 1941. Three million German troops, along with 3,000 tanks, 7,000 artillery guns, and 2,500 airplanes, advanced on a 1,000-mile-long Russian border. More than 4 million Russian people were evacuated. Retreating Soviet forces blew up their own buildings and destroyed crops and food reserves. Mines were flooded and supply depots were destroyed. The Germans moved quickly into Ukraine, where they were at first seen as liberators freeing Ukraine from their enemies in Poland and the USSR. The delusional Ukrainian leaders were arrested and sent to concentration camps. In the fall of 1941, the Nazis began mass killings of the Ukrainian Jews. In the ruthless massacre, 1.5 million people perished and 800,000 more were displaced to eastern cities. In Kyiv, 34,000 people were killed in the first two days of the German occupation. Approximately 2.2 million Ukrainians were taken from Ukraine to Germany to work as slaves.

In a major turn of events, the Soviets defeated the Germans in Stalingrad in 1943 and began advancing to the west. In November of 1943, the Soviet Red Army moved to Kyiv. By the spring of 1944, all of Ukraine was again under Soviet control. Ukraine's western boundaries were redrawn, and after a mutual land and population exchange, the ethnically and politically drawn border between Poland and Ukraine was at last clarified and accepted. In 1945 Ukraine became a charter member of the United Nations and signatory to UN treaties with Italy, Finland, Romania, Hungary, and Bulgaria.

While Ukraine was politically well positioned after World War II, the devastating losses in the war were far-reaching. With nearly 7 million Ukrainians killed in the war and millions more living in Russia and Poland, the population in Ukraine had dropped by 25 percent. Seven hundred cities and 28,000 villages were destroyed in the war. Industrial plants and agricultural operations and equipment were decimated. However, the importance of the region was evident, and Stalin moved quickly to restore production of essential goods in Ukraine. Industrial output reached prewar levels within five years. Agricultural production would take more than a decade to recover. Adding to the postwar misery for Ukrainians, 1 million people died from starvation in a 1946 famine. All through the rebuilding process, Russian Secretary Nikita Khrushchev reimposed oppressive totalitarian control over Ukraine.

After Stalin's death in 1953, Khrushchev's advancements brought limited relief to the Ukrainians. Repressive totalitarian policies subsided for the citizenry, but only for those who strictly adhered to the party line. The formation of a limited, decentralized government in Ukraine brought new confidence back to the Ukrainian Party and government leaders. Amnesty was granted to hundreds of thousands of Ukrainian people released from concentration camps. Commerce and cultural events and activities resumed for the Ukrainian people.

Toward the end of Khrushchev's reign in 1961, the dark trend toward "Russification" had reemerged. Ukrainian language instruction in schools was once again curtailed. Russian-Ukrainian borders diminished in significance under a theory of "fusion of nations." Totalitarian oppression came soon afterward, and clandestine groups secretly opposing the Russian government reemerged. When the Russian secret police discovered dissident groups, their members were imprisoned or executed.

A purge of Ukrainian educational and cultural institutions continued through the 1960s and '70s. In 1982 the 325th anniversary of the reunification of Ukraine with Russia was celebrated, along with the 1,500th anniversary of the founding of the capital city of Kyiv. The economy suffered in the 1970s and '80s. Agricultural production was in decline and affected by recurring droughts. Collective farming and excessive centralized demands on agricultural outputs added to the misery for Ukrainians. Coal mining and other industries also experienced declining growth.

In April of 1986 the Chernobyl nuclear plant, located northwest of Kyiv, experienced major failures while testing its water cooling system. The nuclear reactor overheated, blowing off the 1,000-ton concrete-and-steel roof and releasing 400 times more radiation than the Hiroshima nuclear bomb. The worst nuclear accident in world history exposed hundreds of thousands of people to radiation levels that would affect their health in the years ahead. Dozens of plant workers died in the first few days. Many others would die later from thyroid cancers and other diseases attributable to radiation exposure.

Except for a brief period of independence between 1918–1920, Ukraine was dominated by Poland and Czechoslovakia to the west and the USSR to the north and east. When the Soviet Union collapsed in 1990–1991, the Ukrainian Soviet Socialist Republic finally gained full independence and changed its official name to Ukraine. Despite urging from US President George H. W. Bush to remain within the USSR, a Ukraine referendum on December 1, 1991, yielded an 84 percent voter turnout with 90 percent of the voters endorsing the independence of their country. One week later, Ukraine, Russia, and Belarus formed the Commonwealth of Independent States (CIS). After the USSR was formally disbanded, Ukraine was still struggling as a nation; however, it was now a recognized member of the international community of nations.

The issue of Ukraine having a significant cache of nuclear weapons was a concern for the United States. Following the Chernobyl disaster, the Ukrainians did not want to be the third-largest nuclear power country in the world. With serious reservations, the country's leaders agreed to divest the country of its nuclear arsenal, but only after receiving guarantees of security for its country and financial compensation for the high costs associated with the dismantling and disbursement of the weapons. In May of 1992 Ukraine signed the Lisbon Protocol, in which Belarus, Ukraine, and Kazakhstan would destroy all nuclear weapons or transfer control of any remaining nuclear weapons to Russia.

The Ukrainian port city of Sevastopol was the front line for disputes between Ukraine and Russia in 1992. Ukraine had claimed ownership and control of the Black Sea fleet of Russian ships. Russia responded with a decree that the fleet had always been and would forever be a naval asset of the Soviet Union. In June of 1992 Russian President Boris Yeltsin agreed to a three-year joint administration agreement for the naval fleet. Eventually the fleet was divided between Russia and Ukraine, with Russia keeping most of the assets in exchange for Ukrainian debt forgiveness. Later, in 1997 Russia commenced a 20-year lease from Ukraine, of the port's naval facilities in Sevastopol.

The issue of the administration of the Crimean port at Sevastopol was contentious back in 1954 and throughout the 20th century. In 1991 the mostly Russian-speaking Crimean Peninsula was granted status as the "Autonomous Republic" of Ukraine. Two decades later, on March 6, 2014, in a questionable election, the Crimean Parliament proposed a referendum to secede from Ukraine and join the Russian Federation. Naval dominance in the Black Sea would be back in Russia's complete control. Western countries condemned the transfer and viewed it as a threat to regional stability.

The 2014 referendum in March did not change Kyiv's position that Crimea was still a part of Ukraine. Irregularities were noted in the election process. Multiple ballots were cast by individual voters. It was reported that 100,000 ballots pre-marked as a yes vote were seized by the Ukrainian police. Two months after the March referendum, a Human Rights Civil Society released a report citing that actual voter turnout was less than 50 percent, with only half of the voters choosing annexation by Russia. The European Union sided with Ukraine on the control of Crimea and placed sanctions on Russian companies and individuals. Russian President Vladimir Putin, then in his third term, supported the dubious election and the referendum as the "will of the people."

In February of 2014, masked gunmen took over the Crimean parliament building and raised the Russian flag. Russian lawmakers in Crimea removed sitting government officials and instituted the Russian Unity Party, with Sergey Aksyonov as the Crimean prime minister. In a move that Russian President Putin called "protecting the Russian people and assets in Crimea," Russian troops moved into the peninsula. Ukraine evacuated 25,000 Ukrainian military personnel and their families as the Russian troops moved to the port city of Sevastopol and into military bases around the Crimean Peninsula.

By mid-April of 2014, Russian President Vladimir Putin declared the annexation of Crimea to be a victory. Russia began moving military troops to the region and threatened a nuclear response if they were opposed. NATO also believed that Putin was deploying nuclear-capable weapons to Crimea. Russian troops and Russian-speaking separatists in the eastern region began the armed conflict with Ukraine in the area known as the Donbas, at the eastern border between Ukraine and Russia. Russian militants occupied office buildings and took control of border crossings. The war in Donbas was underway and by May of 2014, 40,000 Russian troops had advanced to the eastern border of Ukraine. Donetsk and Luhansk Republics and 3.6 million Russian-speaking residents of the Donbas are part of

Ukraine. However, like Crimea, Russia has always considered the Donbas to be a Russian territory.

Russian and separatist forces fought for control of the Ukrainian-controlled Donetsk airport. The Russian forces and Donetsk People's Republic (DNR) volunteer fighters eventually gained control of the airport in July of 2015. Fifteen hundred people died in the yearlong effort to control the Donetsk airfield. In response to setbacks in the Crimean invasion, Putin deployed more trucks and troops in what was being called a humanitarian mission. The contents transported by the convoy were discovered by Ukraine's Defense Council to be arms and ammunition, and Ukraine declared the mission to be a direct invasion of Ukraine.

In August of 2014, the small Ukrainian city of Amvrosiivka was occupied by Russian paratroopers and 250 armored vehicles. Ukrainian forces responded by shelling the armored caravan and capturing 10 Russian paratroopers. Later in August, a column of Russian tanks, howitzer long-ranged weapons, and 30 troop carriers entered southeastern Ukraine in what was described as an effort to liberate the Ukrainian city of Mariupol. Approximately 35,000 Russian-backed separatists and 300 Russian troops also seized other cities in the Donbas of southeastern Ukraine, including Luhansk and Donetsk Oblasts.

Following the 2014 occupation by Russian forces and Crimea's questionable election to secede from Ukraine and join the Russian Federation, the Russian-speaking state of Crimea remained under Russian influence, but was still recognized by the United Nations and the United States as an autonomous Crimean republic of Ukraine. Crimea's location on the northern coast of the Black Sea provided Russian forces with access to the Baltic Sea and the Mediterranean. The sea routes are both militarily beneficial and economically significant, with access to nearby Turkey and Romania. Under a mutually arranged lease, Russia continued to maintain the naval fleet in the Crimean city of Sevastopol, giving Russia military prominence in the area and ready access to the Mediterranean Sea. Not being subject to freezing over like other Russian ports, the warm-water port city is also an important strategic asset for Russia's naval fleet.

The Russian-Ukrainian conflict continued with approximately 34,000 Ukrainian troops defending the region against 36,000 Russian separatist forces. As many as 10,000 of the rebel separatists were actually Russian soldiers. As many as 1,000 members of the Russian intelligence agency had also infiltrated Crimea and were providing electronic jamming equipment to protect the Russian artillery from Ukrainian counterattacks. The separatist rebels also had unmanned aerial surveillance that provided timely information about the size and location of Ukrainian forces.

Drones and jamming technology supplied by Russia, along with the use of Russian tanks and artillery by the separatists, refuted claims made by Russia that it was not in the fight in eastern Ukraine for any reason beyond providing humanitarian support. Captured Russian documents revealed that covert financial support was also coming from Russia. Plans for a Russian invasion and occupation of eastern Ukraine and the annexed Crimean Peninsula were also discovered, as well as detailed public relations messaging to justify Russia's actions. In March of 2015 a report from the Royal United Services Institute (a British defense and security think tank) revealed that as many as 10,000 regular Russian combatants were in Ukraine and had been there since the last months of 2014. The report stated that by March of 2015, Russian troop levels reached 42,000. Casualty numbers were difficult to obtain. The United Nations Human Rights Office reported in September of 2015 that as many as 8,000 people had been killed in the conflict.

Russia continued to assert that their mission was to provide humanitarian relief to Russian separatists in eastern Ukraine and to defend against Ukrainian terrorist strikes at the Russian border. This narrative conflicts with Russian railway traffic data collected from 2015 records that showed manifests for thousands of tons of high explosives and weapons being transported into Ukraine. Skirmishes and the deaths of Russian infiltrators in 2016 were used by Russia to shore up their arguments that Ukrainian terrorists were the aggressors at the eastern border. Russia disseminated this argument to the international community as justification for a buildup of Russian forces at the border.

The United States, in April of 2015, expressed concern and was critical of Russia's positioning of air defense systems at the Russian border city of Belgorod and within 50 miles of the second-largest Ukrainian city of Kharkiv and its 1.4 million residents. The city was Ukraine's capital before it was moved to Kiev in 1938. With a land area of 135 square miles, it is comparable to the US city of Atlanta in the state of Georgia. Kharkiv is home to Freedom Square and numerous historically and culturally significant cathedrals, theaters, and museums. Unfortunately, it is also destined to remain a focal point in the ongoing war with Russia.

In what is known as the Kerch Strait incident, rising tensions over the use and control of the waterways and eastern Ukrainian ports peaked in 2018 when three Ukrainian ships crossing from Odessa to Mariupol were fired on by Russian warships. Two dozen Ukrainian sailors were detained by Russian forces. The water route provides an important trade link between eastern ports in the Azov Sea and the Black Sea. Russia assumed control of the water routes after the

2014 annexation of the Crimean Peninsula. The Ukrainian parliament responded by declaring martial law in Ukraine's coastal cities.

Ukrainian soldiers in the Donbas territory continued to do battle with Russian separatist forces. More than 100 Ukrainian soldiers were killed in combat in the region in 2019. In May of that year, Ukraine elected Volodymyr Zelenskyy to the presidency of Ukraine. President Zelenskyy was elected on a promise to end the war. By December of 2019, a prisoner exchange was in progress, with more than 200 soldiers swapped by Ukraine and pro-Russian separatists. As the war appeared to taper down, 50 more Ukrainian soldiers were killed in combat in 2020.

In the buildup toward the 2022 war in Ukraine, Russian President Vladimir Putin accused Ukraine of promoting Russophobia. He went on to warn that Ukraine was building a case for future genocidal actions against the pro-Russian population in Ukraine. Putin's claims were rejected by the international community as false and baseless. Putin went on to argue that Ukraine was never a legitimate sovereign state. Ignoring Ukraine's 1,500-year history, Putin asserted that past actions taken by Vladimir Lenin and Nikita Khrushchev improperly created the state of Ukraine. He falsely accused Ukrainians of being neo-Nazis, which is puzzling given that President Zelenskyy is Jewish and several of his family members died fighting the Nazis while serving in the Soviet army.

From December of 2021 right up to February of 2022, the Russian ambassador to the Czech Republic and Russia's foreign minister denied that Russia had any plans to invade Ukraine. From March to October of 2021, Russia amassed an invasion-sized military force near the Ukrainian border with Russia, in the bordering country of Belarus. In sharp contrast to the messaging from Moscow, the US provided evidence of

Russia's invasion plans. Satellite photographs clearly showed Russian battalions, tanks, and artillery positioned near the northern and eastern Ukrainian borders.

Prior to the February Russian invasion in 2022, fighting between Ukrainian forces and Russian separatists was escalating in the Donbas (Donets Basin) region of southeastern Ukraine. Emergency evacuations were underway in the Ukrainian cities of Donetsk and Luhansk. The population of Luhansk is less than 400,000 and Donetsk has a little over 900,000 residents. The entire Donbas region, a territory the size of the US state of Maryland, is home to more than 4 million people. Forty percent of that population identify themselves as Soviet Russians and the predominant language of the working class there is Russian.

The Russia-Ukraine war in 2022 has displaced more than half the Donbas population. At least 1 million people evacuated to Russia. The area has been under the control of pro-Russian citizens for the last eight years, and over half the people there still consider the area an independent Soviet republic. The importance of the Donbas region extends back to the 17th century. Today it is a highly industrialized area, with the fourth-largest coal reserves in all of Europe. Russia invaded the Donetsk and Luhansk Oblasts in February of 2022, and by July 3, Mariupol, Sievierodonetsk, Lysychansk, and Rubizhne were under Russian control. The attacks on Mariupol began in February and 95 percent of the city was destroyed. The bombing and fighting resulted in the death of 22,000 civilians.

In May and June of 2022, Russian forces attacked and bombed assisted-living facilities, railway stations, shopping malls, and apartment buildings, while steadily gaining control of dozens of eastern Ukrainian cities. On July 3 Russia captured Lysychansk, and the Luhansk People's Republic declared complete control of the Luhansk Province (Oblast). The Ukrainian army fought fiercely and defended the country with artillery and ground forces, but they were outgunned by Russia's artillery by 10 to 15 times. Heavy shelling of the Donetsk Oblast in the cities of Sloviansk and Bakhmut in early July has destroyed the city's buildings and infrastructure. The fighting in December 2022 has been reduced to trench-type warfare, resulting in hundreds of soldiers and paramilitary fighters on both sides being killed daily in what is now known as the bloodiest battle in the 21st century.

The Ukrainian army continues to attack Russian supply lines and ammunition depots. Additional Western-supplied long-range artillery weapons have allowed Ukraine to take back portions of some cities. They also gained the ability to reach well behind Russian and DPR (Donetsk People's Republic) front lines and bomb more ammunition depots and troop locations. July represented a turning point in the Ukraine war. The Russians seemed to have stalled, but according to the Institute for the Study of War (a United States–based think tank), they were just taking an operational pause to refresh troops and supplies.

The war in Ukraine continued through 2022, and the losses on both sides of the conflict were significant. In the months of April through June of 2022, more than 12,000 Ukrainian fighters and 8,000 Russian and separatist forces were killed. Civilian casualties in the Donbas fighting are approaching 3,000. Thousands more have been injured. Russian President Putin shows no signs of backing down from the Ukrainian war. He has lost all standing on the international stage. The citizens of Russia may eventually learn the truth about the war. For now, they are being told that Ukraine is the aggressor and a threat to their country. While it is true that eastern Ukraine has Russian-speaking citizens living life as Russians, they want freedom and not annexation. The narrative that the invasion is a liberation will be difficult—if not impossible—to substantiate when the truth surfaces in Russia. The first offensives in February on 3 million people (about the population of Arkansas) in the capital city of Kyiv made it clear that Russia and Vladimir Putin intend to take over all of Ukraine.

On August 24, 2022, the death toll from the deadliest attack in months rose to 25 when Russian missiles destroyed a train station and bombed residential areas. Moscow claimed it had foiled a new terror plot. At least two children were among the dead, and more than 30 people were injured. The missile strikes took place on the Ukrainian Independence Day. The date marks 31 years since the country declared independence from the Soviet Union. Ukrainian President Volodymyr Zelenskyy responded with this statement to the world: "There are no such bombs that can erase freedom, and there will never be such missiles that can break the will of the people who believe in themselves." In the late summer months of 2022, Ukrainian forces began regaining control of cities in northeastern territories, near the major city of Kharkiv. Thousands of Russian soldiers were isolated as Russian reinforcements and supply routes were cut off by the Ukrainian army.

February 14, 2023, marks Valentine's Day and the 358th day of the war in Ukraine. Ukrainian forces have been fortified by the influx of billions of US dollars that brought sophisticated artillery and ammunition to the front lines of the war. More than 300 heavy tanks have been promised by multiple countries. Poland is supplying 60 tanks, and recently committed to supplying 14 additional German-made Leopard tanks. Ukraine continues to ask for long-range missiles and air support to break the Russian supply lines and combat Russia's deadly bombing campaign. Russia continues to control Crimea and the northeast region of Ukraine, extending from Luhansk to the north and Mariupol in the south. Continuing support from Western and NATO countries, coupled with the Ukrainian commitment to defend their country, projects a protracted timeline for the conclusion of the fighting in Ukraine.

The tenuous and potentially volatile relationships between the United States, Russia, and China are center stage, posing an existential threat to the security of the United States and other allied countries. European countries are slowly shifting the dynamics of power as they coalesce in support of Ukraine in the unprovoked Russian invasion. With Sweden and Finland now seeking membership in NATO, the pressure along the Russian border will cause Russian President Putin to react in unpredictable ways. A peaceful and mutually beneficial outcome in the war in Ukraine is highly unlikely. The impact of the war, soaring inflation, and a post-COVID decline in the economies of the US, Russia, and China has led to even more instability across the globe. The war and growing tensions among Russia, China, North Korea, and the US, coupled with the violent agendas of foreign and domestic terrorists and maniacal power-seeking authoritarian leaders, are creating uncertainty, hate, and fear in populations around the world. The international sociopolitical pot is not just being stirred; it is boiling and about to explode!

2021

If you find yourself at death's door, do not open it. In May of 2021 I had a cold. It was the standard issue: runny nose, sore throat, and cough. Four months later I still had a cold. Not a sickly feeling, mucus-hacking cold—just a cough and fatigue and shortness of breath. My primary physician referred me to a radiologist for a CT scan of my lungs. I looked it up. It is more specifically defined as a computed tomography scan of the chest. This would be the first of many trips to the online dictionary as I expanded my medical vocabulary through the month of September.

Following the lung CT scan, the radiologist posted an impersonal medical assessment of his radiographic findings on my Mayo Clinic web portal and permanent medical record. I opened the site and went straight to the posted test results and radiology images. There were 1,147 images. I looked at every one of them and the process yielded nothing to me. The next page said it all. Autrey, Ronald A. (Mr.) DOB: 28-Dec-1952. I was thankful that there was no dash after the birth year. The next few lines of text were more ominous. "Diffuse bronchitis with fibrotic interstitial lung disease and desquamative interstitial pneumonia or hypersensitivity pneumonitis. Right upper lobe represents confluent fibrosis and focal nodular distortion." The next lines read like a review of my musical vocal talents. I had "heterogeneous mosaic attenuation." Except for the addition of "calcified granulomas and fissural lymph nodes," it sounded like something good. It was not. In fewer words, my lungs were inflamed and I had an interstitial lung disease (ILD) known as pulmonary fibrosis.

Now I had to look up a larger basket of medical terms, and I wish that I had not done so. A trip to the World Wide Web set me into a downward spiral that took my breath away. I stopped looking up the medical terms. I am thankful they did not give me a tattoo reading: "Use or Freeze by 12/31/23." Fortunately, after 12 months the follow-up scans showed no signs of progression. This static non-idiopathic condition could change without explanation or be maintained for years. For now, I will live on and continue my literary quest to write the next great American novel.

The Final Frontier

J ust as I was beginning to think that I was finally safe from prematurely dying, I stumbled into a new treacherously ominous threat that has the potential to bring instant death to one or more, or all of us. Unlike the brutal demise that people witnessed in the invasions by rapacious Scandinavian Vikings as they brutally pirated and plundered unsuspecting Europeans in the 8th century, the existential threat in the 21st century may come from the sky or the hidden caverns beneath the sea.

Humans on planet Earth have pondered the existence of life on other planets and solar systems for millenniums. Could it be that we are not the most supremely intelligent and advanced species in our universe? Are we subject to erasure by some unknown and possibly invisible living force? Could it be that planet Earth is simply another repository of minerals and gases that will one day be collected by roving space travelers? Are we another incidental creature in a conglomeration of parasitic enclaves distributed throughout an infinite and soulless plasma of time and space? If the limitless power of technology is applied at multiples of warp speed, then our demise may be a quick, effortless, and perhaps meaningless extinguishment of life on earth.

On May 17, 2022, the United States Congress held the first of a series of meetings to review and discuss what is known about unidentified aerial phenomena, or UAPs. The committee reviewed video and audio collected from sightings by military and civilian aircraft. Documented sightings and photographs were also discussed. Military and civilian aircraft pilots have witnessed and recorded UAPs that demonstrated unfathomable speeds and maneuverability. We have no crash sites or alien bodies stored in a secret lab. Or do we?

Congressman Tim Burchett spoke out at the congressional hearing and claimed the US government has more physical evidence that they are withholding and covering up. He claims to have reports from multiple unnamed sources that say the government has material from crashed alien spacecrafts. There are also claims that UFOs have demonstrated the ability to disarm our nuclear arsenal. The first hearing was flawed because the testimony came only from government officials and not the people involved in the actual sightings. Short videos were played, but had an inferior quality and could not be examined frame by frame. We do know there is a lot more evidence available from early sightings and phenomena, going back to the 1950s and '60s. Hopefully, future hearings will be more transparent with the addition of firsthand reports, videos, and photographs.

Since the first congressional hearing, scientists and other observers are speaking out about their own experiences and findings. There are reports that the CIA has a stockpile of physical evidence stored at civilian contractor sites, and that it is funding research and analysis of the data collected from individuals that have been affected or sickened by contact with alien artifacts from crash sites. New evidence and theories will most likely continue to surface as we remove the stigma associated with people who share their experiences with UFOs and UAPs.

You could argue that if there were alien manned aircraft visiting our planet, why haven't they landed? Why isn't there more evidence of contacts with planet Earth and its inhabitants? One argument is that aliens may not have the same physical characteristics of a human body. They may also possess transformative powers or the ability to project matter or images that confound our attempts to detect and document their existence. One analogy made by research scientist Gary Nolan, of Stanford University, presents as follows: "When you move into or visit a new home, do you stop and talk to the ants or the rodents in and around the house? Do you even think about their existence?" If you did stop and talk to the ants, what would you say? How would you explain the applications of Instagram or Facebook or space travel?

Nolan goes on to explain that the UFO/UAP data is real. Observers have documented real-life evidence of their experiences. What is impeding our understanding of the phenomena is that our body of scientific knowledge and our laws of physics cannot explain the data. What we do know for certain is that we do not know for certain what and who the aliens are, and if there are any such things at all. The congressional committee is operating under the auspices of concerns for national security and the protection from unknown threats. The theory that scientists should first look at the simple evidence at hand—before spending significant efforts on ethereal possibilities—is a good rule for this committee. Exhaust the investigation of what we know, and then perhaps we can project what our risks may or may not be from outer space.

The concerns about extraterrestrial beings and their intentions may well be moot. Our destruction will more likely be brought about by our own international conflicts. The technology that destroys us may be as simple as the spy balloon that drifted slowly across the continent in February of 2023. The gravitational deployment from a balloon dropping electromagnetic, chemical, biological, or radioactive materials is enough to destroy at least the current generation of human life.

We as a people are accustomed to making assumptions and creating beliefs in things and concepts that we cannot measure, touch, or see. I believe in God, the Creator of the universe. I cannot prove the existence of God or the angels. I have exhausted the examination of physical evidence pertaining to what we know about Christianity and the divinity of a chosen path in life that respects and believes in the omnipresence of one Creator. As for me, I will not lose sleep over any fears about invaders from space. Today I thank God for my simple existence. If I am to be eradicated by some unknown powerful enemy, then I shall pass peacefully into the hands of almighty God, and dwell in the kingdom of light and love for eternity. Amen.

Epilogue: 2022, the Finale

The 23rd year of the third millennium is a capstone year in several ways. It is the concluding chapter of this book's 73-year journey through life on planet Earth. I hope the selected chronicles of my life inserted into the timeline added some street-level contrast to the incredible events that unfolded around the globe. Reliving the events in my life crafted a realization that I was continually blessed in so many ways. The gift of my life from our Master Creator in 1952 was the starting point for an amazing and satisfying personal existence. The things I was able to experience and accomplish filled a dreamlike microcosm that moved through the decades. The joy and intrigue of my human existence played on in my head like a story that was being written each day.

When I was as young as four, my thoughts were an ageless tapestry of contemplations. Each day came with new adventures, and very few challenges were too steep to overcome. I was fortunate and blessed to have lived in the American Dream as my family evolved in a continuously improving lifestyle that ultimately reached pinnacles beyond our collective expectations. My parents were decent, hard-working Christian people who shared their dream with four children. At this writing our parents are alive and well, and entering their ninth decade of living and 74 years of marriage. All the Autrey children are successful in different ways, and we continue living charmed lives in the idyllic settings of North Florida.

Another summit in this timeline is the conclusion of my affiliation with the world of business. I had the unique experience to begin a career with a company at the lowest rung of employment and rise to be the chief executive and chairman of one of the most iconic and successful electrical construction companies in the world. I followed in my dad's footsteps throughout the last 48 years. My years in project management and executive management positions were personally rewarding to me and provided my family with an exceptional lifestyle. I stepped down as CEO in 2012 and remained as chairman of the board for an additional 10 years. For the past decade I have been able to enjoy an enviable standard of living, with worldwide travel and amazing experiences that continue today. When I was a young man on a path of constantly going places and experiencing new things, my mother would tell me, "You need to slow down, or you won't have anything to do when you're older." She may well have been right. As I turned 70 years old, only a few things remained on my wish list.

Over the next few years I hope to complete more books about living and life on earth. My work will turn inward to a study of the physical and mental mechanisms of human thoughts and habits that manifest both beauty and havoc in our ability to coexist with one another. The ongoing struggles mankind imposes on humanity continually threaten our future existence. In another millennium or less, we may just be another layer of organic remains in the crust of the planet. For now, I will focus on my remaining years and family, and assist them in their journeys through life. My wife of 42 years has been a life partner who stood by me in my strongest and weakest moments. We have been blessed with three children and four grandchildren. The Autrey family tree has branched so far and wide, it will take a study of ancestry to document the hundreds of living relatives. As a family we are strong and will try to weather whatever storms may be on the horizon. For me, I am very thankful for the gift of life and living.

See more of Ron's World at AutreyResearch.com.

www.ingramcontent.com/pod-product-compliance
Lightning Source LLC
Chambersburg PA
CBHW020437130626
46549CB00001B/186